Critical praise for this book

'Steve Kettell provides an incisive and important account of how the decisions made around the invasion of Iraq were not simply an aberration from the usual processes of British democracy; they were, rather, a vivid illustration of what has happened to British politics, clustered around a few personalities whose actions are shielded from proper public scrutiny. Thoroughly researched, this is the best book yet on how the disastrous decisions were taken to support Bush's war on Iraq, and how the politicians tried in vain to cope with the collapse in public confidence afterwards.' – Dr Glen Rangwala, University of Cambridge

'Steven Kettell's claim is stark: that, unlike the majority of his electorate, Tony Blair was committed to regime change in Iraq well before 9/11, and welcomed the invasion as a way of enhancing Britain's global role. If true, this claim underscores the importance of another: that all this was possible only because of the centralised, hierarchical and elitist nature of a British political system in need of total participatory overhaul. Controversial and provocative, this book adds an important new dimension to the contemporary debate on UK politics, and deserves to be widely read.' – David Coates, Worrell Professor of Anglo-American Studies, Wake Forest University, North Carolina

'This book provides a clear and accurate account of how Tony Blair and his entourage got Britain into Iraq. I agree with Kettell's argument that this was only possible because of the undemocratic and elitist nature of the British state.' – The Rt Hon Clare Short MP

'The Iraq war, its causes and its consequences, has produced a number of powerful books. This latest addition provides a comprehensive, readable and intelligent look at the ramifications of the sorry tale for British and international democracy.' – John Kampfner, editor of the *New Statesman*

'Kettell's book, though partisan, is impressively thorough and well-researched. Not all will like his conclusions, but it is nevertheless a persuasive and important contribution to the debate on the biggest question-mark of the Blair premiership.' – Dr Anthony Seldon, Brighton College

'This important book not only effectively counters the myths surrounding British policy towards Iraq, it also reveals the elitist and centralised nature of the political system and foreign policy-making more generally. It is a must-read for anyone entertaining the notion that our system is democratic or that foreign policy is made in the public interest.' – Mark Curtis, author of *Unpeople: Britain's Secret Human Rights Abuses* (Vintage, 2004)

About the author

Steven Kettell is a lecturer in the Department of Politics and International Studies at the University of Warwick. His research interests are focused primarily in the fields of British and international political economy. His first book, entitled the *Political Economy of Exchange Rate Policy-Making*, was published by Palgrave in 2004. He is also a founder and Executive Editor of the journal, *British Politics*.

About this book

Britain's participation in the Iraq war defines one of the most tumultuous periods in its political history. Driven by a desire to enhance the influence of the British government on the world stage, the decision to support the US-led invasion has severely disrupted the stability of international relations, produced rising disenchantment with the domestic political process, and threatened to undermine the continued viability of the New Labour project.

Yet these developments are also indicative of a far deeper malaise. Highlighting the relatively sparse mechanisms available for scrutinising and checking the actions of the executive, the events surrounding the war have clearly exposed the flaws and weaknesses inherent in the British democratic system. Underpinned by the principles of hierarchy, centralisation, and elitism, British democracy is characterised by a deep-seated adherence to a top-down style of policy-making at the expense of more participatory and accountable forms of governance. With these limitations having been further amplified by the internal structures of the New Labour government itself, the consequences have left an indelible mark on Britain's political landscape.

Dirty Politics?

New Labour, British Democracy
and the Invasion of Iraq

Steven Kettell

Zed Books
LONDON AND NEW YORK

Dirty Politics? New Labour, British Democracy and the Invasion of Iraq
was first published in 2006 by Zed Books Ltd,
7 Cynthia Street, London N1 9JF, UK and
Room 400, 175 Fifth Avenue, New York, NY 10010, USA
www.zedbooks.co.uk

Cover designed by Andrew Corbett
Set in 10/13 pt Goudy by Long House, Cumbria, UK
Printed and bound in Malta by Gutenberg Ltd

Distributed in the USA exclusively by Palgrave Macmillan, a division of
St Martin's Press, LLC, 175 Fifth Avenue, New York, NY 10010

A catalogue record for this book
is available from the British Library

US Cataloging-in-Publication Data
is available from the Library of Congress

ISBN 1 84277 740 8 (hb)
ISBN 1 84277 741 6 (pb)
ISBN 978 1 84277 740 4 (hb)
ISBN 978 1 84277 741 1 (pb)

Contents

For my wife
Marie

Acknowledgements

First of all I would like to thank my colleagues in the Department of Political Science and International Studies at the University of Birmingham, especially Peter Kerr, Colin Hay, and David Marsh, for all their insightful thoughts and assistance to me during the course of writing this book. Similar thanks must go to Anna Hardman, Mandy Woods, Kate Kirkwood, Pat Harper and the external reviewers at Zed, whose suggestions and comments were always helpful and inspiring. On a more personal note, I would also like to express my deepest gratitude to my family for everything they have done throughout the last few years, and without whose help this book would never have been possible. The one to whom I am most indebted of all, however, is as always my wife, Marie, who has put up with more long hours, bad moods, and general slovenliness than anyone has a right to expect. It is to her, therefore, that this book is dedicated.

Preface

The events surrounding the war in Iraq acutely expose the centralised, hierarchical, and elitist nature of British democracy. Deeply embedded within the ideational and institutional contours of its political system, these underlying norms and values have shaped and influenced the emergence of New Labour and its governing strategy. Based on a desire to project British power across the world stage, a key component of this strategy involved the pursuit of regime change in Iraq as a means of re-ordering the global political economy in line with Britain's 'national interests'. Facilitated by Britain's constitutional architecture, this policy was developed in an informal, secretive, and tightly controlled manner, involved persistent and ongoing attempts to regulate the flow of politically sensitive information, and utilised the supposed benefits of strong and decisive leadership as a means of shaping the course of political debate. Although the war was opposed by the majority of the British people, these measures not only helped to reduce scrutiny of the government's actions, but effectively enabled it to avoid the ultimate sanction of accountability itself.

Abbreviations

CIA	Central Intelligence Agency
CBW	Chemical and Biological Weapons
DIS	Defence Intelligence Staff
DOP	Ministerial Committee on Defence and Overseas Policy
ECGD	Export Credits Guarantee Department
EU	European Union
FAC	Foreign Affairs Committee
HCLC	House of Commons Liaison Committee
IAEA	International Atomic Energy Agency
ISC	Intelligence and Security Committee
ISG	Iraq Survey Group
JIC	Joint Intelligence Committee
MoD	Ministry of Defence
NATO	North Atlantic Treaty Organisation
PAC	Public Administration Committee
SCI	Senate Committee on Intelligence
THI	The Hutton Inquiry
UN	United Nations
UNMOVIC	United Nations Monitoring, Verification and Inspections Commission
WMD	Weapons of Mass Destruction

1
Introduction:
A Sign of the Times

A case of dirty politics?

In March 2003 Britain joined forces with the United States of America to launch an invasion of Iraq. The official aim in so doing was to rid Saddam Hussein of his weapons of mass destruction (WMD) and to help reduce the prospects of a devastating confluence between rogue states and the forces of international terrorism. The ramifications of this conflict, however, proved to be far wider than anyone could have predicted. Indeed, the events surrounding the war have since not only come to define the era of Tony Blair's premiership, but are now seen to demark one of the most tumultuous periods in Britain's entire political history. Amidst allegations that the country was misled over the reasons for going to war and that senior government figures wilfully misused intelligence in order to drag Britain into the conflict, and with question marks continuing to hang over the legality of the invasion, the government's decision to pursue a policy of regime change in Iraq has produced a corrosive loss of trust and a rising level of disenchantment with both the New Labour government and the domestic political process in general.

The broader effects of the war have also been nothing short of devastating. In financial terms alone, the costs of the invasion have reached extraordinary heights. By the end of August 2005, they had amounted to more than £3 billion for Britain and to more than $190 billion for the United States, enough to have funded anti-global hunger efforts for seven years, or to have immunised every child in the world for over six decades.[1] In more directly human terms, the cost of the war has also been staggering. In the thirty-one months since the invasion was launched, more than 2,000 US soldiers had lost their lives in the conflict, almost 100 British servicemen had been killed, and the civilian death toll had reached anything up to, and had perhaps even exceeded, 100,000.[2] In addition to this, the attempt to introduce a 'Western-style' liberal democracy into Iraq has also proved to be highly problematic. Despite a relatively successful parliamentary election, the process of drawing up a new constitution has posed an array of deeply entrenched political dilemmas for the new Iraqi state. With widespread concerns about the future role of Islamic law, with question marks about the extent of its commitment to upholding human, and especially women's rights, and with disputes raging over the structure of proposed federal arrangements (fiercely opposed by Iraq's Sunni minority on the grounds that this would lead to a loss of revenues to the oil-rich Kurdish and Shi'ite dominated regions), the future integrity, cohesion, and stability of the Iraqi nation itself remains far from certain.

The impact of the war upon the international political economy has been greatly damaging. In opening up a series of fissures within the world system, the invasion of Iraq has not only served to undermine the United Nations, to embitter relations between Europe and the United States, and to heighten antagonisms between the West and the Muslim world, but has also arguably increased the level of global instability and disorder that has characterised the twenty-first century thus far. Indeed, for all the efforts of a war ostensibly designed, at least in part, to deal with the dangers of international terrorism, the threat of terrorist activity itself appears to be undiminished. In July 2005, this was vividly demonstrated in London by a series of al-Qaeda–inspired bombings, the worst terrorist attacks ever to take place on the British mainland.

Yet insofar as Britain itself is concerned, whatever the events surrounding the invasion of Iraq might reveal about the behavioural shortcomings of a particular government, they are also indicative of a more general, and far deeper, malaise within its democratic system. Put simply, the fundamental issue to have emerged from the war is not that senior members of the New Labour establishment have managed to ride roughshod over the general will of the British public and have managed to subjugate the processes of the political system with impunity on a matter of such importance. The real issue, rather, is what this episode reveals about the nature of the political system itself—namely, that the enactment of the public will is not, and has never been, the purpose of the British polity. On the contrary, in many ways the British democratic system represents the very antithesis of such aims. Founded on intractably and deeply entrenched principles of centralisation, hierarchy, and elitism, this is characterised by a deep-seated adherence to a model of government marked by a strong

2

and relatively unfettered executive at the expense of a more responsive and participatory form of decision-making. What the events surrounding Britain's involvement in the Iraq war demonstrate, then, is not so much the failure of British democracy per se, as the enduring success of its elitist underpinnings. While the day-to-day ephemera of political life itself may be a dirty affair, the vitiated state of its foundations is far more deeply ingrained.

Analysing the war

Conventional accounts and explanations of Britain's participation in the Iraq war tend to revolve around two central themes. The first of these is that this was primarily the result of Britain's general subservience to the United States. In its standard format, this view contends that the New Labour government, and Tony Blair in particular, acted in varying degrees as 'poodles' to the neo-conservatives in Washington, fuelled by a post-9/11 desire to enforce regime change in Iraq as part of a broader mission to assert America's global hegemony. In effect, it is argued that senior government figures deliberately misled the country and Parliament about the threat posed by Iraq's weapons of mass destruction in order to demonstrate Britain's commitment to remaining the chief ally of the United States, and to provide the Bush regime with the political fig leaf of a coalition partner in its international misdemeanours.[3] In the second and contrary interpretation, it is argued that senior figures in the New Labour establishment (and, again, especially the Prime Minister) were genuinely and fervently convinced that the path to war with Iraq was the right way of dealing with the new global security threats deriving from the unholy trinity of WMD, rogue states, and international terrorism. While varying degrees of doubt also remain as to the extent to which the main actors involved may or may not have engaged in deceitful activities in order to strengthen the case for war, it is not therefore doubted that the underlying intentions in this regard were sincere, nor that their convictions were real.[4]

Beyond these contrasting interpretations, however, analyses of Britain's participation in the Iraq conflict are broadly convergent on the issue of its domestic political impact. Generically, the various machinations through which the government's Iraq policy was developed and carried out are seen to provide a form of 'barium meal', neatly exposing and illuminating the various flaws, shortcomings, and weaknesses that exist within the British system of democracy. In turn, such an analysis leads to the conclusion that the way to revitalise and reinvigorate democracy in Britain is through a medicinal series of reforms designed to strengthen the powers of Parliament, and to temper the dominance of the executive branch.[5]

While such analyses are undoubtedly both important and insightful, these interpretations of Britain's involvement in the Iraq war are nevertheless problematic. Primarily, this is due to the overly privileged role that is accorded the individual actors who were involved in driving the project forward. This has led to explanatory accounts being constructed on the basis of the assumed intentions, values, beliefs, and personalities of Tony Blair, George W. Bush, and their respective aides. While these accounts acknowledge that such individuals did not have a completely free hand to do as they would like, the formative context within which the decision to go to war was made is nevertheless thought to have been comprised of essentially contingent and subjective factors, including the desires of the Bush administration, the views and the relative flammability of the Labour backbenches, the attitude of ministerial colleagues and special advisors, the worldview of Tony Blair himself, and the more general state of domestic public opinion. Although these are all clearly important to any analysis of the conflict, the main problem with such an actor-based approach is that this ultimately tends to produce a descriptive account of events which has little or no consideration for the broader structural context in which these key actors were themselves situated, nor of the way in which this affected their respective views, proclivities, and political behaviour.

In contrast, the argument of this book is that the development of the Iraq policy was fundamentally conditioned by the underlying structural architecture of the British political system. This is based on a series of deeply entrenched norms and values pertaining to a centralised, hierarchical, and elitist style of government, producing a model of democracy characterised by the apotheosis of strong and decisive leadership, by a limited notion of representation, and by a relative paucity of effective checks and balances on the use of executive power. In turn, these ideational and institutional contours have exerted a key formative impact upon the emergence and development of New Labour. Fuelled by the experience of operating from within the confines of the British political system, and especially by the repeated electoral failures between 1979 and 1992, senior party figures became convinced that success could only be ensured through a process of internal restructuring designed to establish conformity with its elitist principles. Following an intensive process of reform, by May 1997 the Labour party was now fully equipped and willing to capitalise on the centralised and relatively unfettered nature of power within the British state. The stage was set, then, for these behavioural norms and values to be elevated to an entirely new level.

This has been reflected in both the style and the substance of New Labour's governing strategy. In essence, this has sought to enhance Britain's position within the international political economy, to sustain the government in power, and to maintain a sufficient degree of operational freedom for members of the core executive. New Labour's domestic strategy has been based on a neo-liberal economic programme embedded within a support mechanism of 'depoliticisation', accompanied by a strong emphasis on internal party discipline, centralised decision-making, and an ongoing programme of media management designed to regulate the flow of politically sensitive information. In its external dimension, New Labour's strategy has focused on the promotion of international free markets, the provision of diplomatic and military support to key allies, and an attempt to position Britain as a 'transatlantic bridge' between Europe and America. This has been coupled with an interventionist foreign policy designed to align the contours of the world order with those of Britain's geo-strategic interests and to project British power and influence across the international stage.

The analysis of New Labour's Iraq policy thus needs to be considered in relation to the broader aims and objectives of this governing strategy. Doing so opens the way for a somewhat contrasting view of these developments. This shows, first, that senior government figures, and Tony Blair in particular, did not act out of their subservience to the United States, but were in favour of regime change in Iraq prior to the rise of the Bush administration; and, second, that the policy was not simply motivated by a desire to address the issues of rogue states, terrorism, and WMD, but was focused on the broader foreign policy goals of shaping the global political economy with a view to enhancing Britain's international position. Moreover, at each and every stage during the course of events, the underlying principles of centralisation, hierarchy, and elitism were clearly discernible in their impact, both in facilitating the development of the Iraq policy through the structural dynamics of the British state and through their utility for the governing authorities as an effective means of justifying their actions.

Argument and format

That the New Labour government was keen to adopt an assertive foreign policy was evident from the outset. While the prospect of pursuing an

5

increasingly hard line against Iraq (including support for regime change) was forestalled only by a lack of political and legal abutments, the government's interventionist stance was progressively entrenched by a series of military campaigns. This involved four days of air strikes against Iraq in December 1998, an ostensibly humanitarian crusade against Yugoslavia in 1999, and an equally progressive skirmish in Sierra Leone the following year. With the rise of the neo-conservative Bush administration, however, and particularly following the terrorist attacks of 11 September 2001, the issue of Iraq was catapulted up the political agenda. This now presented Washington with the opportunity to pursue a 'new-imperialist' strategy designed to enforce the global pre-eminence of the United States, and presented senior figures in the New Labour hierarchy with the political space required to pursue a tougher line against Saddam Hussein. Buttressed by further military action in Afghanistan, a key aim in deposing the Iraqi regime was that this would establish the credibility of core Western powers in the 'war on terror', would deter any potential transgressors from stepping out of line, and, through the associated spread of 'freedom' and 'democracy', would help to establish and maintain an international order more attuned to the interests of the world's main capitalist nations.

Having apparently agreed to support this policy of regime change during discussions with George W. Bush in the spring of 2002, Tony Blair and a small band of officials readily set about devising a strategy to create the political and legal conditions required to justify military action. This involved a focus on the issue of WMD, the use of the United Nations (UN) as both a cover and a trap for the ensuing manoeuvres, and a sustained propaganda campaign based around a deliberate hyping of the threat posed by Iraq in order to convince domestic and international opinion of the need for firmer measures. Central to this was the production of the now-infamous 'September dossier', which revealed a pattern of unduly close relations between the intelligence services and New Labour officials, and which provided the main source for the controversy surrounding the government's use of intelligence material. Throughout this time, neither the Cabinet, Parliament, nor the general public had any knowledge of, or influence over, the underlying developments that were now driving the policy forward.

Indeed, while international support was now mobilised behind a UN resolution authorising a renewed programme of weapons inspections, domestic opinion remained largely reticent about the government's motives. In response, Downing Street's inner circle began to place a growing emphasis on the humanitarian imperatives for military action, highlighting the apparent benefits of strong and decisive leadership in a concerted attempt to make a virtue out of what was now the Prime Minister's increasingly well-worn vice. With tensions rising inside the UN Security Council, New Labour officials also turned their hand to misrepresenting the position of the French government in order to establish a reliable scapegoat for the impending failure to secure explicit UN approval for the use of military power. This was also accompanied by a controversial strengthening of the Attorney-General's legal advice on the use of force and by an intensive deployment of internal party discipline in order to persuade Parliament to endorse the decision to go to war in spite of large-scale public opposition.

Although the immediate conflict was over relatively quickly, political difficulties over the failure to discover weapons of mass destruction in Iraq led to the adoption of an equally intensive postwar management strategy. At the centre of this was a concerted attempt to frame the political debate by misrepresenting allegations being reported by the BBC journalist Andrew Gilligan concerning unease within the intelligence community about the government's use of classified material in the run-up to the Iraq war. This was accompanied by a strong desire to ensure that the identity of the source for the BBC's story, Dr David Kelly, made its way into the public domain. Since it was felt in official circles that Gilligan had misrepresented Dr Kelly's views, this disclosure would enable the government to effectively discredit the BBC's allegations, and would thus exonerate the government from having deliberately misused intelligence in order to strengthen the case for military action.

Also central to this postwar strategy was an ongoing attempt to constrict any open investigation into the political circumstances behind the invasion of Iraq. An inquiry into the decision to go to war by the Foreign Affairs Committee (FAC) was denied access to whole swathes of official information which, in contrast, the centrally appointed and secretive Intelligence and Security Committee (ISC) was permitted to examine in the hope that this would lead to it clearing the government of misusing intelligence. In a similar fashion, the subsequent Hutton and Butler inquiries were also constrained within tight terms of reference designed to avoid any examination of the political context behind the decision to go to war. In so doing, the New Labour executive was able to shape the course of political debate and to undermine the ability of Parliament and the wider public to effectively scrutinise its actions.

Following the publication of the Butler Report, the government embarked on an intensive drive to redirect the political agenda back onto domestic issues and to promote the advantages of a strong and decisive executive. The results, however, were less than convincing. Yet even with the issue of Iraq refusing to leave the headlines, and with questions over the Prime Minister's conduct continuing to bedevil Downing Street, widespread public hostility towards the government was sufficiently contained for New Labour to secure a third consecutive victory in the general election of May 2005. Having achieved this with the support of little more than a fifth of the British electorate, though, the sound of success rang distinctly hollow.

And so too, it would seem, ring hopes for a programme of meaningful political reform. Given the enduring nature of the underlying norms and values encased within the British political system, it seems highly unlikely that the kind of reform agenda being promoted by many observers would lead to the kind of radical and extensive changes that would be required in order to establish a fully responsive and accountable form of democratic governance. Rather, since any changes would necessarily be developed from within the confines of the political system itself, it is highly likely that these would be effectively constrained and diluted by the various pressures that this creates. The result, in effect, would be to treat the symptoms rather than the deep-rooted causes that so ail British democracy, while leaving the underlying norms and values of the political system itself untouched. While measures to strengthen Parliament would be an undeniable improvement upon the present state of affairs, such a step would not of itself dissolve the essentially paternalistic ethos which pervades Britain's governing system, and would not automatically lead to a more representative and participatory form of policy-making. While such a pessimistic conclusion may not come to pass, such negativism nevertheless seems strangely suited to the days in which we live. That this is so at the dawn of the twenty-first century is indeed a sign of the times.

The format of this book is as follows: Chapter Two details the underlying structures of British democracy, and examines the way in which this has conditioned the emergence of New Labour's governing strategy. In Chapter Three, the background context of the Iraq issue itself is examined. This chapter charts the interrelated themes of the emergence of the Iraqi threat from the 1980s, the development of New Labour's foreign policy, and the rise of the neo-conservative Bush administration in the United

States. In Chapters Four and Five, the analysis focuses on the course of events from the aftermath of 9/11 through to the parliamentary decision to endorse the invasion of Iraq in March 2003. The central theme is the development both of the policy of regime change and of the accompanying strategy to establish legal and political cover for this move by emphasising the issue of Iraq's WMD, by seeking to deal with the issue through the United Nations, and by pursuing a concerted propaganda campaign designed to persuade international and domestic opinion of the need for firmer action against Saddam Hussein. In Chapter Six, the analysis deals with the government's strategy for managing the postwar situation by attempting to discredit the allegations being reported by the BBC through the public disclosure of Dr Kelly's identity. Chapter Seven covers the subsequent events ranging from the publication of the Hutton Report through to the terrorist attacks of July 2005. It examines the government's ongoing efforts to shape the course of political debate and to direct attention back towards a domestic agenda amidst persistent controversy over the events surrounding the Iraq war. In the final chapter, the significance of this policy episode for both the nature and the future of British democracy is drawn.

2

The Democratic Consequences of New Labour

The institutions and processes of the British political system are conditioned by the underlying principles of centralisation, hierarchy, and elitism. These pertain to a model of democracy characterised by the virtues of strong and decisive government, by a limited notion of representation, and by a relative paucity of checks and balances on the use of executive power. Having been forced to conform to these principles in order to gain electoral success, the Labour party in office has since amplified them to new commanding heights. The result has been the adoption of a governing strategy based on a framework of neo-liberal economics, intensive media management, highly centralised decision-making, and rigorous internal party discipline. Externally, these themes have been reflected in the pursuit of an interventionist foreign policy set within a transatlantic framework, designed to project British power and influence across the world stage.

The British political tradition

The endurance of the British political system cannot be doubted. In circumstances in which others have been swept away by the tides of war, folly, and revolution, the central institutions of the British state have stood as pillars of continuity, pitched upon their island home amid the unremitting seas of change. Frequently cited, though no less accurate for that, it is perhaps this gradualist and evolutionary character of the British polity that more than anything else has served to mark it out among its number. While stasis for its own sake does not rule, it is through the prism of stasis, as a rule, that the political life of the nation is reflected.

Traditional analyses of the British political system, however, suffer from two main deficiencies. The first of these is the disaggregated and fragmented manner in which the subject has often been approached. Focusing on the various individual components of the system themselves, such as the role of the Prime Minister, the inner workings of Parliament, the electoral system, and so on, most studies in this area have sought to expand knowledge of such matters as topics in their own right, as opposed to viewing them in a holistic manner as integral parts of a unified whole. Useful though such analyses are, this dislocation thus militates against an understanding of the systemic interconnections that exist between these various components. In turn, this precludes a broader examination of the way in which the institutional structure of the British political system conditions and influences the actions of those who operate within it.[1]

Conversely, although there are some notable exceptions to this general trend, more holistic accounts of the British political system are also subject to various difficulties. One of the most significant of these is that its institutional structure is frequently treated as a simple agglomeration of its constituent parts. Although this enables the various mechanics of the system to be discerned in much the same way that one might draw up a series of technical blueprints, the central weakness of this approach is that it remains overly descriptive and affords scant consideration to the crucial role of ideational factors in both the construction and the operation of the system itself. However, since it is the ideas and perceptions held by actors about their situational environment which form the basis for, and which thereby mediate, their political behaviour, this analytical gap also precludes a fuller understanding of the way in which the British system operates. Further still, where holistic analyses have sought to incorporate ideational elements, these have tended to present the norms and values which underpin the system as having largely derived from, and as therefore being in harmony with, the political culture of the British nation itself. In essence, this offers a predominantly static and idealised interpretation of Britain's political development, with no recognition of any challenges that may have emerged from alternative beliefs, and with no explanation as to how such challenges have been contained.[2]

Indeed, contrary to their own self-image, political institutions are by no means neutral or objective. Given that they are the product of human agency, their configuration will invariably embody certain assumptions about the range and type of tasks that are thought necessary to be performed, as well as the particular way in which they are to be undertaken. These ideational underpinnings, manifest in the various rules, procedures, and lines of authority contained within the institutional structure, thus imbue it with a form of strategic or selective bias. While not predetermining any specific outcome, this will thus serve to privilege certain types of practices, ideas, and interests over others, and will thereby also condition the kind of strategies that are employed by political actors as they seek to pursue their aims. This bias is made all the more pervasive by the way in which institutional structures also act to shape the self-identities of agents themselves. As actors don particular labels and assume particular roles such as 'backbencher', 'minister', 'Prime Minister', and so on during the course of their daily life, they do so replete with all the appellative norms, values, and behavioural expectations that accompany such titles. Although this does not, of course, mean that all agents performing the same role will act in precisely the same way, the result, nevertheless, is to further influence the various self-interests that are perceived, as well as the range of strategies that will be deemed suitable for their pursuit.

In turn, while these strategic activities will impinge upon and modify the institutional environment over time, given that the most successful strategies are likely to be those which conform to its dominant norms and modes of behaviour, this selective bias will also exert a strong gravitational pull on its overall pattern of development. Although the interjection of unforeseen and contingent factors will undoubtedly play a role, and although the possibility of radical transformations cannot be discounted, the underlying tendency will therefore be towards a developmental trajectory that reproduces the dominant norms and values on which the political system is based.[3]

The dominant ideas and behavioural modes which underpin the British political system pertain to a distinctive political tradition based around a centralised, hierarchical, and elitist form of governance. This is characterised by a concentration of executive power and authority, supported by relatively weak mechanisms for enforcing scrutiny and accountability, by a limited notion of representation, and by an emphasis on the virtues of 'strong', 'decisive', and 'responsible' leadership. Over the centuries, these ideational rivulets have carved deep institutional grooves into Britain's political landscape. Indeed, one of the main reasons for the endurance of elitist government in Britain is the historical continuity of its political institutions. While many of Britain's liberal-democratic relatives have endured periods of sharp dislocation and an enforced wholesale reordering of their political structures, the constitutional architecture of Britain has thus far managed to avoid any far-reaching and fundamental redesign.[4]

The result is that the core components of the British political system have remained substantially intact since the pre-democratic era, effectively entombing its dominant norms and values, and enabling them to endure the passage of time with only superficial modification. While the evolution of the British political system has, at times, been far from the model of harmony and consensus that is sometimes portrayed, challenges to the prevailing order have been successfully negotiated by the governing authorities through a judicious mix of suppression and careful accommodation. Their success in this has effectively served to neutralise any radical impulses, and has allowed the old structures of power and authority to survive relatively unscathed to the present day.

The origins of elitism

In broad terms, the origins of the British political system can be usefully traced back to the Norman conquest of the eleventh century. This produced a unified system of territorial government and administration, a common language, and a centralisation of power and authority in the hands of the reigning monarch. Buttressed by the ideological doctrine of the 'divine right of kings', this personalised notion of sovereignty was diluted only by the right of Parliament, as formalised in the Magna Carta of 1215, to be consulted on certain high matters of state, such as the raising of taxation for the purposes of war. The determination of policy was, quite literally, the prerogative of the reigning monarch, and the role of Parliament was, for the most part, simply to act as a rubber-stamp for royal decisions. Although tensions between the Crown and Parliament were relatively well contained over the next few centuries, the underlying antagonisms resulting from the monarch's financial dependence upon his or her wealthier subjects sharpened considerably during the seventeenth century. Following an ill-starred combination of severe economic depression and an unpopular attempt by Charles I to raise taxes for the pursuit of military endeavours in Europe, a long and bloody civil war descended upon the kingdom, culminating in a royal execution and in the establishment of a parliamentary republic under the dictatorship of Oliver Cromwell. Accompanying this regicidal turn, the emergence of radical pressures for a more egalitarian and participatory form of governance, fronted by groups such as the Diggers and the Levellers, also attracted a severe response from the state. In this case, the threat posed to the newly ascendant interests of the parliamentary elite was firmly and decisively

13

dissipated by a campaign of brutal suppression initiated on the grounds of enforcing social and political order.[5]

Following a brief restoration of the monarchy and an attempt by James II to re-establish the doctrine of absolutism after Cromwell's death, the ongoing struggle between the Crown and Parliament was resolved in favour of the latter during the Glorious Revolution of 1688. But even so, the outcome resembled an accommodation more than it did a full-scale dethroning of the *ancien régime*. While the power and authority of the monarchy itself had now been transferred to Parliament, the reality was that political control had now effectively passed to the landowning aris-tocracy, whose dominance of Parliament was buttressed by a highly restrictive franchise and by a widespread belief in the immutable nature of social hierarchy. At the apex of this, naturally, stood those whose wealth and refinement made them perfectly suited to the grand purpose of ruling a nation.

Importantly, then, despite a shift in the perceived role of Parliament from being a forum to represent the respective territorial interests of the kingdom to one whose overriding duty was to advance the 'national interest', or the 'common good', the new constitutional order dutifully continued to uphold the independence of government and its primacy in determining policy. In 1774 this was given its popular and ideological coherence by Edmund Burke, who insisted that Members of Parliament should not be bound to merely reproduce the views of their constituents in a delegatory fashion, or to be thus responsive to the popular whims of the day, but that they instead needed to be autonomous and free to act in accordance with their own views and consciences. The main reason for this, claimed Burke, was that the government required a certain freedom of manoeuvre in order to be able to perform effectively and to be able to take and implement the difficult and unpopular decisions that would invariably be needed to protect the interests of the nation.

While relatively stable, these 'harmonious' constitutional arrangements eventually came under increasing pressure during the nineteenth century. Revolutionary forces unleashed by France and America, huge social changes wrought by industrialisation, a progressive decline in the power of the landed aristocracy vis-à-vis that of the rising bourgeoisie, and an accom-panying growth in the popularity of liberal ideas concerning the political and economic organisation of the country all gave renewed impetus to calls for a more open and democratic political system. The response from the governing authorities, however, was one of both coercion and concession.

14

While more radical elements such as the Chartists and the early forerun-
ners of the trade union movement were now subjected to a policy of sustained repression, the franchise itself was gradually widened in the hope of
weakening any pressures for more radical political change. This culminated
in the advent of universal adult suffrage, marking Britain's emergence as a
fully liberal democratic state in the decade after the First World War.

Yet despite this, the emergence of mass democracy in Britain did not
lead to a wholesale transformation in its system of government. Rather, by
successfully absorbing the more moderate thrust of the democratic challenge, and by effectively marginalizing its radical impulses, successive
British governments worked to sustain the pre-existing structures of power
and authority, as well as the ideological norms, values, and practices
embedded within the British political system. Indeed, these were further
enhanced by the prevailing beliefs and actions of the newly ascendant
liberals themselves. Despite proclaiming a commitment to universal equal-
ity under the rule of law, nineteenth-century liberal thought also upheld a
hierarchical conception of society in which the chief determinant of ruling
ability was now the ownership of private property. Moreover, since it was
now possible for this natural order of things to be subverted through the
ballot box, liberals also remained keen to uphold the traditional and
limited Burkean notion of representation and to safeguard the autonomy
of the government against potential encroachment from the electorate.
Although the expansion of the franchise marked a discernible shift towards
the notion of 'the people' as the proper basis for democratic representation, the overwhelming majority of liberals thus continued to adhere to the
underlying practices and conventions of Parliament as the sole site and
repository of legitimate political action. In so doing, the primacy of executive independence in determining and implementing those policies
deemed best suited to further the 'national interest' remained firmly
intact.

Structure and strategy

Britain's historically conditioned political system is made up of several
interlocking components. Conventionally, these are thought to combine in
a distinctly Panglossian way, matching the advantages of strong, decisive,
and responsible government with clear lines of accountability in order to
provide the British people with the best of all possible polities. Free, fair,
and regular elections to Parliament ensure that the will of the British

people is openly expressed and represented; the use of the 'first-past-the-post' (or simple plurality) electoral system serves to produce a single-party majority government with both the mandate and the capacity to govern effectively; the prevailing two-party system sustains an institutionalised opposition and offers voters an alternative choice of government; and the doctrines of ministerial and collective responsibility ensure that members of the executive are held accountable to Parliament, and thence to the British people themselves. All this, too, is set within the overarching framework of an uncodified constitution, enabling an adaptive and a pragmatic, rather than an ideologically dogmatic, response to any adverse circumstances that may arise.[6]

The reality behind this institutional idyll, however, is altogether different. In contrast to its idealised self-image, in practice the British political system combines the worst elements of supreme executive power with a relative paucity of effective checks and balances on its use. Members of the executive are subject to few formalised mechanisms of regulation and are effectively constrained in their activities only by the informal conventions of Parliament, by the pressures of internal party politics, by the effectiveness of the opposition parties, and, given the need to secure re-election, by the broad state of public opinion more generally. Despite draping itself in all the refinement of democracy, the self-proclaimed 'Mother of all Parliaments' is notably lacking on matters of substance.

One of the main cornerstones of Britain's political arrangements is the first-past-the-post system of voting in Westminster elections. A system that is shunned by practically every other nation calling itself a democracy, first-past-the-post is virtually guaranteed to bestow a majority of seats in the House of Commons upon one political party, to effectively disenfranchise large swathes of the population through the phenomena of wasted votes and safe seats, and to produce grossly disproportionate and unrepresentative outcomes. While no government since the 1930s has managed to secure more than 50% of the vote in a general election, the electoral scorecard since 1945 has bestowed an average majority upon the ruling party of seventy-six, or some 55% of the seats, with an average of just 44% of the vote. Once the level of turnout itself is taken into consideration, the Westminster electoral system has, for the most part, returned British governments to power with an average support of less than a third (32.6%) of the entire electorate.[7]

Once a party has secured a comfortable majority in the House of Commons, the ensuing reign of its executive is generally unrivalled within

16

the liberal-democratic fold. Of the available mechanisms for scrutinising the executive and for holding its members to account, the process of parliamentary questioning remains limited by the constraints of time and by the executive's tight control of official information, while the effectiveness of parliamentary select committees is also curtailed by their composition along party lines, by their inability to scrutinise either ministers or senior civil servants without government permission, by their lack of power to compel the disclosure of 'sensitive' information, and by their limited means of sanction, which are restricted to the mere issuance of a report which may or may not be raised for debate in Parliament. In addition to this, parliamentary debates and votes themselves are also tightly constrained by the all-pervasive strictures of party discipline. Since most MPs are dependent on the support of their party for a successful career on the greasy pole, and since failure to abide by the wishes of the leadership can result in a loss of promotional opportunities or even political excommunication, the result is to create mass ranks of MPs who are little more than docile lobby-fodder for their respective oligarchies. While periodic backbench revolts can complicate the executive management of Parliament, more often than not the effect is to create the impression of parliamentary power while leaving the underlying reality of executive dominance unchecked.

Indeed, the pressures of strong party discipline are themselves derived from the structural characteristics and behavioural norms of the British political system. Since parliamentary convention dictates that its business be undertaken in a combative and combustible atmosphere, since the effectiveness of a political party is dependent upon its ability to muster sufficient parliamentary troops either in support of or in opposition to legislation put forward by the executive, and since the parameters of political discourse in Britain (and especially within the Whitehall village) are similarly dominated by the perceived virtues of strong, decisive, and responsible government, it remains a reliable rule of political thumb that undisciplined and disunited parties are not only ineffectual, but also suffer for their sins at the ballot box.

Further still, the centralising aspects of the British political system also course throughout the executive itself. Belying the constitutional niceties of Bagehot, the machinations of the Cabinet remain subject to the extensive powers of the Prime Minister, who, in his or her role as head of the executive, effectively stands as a latter-day monarch at the apex of the British state. While the precise nature of the Prime Minister's control remains

conditional upon the ongoing support of his or her Westminster colleagues, and especially those within the Cabinet, the lack of a formalised
constitution and the ability to exercise key powers under the royal prerogative together give a wide degree of latitude to the holder of the position.
This enables the incumbent, *inter alia*, to appoint and dismiss ministers, to
make appointments to the senior civil service, the House of Lords and
committees of inquiry, to direct the operation, agenda, and discussions of
the Cabinet itself, to endorse international treaties and agreements (subject
to few, if any, parliamentary constraints), to deploy and direct the British
armed forces, and to determine the date of the next general election,
subject to a maximum five-year period.

Yet despite this centralisation of power and authority in the hands of the
executive branch, the process of state management itself remains difficult
and contentious. One key source of tension stems from the need for the
governing authorities to maintain an image of democratic integrity in
order to preserve the political legitimacy, and hence the continued viability, of their rule. This, however, exposes the government to the demands
and expectations of the domestic populace and gives rise to competing
views as to what constitutes the 'national interest' at any given time.
Although the initiation of policies designed to promote the national good
remains the prerogative of the executive, the 'national interest' itself cannot,
in an ostensibly democratic polity, be defined without recourse to the
broader attitudes, desires, and opinions of the British Parliament and its
electorate. While this does not mean that the government is obliged to
simply reflect or to abide by the caprice of the masses, these pressures do
at least oblige it to construct a policy programme that appears to be
sufficiently compatible with both the desires of the central executive and
the demands of public and parliamentary opinion.

On a broader level, the constraints imposed on Britain's governing
authorities by the internal architecture of the state are also conditioned by
a variety of international factors. These include Britain's membership of
supranational organisations such as the European Union and the United
Nations, its commitment to abide by treaties such as the Geneva Convention and the Kyoto protocol, and its pattern of multilateral alliances,
including NATO and the 'special' relationship with the United States.
More generally, since the authority and credibility of the government also
depend upon the provision of economic prosperity and political stability,
state managers are compelled to try and acquire the best possible position
for the state within the global political economy. While this puts pressure on

the government to maintain and improve the competitiveness and dynamism of the domestic economy as a site for capital expansion, it also involves the use of measures to shape the contours of the world system as a whole, in order to promote Britain's national interests on the international stage.

To assist them in these various tasks, key state managers can be usefully said to devise a political, or a governing, strategy. This will identify the central challenges that are faced at any one time and will provide a more or less coherent means of dealing with them rooted in the state managers' perception of the domestic and international context in which they are operating.[8] The development of such a strategy will also be conditioned by an assessment of the relative successes and failures of previous strategies, will be adapted as circumstances change, and may prove overall to be a fractious affair. Not all members of the executive may be in full agreement as to its content, or even involved in its formulation, and the final result may itself provide an uneasy mixture of contradictory policies and competing ambitions. Nevertheless, an emergent strategy will necessarily comprise both internal and external policy measures designed, in essence, to merge the two key subjective goals of gaining both freedom of manoeuvre and re-election to high office with the more objective concerns of augmenting Britain's relative position within the global political and economic system.

The rise of New Labour

The emergence and development of New Labour since the mid-1990s has been fundamentally conditioned by the dynamics of the British political system. Following a quartet of consecutive election defeats at the hands of the Conservative party, in 1994 key figures in the Labour party, by then under the tutelage of Tony Blair, determined that the key reasons for this failure stemmed from a lack of firm leadership and internal discipline, coupled with the pursuit of unpopular and impractical policies that had been persistently foisted upon the party by its immoderate left-wing elements. Given the selective bias of the British political system towards well-ordered, hierarchical, and centrally managed parties, these factors were thought to have alienated crucial sections of the electorate (most notably the voters of Middle England), to have created internal splits and dissonance, and to have therefore undermined the credibility of the party as an effective governing force. On the basis of this analysis, a small coterie of senior party officials based around Tony Blair, Gordon Brown (the shadow Chancellor), Peter Mandelson (the party's Campaign and Communications Director), Alastair Campbell (Blair's press spokesman), and Phillip Gould (his opinion-poll advisor) embarked on a mission, known as 'the project', to transform the party into a ruthless electoral machine. This was based upon three main components: a policy shift to what was now considered to be the centre ground of British politics, an unyielding emphasis on the need for constant media management, and the establishment of strong, centralised party discipline and control.

Building on the reform process that had been initiated by Neil Kinnock during the mid-1980s, the first of these aspects involved charting a political course back towards the centre ground in an attempt to construct a broad-based appeal and to re-establish the credibility of the party as being 'fit to govern'. In domestic terms, this political strategy has entailed a fundamental rejection of old-style Keynesian social democracy and the devout acceptance of a fervently neo-liberal framework in an attempt to minimise the direct involvement of the state in economic affairs, and to expose the British economy to the competitive disciplines of the free market. Behind the softening rhetoric of the Third Way, with its discourse of inclusiveness and socially progressive politics, the core elements of the Thatcherite project have been extended and entrenched by the New Labour government. This extension has included a progressively larger role for the private sector in public-service provision, an unremitting emphasis on the need for 'prudent' financial management, an ongoing process of public-sector and welfare-state modernisation, and the maintenance of trade union reforms designed to provide the most lightly regulated labour market in the Western world. All of this, too, has been undertaken against a backdrop of widening social disparities, including some of the highest levels of poverty and inequality seen anywhere within the European Union.[9]

To further strengthen its neo-liberal credentials and to further enhance the power and autonomy of the centre, New Labour has successfully embedded its commitment to the free market within a support mechanism of 'depoliticisation'. This includes the operational independence of the Bank of England, a series of self-imposed fiscal rules designed to constrain the level of public debt, and a strident emphasis on the constraints imposed by the processes of globalisation and EU membership, both of which have been presented as external imperatives to which the British state must adjust or perish. In this way, by distancing the government from key economic decisions, and by presenting this disengagement as a prerequisite for macroeconomic stability, efficiency, and long-term growth,

New Labour's political strategy has served to reduce the accountability of the governing authorities for potentially contentious issues and has further insulated the executive from the pressures of public opinion.[10]

Accompanying the emphasis on free-market economics, the second component of New Labour's political strategy has involved the deeply ingrained use of media-management techniques as a way of effectively promulgating the party message, managing public opinion, and controlling the political agenda. Initially deriving from methods employed by the US Democrats during the successful Clinton campaign of 1992, this media management has included the almost-routine use of leaks, briefings, and spin, a strong focus on the presentational aspects of government policy, and the transformation of party conferences, so long the bastion of left-wing dissent, into stage-managed events designed specifically for media consumption. Alongside this, an unrelenting emphasis on the need for strict party discipline also helps to convey the impression of unity and a sense of political purpose. This involves putting intense pressure on MPs to propagate the party line at every opportunity, as well as the regulation of ministerial output through the central channels of Downing Street. In the Ministerial Code adopted just two months after the 1997 general election, ministers were warned that the 'policy content' of speeches and media interviews, 'the timing and form of announcements' and any 'new policy initiatives' would all need to be cleared through the Number 10 press office, controlled by Alastair Campbell.[11]

Aligned with this emphasis on media management has been a correspondingly high reliance on special advisors. These constitutional hybrids, resembling a centaur-like mix of civil servants and overt political activists, have practically doubled in number since New Labour came to power in 1997, with around half operating within the central organs of Number 10 and the Treasury. Widespread concerns that this influx has led to a politicisation of Britain's traditionally 'neutral' civil service—an anxiety heightened by the government's persistent refusal to specifically delineate the role of special advisors in a Civil Service Act—have also been matched by concerns about their apparent lack of accountability. Although special advisors perform a directly political function for the government, their appointment nonetheless remains beyond the investigatory purview of the House of Commons. This was perfectly encapsulated within forty-eight hours of the 1997 election victory by the use of the Crown's prerogative powers to create entirely new roles for Alastair Campbell and Jonathon Powell (Blair's Chief of Staff), and to bestow upon them wide-ranging powers, including, in Campbell's case, the ability to issue direct orders to civil servants.[12]

In a further corollary of New Labour's authoritarian tendencies, the third element of its political strategy has been founded on a perceived need to firmly centralise control within both the party and the government itself. To this end, the power of the trade unions has been progressively eroded, and the policy-making roles of the annual conference and the National Executive Committee have been formally reduced, while the influence of the Prime Minister's Office has steadily grown to match Blair's presidential style of rule. Reflecting this, the power and status of the Cabinet, too, have been correspondingly diminished. Ministerial opposition to the Prime Minister is frequently discounted and major policy decisions, such as Bank of England independence, the construction of the Millennium Dome, the now-abandoned referendum on the European constitution, and the development of the Iraq policy, are frequently made without any substantive ministerial discussion. Notwithstanding the peculiar schism between Tony Blair and Gordon Brown, which saw the latter secure broad swathes of independence over economic affairs in return for conceding the party leadership under the terms of the 1994 'Granita deal',[13] key executive influence has now congealed around the Prime Minister and a close-knit cabal of trusted aides, producing an informal, 'sofa style' of government that effectively reduces the Cabinet to a mere forum for ratifying decisions that have already been made.[14]

This presidential style, in conjunction with New Labour's numerical dominance in the House of Commons, has also led to a corresponding diminution in the power of Parliament itself. Proposals to strengthen its scrutinising capabilities, such as removing the control of the whip over select committee appointments and providing set time in Parliament for the discussion of committee reports, have been rejected, policy announcements have been almost systematically made via their trailing in the media, and the effectiveness of party discipline, buttressed by Blair's repeated strategy of transforming key votes into measures of confidence in his leadership, has enabled the government to push through a range of controversial legislation such as foundation hospitals, top-up fees, the war in Iraq, and identity cards, despite widespread hostility and fierce opposition from within the party. Indeed, the Prime Minister's own disregard for Parliament is perfectly demonstrated by his voting record in the House of Commons itself, which, at just 5% of all votes, is far and away the lowest for any premier since the early eighteenth century.[15]

Despite assurances that New Labour would 'seek to decentralise and make accountable the institutions of political power in Britain', the power of central government has also been essentially untouched by the apparent democratisation of New Labour's constitutional reforms.[16] While devolution has undoubtedly improved democratic governance in Scotland and Wales, the key executive powers of state remain firmly held at Westminster; the Human Rights Act contains no provision for ensuring that legislation incompatible with the European Convention on Human Rights is actually overturned; the process of House of Lords reform has (at least transitionally) turned the upper chamber into an appointed appendage of the executive; and hopes of a meaningful Freedom of Information Act have been dashed by its wide series of exemptions, which include Cabinet records and ministerial correspondence, policy-making decisions, and anything that is deemed to be prejudicial to 'the effective conduct of public affairs'. Further still, despite the persistent support of two-thirds of the British people, a promised referendum on reforming the first-past-the-post system for Westminster elections has also fallen by the wayside, due primarily to the huge benefits that now accrue to New Labour, given the present geographical composition of the electorate.[17]

Britain in the world

The ideational and institutional contours of the British political system have also conditioned the external dimension of New Labour's governing strategy. While the domestic component has sought to augment the power and autonomy of the executive and to augment Britain's international position through a combination of a free-market agenda, a strategy of media manipulation, and the rigorous enforcement of centralised political control, the external component has also sought to utilise these methods as part of an attempt to project British power and influence onto the world stage. Dramatic changes to the global political and economic landscape over the last fifteen years, however, have increased the complexity of this task. Central to this has been the implosion of the Soviet bloc from 1989, which has transformed the United States into the world's sole remaining superpower, and which has led to the collapse of the bipolar world order that had framed international relations since the 1950s. The ending of the Cold War has also led to a reversal of fortunes for many former Soviet and American client states, most notably those in Central Asia, North Africa, and the Middle East, whose loss of strategic importance now signalled the end of their superpower sponsorship. Cut loose to fend for themselves, lacking robust political and economic structures, and faced with a preponderance of social turmoil, poverty, and ethnic and religious tensions, much of this ex-clientele began to degenerate into 'failed' or 'rogue' states. The result has been to create a range of unstable and disorderly 'frontier zones' within the global political economy. This has posed new dangers to the stability of core zones within the world system, either directly—through illegal flows of people, drugs, money, and weapons—or indirectly—through their effects on regional and global stability and security.[18]

Further changes to the global political economy have made the management of this problem increasingly difficult. On the one hand, the geographical expansion and growing competitiveness of the world economy itself imposes strong financial pressures on nation states, forcing them to engage ever more intently on elevating their global position while making them wary of becoming involved with large, costly, and potentially open-ended foreign enterprises. On the other hand, the expansion of international media coverage facilitated by huge advances in communications technology has also forced nations to pay greater attention to the management of domestic public opinion, especially when issues of war and peace are involved. The combined effect of these pressures has been to provoke the core capitalist nations of the West, and especially the United States, into adopting new forms of imperialist strategies for dealing with the challenges of the new frontier.

In contrast to old-style imperialism, in which colonising powers sought to shape the global environment through conquest, overt subjugation, and direct rule, 'new imperialism' seeks to maintain international order and security without the use of colonies, without the day-to-day risks and burdens of direct administrative management, and without any long-term and costly entanglements. Instead, imperial control today is exerted as much through indirect methods, such as the world's trading and financial systems, as it is through the increasingly short-term use of military power accompanied by ostensibly neutral projects of nation-building. Ideologically justified by recourse to notions of humanitarianism and the benefits of values such as 'freedom', 'democracy', and 'human rights' (ubiquitously presented as the guarantors of peace, prosperity and justice), this new imperialist strategy has provided a means of helping to lock unstable frontier zones into the capitalist world economy, while defending the limited scope of any external intervention on the grounds that this should be restricted to ensuring the installation of self-governance and sovereignty.[19]

Within this overarching context, the specific orientation of New Labour's external policy has focused on promoting the neo-liberalisation of the world economy, the provision of military and diplomatic support to favoured regimes, and the pursuit of an aggressive variant of liberal interventionism in foreign affairs. This has been set within the maintenance of a transatlantic-bridge strategy, designed as a means to enhance and project British power and influence on the world stage by positioning Britain as a pivotal power between Europe and America.

The first of these measures has sought to further entrench the free-market principles of the world economy with a view to creating wider avenues of trade for British businesses and for improving Britain's position within the global capitalist system. Among the various measures adopted are: the attachment of free-trade conditions to government aid for developing countries (albeit under the aegis of ensuring transparency and good governance for host populations); a close engagement in ongoing negotiations to further extend free-market principles through the General Agreement on Tariffs and Trade (the 2001 round of which further strengthened the mechanisms of global neo-liberalism through the creation of the World Trade Organisation); and support for measures to allow developing countries limited access to the single European market in return for a reciprocal liberalisation, deregulation, and opening up of their domestic economies to Western corporations. Moreover, while many of these measures have been persistently rejected by developing countries themselves, and while global inequalities have grown in parallel with the extension of the free market, New Labour nonetheless remains, in Blair's words, 'an unashamed champion of free trade'.[20]

The second principal means by which New Labour has sought to shape the international political economy is the provision of support for Britain's geo-strategic allies. Typically, this has been demonstrated through the export of arms. Despite its early rhetoric about the need for an 'ethical' foreign policy, New Labour has keenly demonstrated its credentials as a disciple of realpolitik by striving to maintain Britain's position as the world's second-largest exporter of arms behind the United States. Poor records on human rights and democracy have also proved to be no barrier to trade, with arms sales abounding to strategically positioned, though often highly repressive, states in the Middle and Far East, including Saudi Arabia, Kuwait, Egypt, Israel, Indonesia, and Turkey.[21] In marked contrast to New Labour's insistence on the need for free-market discipline elsewhere, large portions of Britain's arms exports are also heavily subsidised.

This subsidisation is undertaken through the Export Credits Guarantee Department (ECGD), a largely autonomous agency that provides British export firms with insurance against non-payment by foreign customers. While the department produces no annual report for Parliament, and while its activities are not the subject of routine scrutiny from the legislature, in 2003–4 the ECGD underwrote some £3 billion of exports, a third of which involved arms, and around a quarter of which involved trade from the arms-related aerospace industry. While this provision is frequently justified on the grounds that more than a quarter of a million British jobs are dependent on the arms sector, evidence also demonstrates that these funds would be more productively employed in civilian uses both in Britain and in the host country. This point is especially pertinent in the case of developing countries, which account for more than 85% of Britain's large arms sales, and with the large majority of arms exports covered by the ECGD going to the Middle and Far East. The fundamental purpose of the ECGD, then, is not so much to assist British exporters as it is to advance Britain's geo-strategic interests and, in particular, to maintain its economic and political influence in what remains the most strategically sensitive and oil-rich region on earth.[22]

In another notable contrast to New Labour's emphasis on the impotence of the state concerning the forces of globalisation, the government has also adopted a staunchly proactive and interventionist approach to foreign affairs. Based on an attempt to enhance Britain's power and influence on the world stage by strategically positioning the British state as a transatlantic bridge between the political continents of Europe and the United States, this has led to a series of military interventions, in Kosovo (mid-1999), Sierra Leone (August 1999), Afghanistan (2001), and, of course, Iraq (with air strikes in December 1998 leading to full-blown war in March 2003). Furthermore, despite frequent claims that such interventions have been based on humanitarian motives, the underlying driving force has been the desire to deal with unstable frontier zones as a means of enforcing a Western-orientated global order, and to send a firm signal of intent to would-be transgressors regarding the willingness of Western powers to use force in order to do so. Indeed, New Labour's claim to be acting in support of humanitarian goals such as democracy and human rights clashes palpably with the lack of any support to pro-democracy forces in key ally states such as Saudi Arabia or Egypt, with the government's public provision of diplomatic support for regimes in China and Russia (despite their respective actions in Tibet and Chechnya), as well as with the abject failure to even remotely criticise its principal ally, the United States, in spite of the latter's persistent refusal to recognise the authority of the International Court, and despite its blatant disregard for human rights in its operations at Guantanamo Bay.[23] Moreover, this strategy, in line with New Labour's governing style more broadly, has also been marked by a high degree of centralisation and by its progressive transformation into the personalised domain of the Prime Minister. With economic policy and a broad swathe of domestic issues effectively under the suzerainty of Gordon Brown, it is the sphere of foreign affairs that has proved to be Blair's primary channel for the pursuit of high political ambitions.

Concluding remarks

The centralised, hierarchical, and elitist principles underpinning the British political system are both extensive and deep-rooted. Firmly embedded within the constitutional architecture of the state, these ideational and institutional contours have enabled the pre-democratic structures of power and authority to endure relatively unchanged to the present day. This has perpetuated a form of democracy based on the virtues of strong and decisive government, and on a lack of any robust and significant mechanisms for ensuring the effective scrutiny and account-ability of the executive. By forcing the Labour party to internalise these norms and values in order to succeed politically, and by compelling it to do so at a time when the wider party membership was willing to accept drastic changes in the pursuit of electoral success, the selective bias of the British political system has exerted a key and determining influence on the emergence and development of New Labour. Moreover, by enabling those at the apex of the party to take these centralising principles to new heights in government, the institutional and ideational contours of the British polity have served to amplify and enhance these effects. In both style and content, this has taken New Labour into political terrain where even the less-than-angelic Conservatives, who have not until recently experienced the same profound degree of shock of years spent in the political wilder-ness, and who have not therefore been forced to undergo the same level of internal restructuring, would have been reluctant to tread. The result has been to further bolster the power of the executive and to further diminish the already enervated condition of British democracy.

These centralised, hierarchical, and elitist principles have been at the heart of New Labour's governing strategy. In domestic terms, this has sought to improve Britain's relative position within the global political economy and to augment the freedom of the central executive by utilising a depoliticised neo-liberal framework, unrelenting media manipulation, rigorous internal party discipline, and a distinctly presidential style of government. In a similar fashion, the external components of New Labour's statecraft have also been conditioned by its elitist foundations. Set against the backdrop of an increasingly insecure and unpredictable global environment, these have been principally focused on securing an international extension of free-market principles, providing military and diplomatic support to geo-strategic allies, and pursuing an interventionist policy direction from within the framework of a broader transatlantic-bridge approach. It is in the context of this governing strategy, set within the overarching context of the character of New Labour and the British political system, that the question of Britain's involvement with the war in Iraq needs to be examined.

3

Iraqnophobia

The background context to Britain's involvement in the Iraq war was comprised of three interrelated themes. The first of these was the changing nature of the relationship between the Western powers, chiefly the United States, and the Iraqi regime itself. Its transformation from being a key ally of the West during the 1980s to being an international pariah state embroiled in a long-running dispute with the United Nations provided the wider formative arena in which the events that followed were shaped. The second key theme concerned the foreign-policy approach of the New Labour government. Set within the overarching context of a transatlantic-bridge strategy, this advocated the projection of British power and influence as a way of moulding the contours of the global political economy in line with Britain's national interests. Importantly, this involved the use of military force, principally against Iraq and Yugoslavia, as a means of dealing with instability in world frontier zones and of establishing the credibility of core Western powers. Importantly, while New Labour's foreign policy also favoured the pursuit of regime change in Iraq, such an approach was precluded by various political and legal barriers. The third and final theme behind Britain's involvement in the Iraq war, however—the rise of the neo-conservative Bush administration in the United States—created the opportunity to surmount these obstacles. With senior figures in the US strongly committed to overthrowing Saddam Hussein as part of a new-imperialist strategy for projecting American hegemony, this, along with the events of 9/11, now provided the New Labour hierarchy with the space to drive forward with the government's more assertive foreign-policy ambitions.

Internal affairs

Historically speaking, Iraq's status as one of the world's foremost pariah regimes during the 1990s was a distinctly aberrant position. Indeed, for most of its existence, the cradle of ancient Mesopotamia had served as a key Western ally in the Middle East, forming one of the main channels for the promotion of Great Power interests throughout the region. Forged from the wreckage of the Ottoman Empire during the aftermath of the First World War, the newly created state of Iraq, an arbitrary territorialisation of disparate ethnic and religious groupings, was rapidly transformed into a key outpost of the victorious British Empire. With the discovery of oil firmly ensconcing its geo-strategic importance, Iraq's position as an imperial suzerain continued well after its formal transition to independence in 1932, with the installation of a puppet regime under the rule of King Faisal II providing the means of sustaining British influence. From 1958, however, with the British Empire beating a retreat across the globe, Iraq's Great Power tutelage was gradually transferred to the United States. Anxious to strengthen its own geo-strategic influence in the Middle East, and to repel that of the Soviet Union, the American government embarked on a decade-long series of CIA-sponsored coups and counter-coups, the culmination of which was the eventual ascension of the Ba'ath Party, and its leader General Ahmed Hassan al-Bakr, in 1968. Iraq's new-found status as an American ally, though, would initially prove to be short-lived. In 1972 al-Bakr's decision to nationalise Iraqi oil in an effort to strengthen his domestic power base led the United States, in conjunction with Israel and Iran, to launch a concerted attempt to undermine his regime by providing support to an internal Kurdish insurgency. By 1975 the pressure of the revolt had, at least for the American government, been notably successful. While the lot of the Kurds had not been improved, al-Bakr had been ousted, and Iraq's alliance with the United States was on the way to being restored. Its new leader was Saddam Hussein.

Four years later, Iraq's usefulness to the West was amply demonstrated. Following the 1979 Iranian revolution and the deposing of the Shah (a puppet regime installed by a US- and British-sponsored coup in 1953), Iraq's decision to attack the newly created Islamic state offered a huge opportunity for the United States to re-establish its regional influence. Throughout the ensuing conflict, which lasted for eight years and which resulted in more than a million deaths, the US not only provided Iraq with intelligence and financial assistance, but also helped to develop its unconventional arsenal through the sale of chemical and biological materials. All this, too, was undertaken despite Saddam Hussein's willingness to use chemical weapons for both military and domestic political purposes. In one of the most notorious incidents (though itself just part of the wider 'Anfal' campaign which killed up to 100,000 Iraqi Kurds during the late 1980s), at least 5,000 people were murdered in a gas attack on the town of Halabja during March 1988.

The British Conservative government was no less implicated in the events of the Iran–Iraq war. Although a neutral posture was initially adopted in order to continue the sale of arms to both sides, political criticism that this was helping to sustain the bloodshed led to the establishing of 'guidelines', announced in October 1985 (some nine months after their actual adoption), stating that no orders for defence equipment would be approved that would 'significantly enhance' the ability of either side to 'prolong or exacerbate the conflict'. Following the ceasefire of August 1988, therefore, government officials sought a revision of the guidelines in order to revive Britain's 'defence' exports to the region. As the Foreign Secretary, Geoffrey Howe, astutely observed, there would be 'major opportunities' for British firms in postwar reconstruction, and a 'considerable' opportunity for new defence sales. Within months of the Halabja atrocity, new guidelines stating that the government's policy should be revised in light of the ceasefire had subsequently been adopted, and by the end of the year the government had doubled Iraq's previous annual allowance for arms purchases, extending a £340 million line of credit to facilitate a new wave of procurement. Further still, the guidelines themselves were also interpreted in a liberal fashion, with ministers turning a blind eye to sales of 'dual-use' equipment with the potential for military application being funnelled into Iraq through other Middle Eastern states, especially British allies such as Jordan, Egypt, Kuwait, and Saudi Arabia.[1]

Anxious, however, to avoid inflaming public opinion, which officials presciently reckoned would not support the government helping to re-equip a vicious dictator, the relaxation of the guidelines remained a wholly covert affair, and no public announcement of a change in policy was made until the Iraqi invasion of Kuwait prompted the imposition of a complete arms embargo against Saddam Hussein's regime. Instead, the official line was simply that the guidelines were being kept 'under constant review'. This was later justified by the government on the grounds that a 'high profile announcement' would have provoked a flood of inappropriate export applications, and could have been 'misinterpreted' by other nations, principally the US and 'Arab states'. A far more compelling reason, though, later revealed by a Foreign Office official, was that it would look 'very cynical' if the government altered its guidelines on Iraq so soon after the attacks on Halabja.[2]

The porous nature of the official guidelines eventually came to light in 1992 during the trial of directors from the company of Matrix Churchill, who were accused of illegally exporting machine tools to Iraq for arms production during the late 1980s. With it subsequently emerging that ministers had sought a Public Interest Immunity certificate to withhold information from defence lawyers relating to the changed interpretation of the guidelines, and with the former Conservative Minister for Defence Procurement, Alan Clark, revealing under cross-examination that ministers had eased the export restrictions and were acutely aware of the real nature of the machinery being sold to Iraq, the trial itself sensationally collapsed. In an effort to heal its political wounds, the government quickly established an inquiry, headed by Sir Richard Scott, to examine the issues that the trial had raised. After a lengthy examination, the inquiry finally published its findings in February 1996. Clearing the government of any wrongdoing, the Scott Report found that ministers had not changed the guidelines, but had merely altered their interpretation of them. It declared that the government had 'carefully balanced British export interests alongside wider foreign policy considerations' and concluded that there was 'no evidence of impropriety' in the Matrix Churchill case.[3]

While this added to a growing sense of 'Tory sleaze' in Britain, Saddam Hussein too was by now experiencing life as a pariah. Although Western governments had remained perceptibly unperturbed by Iraq's aggression towards Iran and by the ongoing suppression of its own people, the decision to invade and annex Kuwait in August 1990 transformed Iraq from being a geo-strategic ally into being one of the world's leading deviant regimes. The response from the United Nations, as laid out in Resolution 678, was to authorise member states to use 'all necessary means' (the traditional UN code for war) to eject Iraq from its southern neighbour. On 16 January 1991, with no Iraqi retreat in sight, US-led coalition forces began an offensive known as Operation Desert Storm. In military terms, the campaign was relatively short. After forty-two days of intensive bombing, a ground offensive rapidly tore through the depleted remains of the Iraqi army, and within five days a ceasefire and a withdrawal had been announced.

Much bewailed in later years, however, was the fact that coalition success in the Gulf War was not followed by any direct effort to overthrow Saddam Hussein. Since this would have exceeded the UN mandate and fractured the carefully constructed military alliance, the US government sought instead to depose Saddam by encouraging the northern Iraqi Kurds and the large Shi'a Muslim population in the south to rise up against the regime on the understanding that they would be given the support they required to succeed. But with the revolt under way, US General Norman Schwarzkopf inadvertently conspired to undermine their efforts by agreeing to allow the Iraqi military to continue with the use of its helicopters, thereby enabling it to embark on a brutal campaign of repression. As the hostilities intensified, US President George Bush senior now refused to recommit American troops to assist the uprising. In the words of a White House spokesman, the United States had no intention of becoming involved 'in Iraq's internal affairs'.[4]

Yet with pictures of Kurdish refugees streaming onto the TV screens of Western audiences, the political pressure for action began to mount. In response, the British and American governments set up a series of 'safe havens' in the north of Iraq, later accompanied by 'no-fly' zones in both the north and the south of the country. Reflecting this, the postwar strategy for dealing with Iraq was based on a broader policy of containment. The military restrictions of the no-fly zones (patrolled with intermittent air strikes throughout the rest of the decade) were accompanied by the passing of UN resolution 687, which obliged Iraq to destroy all of its WMD, as well as any related programmes and facilities. To ensure this, a new weapons inspectorate, UNSCOM, was created, and was to have unrestricted access to any sites and individuals it deemed appropriate.[5] In conjunction with this, responsibility for the inspection and destruction of Iraq's nuclear capacity was handed over to the International Atomic Energy Agency (IAEA). Economic sanctions, too, were sustained, banning the export of oil and the importing of non-essential items (slightly eased from 1995) until Iraq had clearly demonstrated its conformity with the disarmament requirements.[6]

Thus began a long-running game of cat and mouse between Iraq and the UN inspectors. While Saddam's regime embarked on a systematic process of concealment, deception, and (as it transpired) the unilateral and secret destruction of its WMD capabilities, the inspectors, for their part, were given secret assistance by the US Central Intelligence Agency (CIA), which provided tips and intelligence in the ongoing hunt for weapons. The chase was also punctuated by a series of periodic crises, in which, after a promising start, the inspections process became increasingly bogged down. In October 1994 an Iraqi threat to cease co-operation altogether was only reversed following the deployment of over 50,000 US troops to the region, while in August the following year the defection of General Hussein Kamel, a senior Iraqi official with responsibility for weapons programmes, revealed that Iraq's WMD projects had been far more extensive than it had previously acknowledged. Nevertheless, in a frequently overlooked disclosure, Kamel also revealed that Iraq's nuclear programme had since been halted, and that its stocks of chemical and biological weapons (CBW) had been destroyed following the Gulf War. In February 1996, following his return to Iraq, Kamel was assassinated, while Iraq's programme of obfuscation and non-cooperation resumed apace.[7]

A global player

In May 1997, with the Iraq crisis continuing to simmer, an apparently new political dawn broke in Britain with a landslide election victory for New Labour. Armed with a majority of 179 seats, the largest since the National Government of 1935, the political tsunami seemed to augur an era of democratic renewal and revitalisation. In terms of foreign policy, however, the underlying aims of the New Labour government remained distinctly familiar. Despite an initial declaration that its policies would now harbour an 'ethical dimension', the primary and far more generic ambition was to shape the global political economy in a manner more conducive to the promotion of the British national interest. This was broadly conceived as the entrenchment of a neo-liberal economic architecture and the maintenance of a stable and secure pattern of international relations in which British influence could be effectively deployed. Indeed, driven by a desire not to be seen as weak on defence, by the increasingly competitive pressures of the global capitalist economy and by the personal values and proclivities of Tony Blair himself, the New Labour government would prove to be a far more assertive proponent of these aims than its predecessor.

In his first major statement on New Labour's foreign-policy objectives, these themes were clearly elucidated by the new Prime Minister. The primary goal, he declared, was to 'make the British presence in the world felt' by combining a 'strong defence' capacity with Britain's pattern of 'historic alliances' to form 'an instrument of influence' for the projection of British power overseas. Praising the British Empire as having been 'a most extraordinary achievement', Blair warned that Britain 'must not reduce our capability to exercise a role on the international stage', and declared that the overriding aim of the government's foreign policy was to maintain Britain's position as 'a global player'. In particular, Blair highlighted the need for firm measures to address a wide variety of international issues generating 'human misery and political instability' in the modern world. While these ranged from the environment, crime, human rights and terrorism to economic reform and international development, the Prime Minister also sought to focus attention on the long-running problem of Iraq. Emphasising the dangers posed to world stability by its persistent refusal to abide by UN resolutions on disarmament, Blair insisted that the government's resolve to deal with the matter was 'unshakeable'. In sum, the clear message was that New Labour's foreign-policy trajectory 'should complement and reflect our domestic goals', as a fundamental part of 'our mission of national renewal'. A policy of promoting 'the values and aims we believe in', enthused Blair, was not merely the altruistic projection of British power, but, by helping to ensure a more favourable international order, was rather a form of 'enlightened patriotism'.[8]

More specifically, the key to pursuing this approach was to be the adoption of a transatlantic-bridge strategy. This was designed to amplify Britain's influence on the world stage by having it act as the key political channel between Europe and the United States, the underlying assumption being that the adoption of closer relations with both would prove to be self-reinforcing. Strong links with Washington, it was supposed, would elevate Britain's influence in Europe, while conversely, stronger ties with Europe would increase Britain's ability to influence the United States. In one fell swoop, the government could increase its sway over the future path of European politics, as well as over the actions of the world's only superpower, thereby enhancing its ability to shape the contours of the global political economy.[9]

In its early days this transatlantic-bridge strategy proved to be markedly successful. The Prime Minister's close relationship with the US President, Bill Clinton, was mirrored by a rapid thawing of relations with the European Union that had grown decidedly frosty during the era of Conservative rule. Notwithstanding the government's ongoing procrastination over the question of joining the single European currency, New Labour officials avowedly pursued a far friendlier course of action, rapidly implementing the Maastricht Social Chapter and signing up to the treaties

of Amsterdam (1997) and Nice (2000). The interventionist strand of New
Labour's foreign policy, on the other hand, soon ran into difficulties. In
particular, proclamations of an ethical dimension were rapidly besmirched
by tensions surrounding Britain's diplomatic support for Russia and
China, and by its export of arms to states with dire human-rights records,
including Indonesia, Zimbabwe, Saudi Arabia, Colombia, Sri Lanka, and
Turkey. The most sensational difficulties over foreign policy, though,
emerged during the 1998 'arms-to-Africa' crisis. This revealed that Foreign
Office officials had circumvented one of their own embargoes by providing
tacit assistance to Sandline International, a private military company
seeking to supply arms to the deposed leader of Sierra Leone (the democratically elected President Ahmed Kabbah), with a view to restoring him
to power.

Regardless of these problems, the government's desire to pursue an
assertive foreign policy remained undimmed. And in no instance was this
clearer than on the question of Iraq, which was by now considered to be
one of the main geo-strategic fault lines in the international political
economy. With the UN inspections process remaining strained, and with
Iraq continuing to pursue a policy of concealment, deception, and
obstruction, senior officials in the New Labour hierarchy grew increasingly
keen to adopt a harder stance. The intelligence picture, though, remained
uncertain. The view of the United States was that Saddam Hussein continued to covet WMD as a means of establishing Iraq's regional hegemony,
but that he would not risk provoking any direct confrontation in the Gulf
for fear of endangering his regime. The assessment of the Joint Intelligence
Committee (JIC), the chief conduit of intelligence material for the British
government, was that 'the vast majority' of Iraq's WMD had now been successfully eliminated by UNSCOM and the IAEA.[10] Nevertheless, towards
the end of 1997 Tony Blair confided to Paddy Ashdown, the leader of the
Liberal Democrats, that the state of the intelligence was 'pretty scary', and
that Saddam Hussein was 'very close to some appalling weapons of mass
destruction'. 'We cannot', he warned, 'let him get away with it. The world
thinks this is just gamesmanship. But it's deadly serious'.[11]

In February 1998 these sentiments were on further display in the
House of Commons. With the inspections process continuing to falter, the
Prime Minister warned that the international community would not 'play
more elaborate diplomatic games' with Iraq, and insisted that 'the most
severe consequences' would follow if Saddam continued to defy the will of
the United Nations. Declaring a policy of inaction to be 'the riskiest option

of all' in the present circumstances, Blair went on to detail his own pre-disposition towards regime change, stating that the use of military action to secure this goal was being ruled out not on a matter of principle, but on the grounds of legal, political, and logistical impracticalities. As he explained:

> Obviously we will do what we can to assist opposition groups in Iraq and to look at ways in which we can undermine Saddam Hussein in any shape or form.... The problem with saying that we should have set some sort of military objective to remove Saddam Hussein ... was that there was not the authority to do so; nor would it have been possible without a massive commitment of ground as well as air forces.[12]

The dispute between Iraq and the inspectors, then, continued to rumble on through the United Nations. Moves by France, China, and Russia to relax economic sanctions with a view to ensuring their eventual dissolution were persistently blocked by the United States and Britain, who, in turn, saw their own attempts at securing stronger measures being given similarly short shrift by their fellow members on the Security Council. In August, with hopes of an end to sanctions beginning to fade, Iraq ceased to co-operate with the UN inspectors. Two months later, President Clinton signed the Iraq Liberation Act, making the pursuit of regime change the official policy aim of the American government.

As tensions over the inspections process continued to rise, so too did the prospects of military action. In November, the threat of US air strikes was narrowly averted at the last minute following the personal intervention of the UN Secretary General, Kofi Annan, who successfully brokered a deal with Saddam for the readmission of inspectors in return for assurances that the sanctions regime would be reviewed. The resumption of inspections, however, was also accompanied by a resumption of Iraqi obstructionism. In December, this led to a further sharpening of the crisis when Iraq continued to refuse access to 'sensitive sites' such as presidential palaces and official residences. The result was the withdrawal of the weapons inspectors, followed by a four-day campaign of US and British air strikes known as Operation Desert Fox.

Progressive war

Blair's involvement in these attacks, the first aggressive use of the armed forces by the New Labour government, foreshadowed the kind of centralised decision-making that would prove to be the hallmark of later events. The key decision to join the US-led operation was made not by the full Cabinet, but by its Defence and Overseas Policy Committee,[13] while Parliament itself was only permitted to record its view on the matter through a vote on the adjournment once British troops had already been committed to action. Furthermore, while Blair insisted that the expressly stated aims of the campaign were to degrade Iraq's WMD capability and to force it to comply with UN resolutions, the Prime Minister's support for a policy of regime change was again clearly apparent. Though emphasising that this was not 'a specific objective' of the air raids, Blair once more revealed that his opposition to the explicit pursuit of this end—a goal that was now being directly advocated by the Conservatives—was based not on its undesirability, but on its current impracticalities. Indeed, while professing to 'agree entirely that a broad objective of our policy is to remove Saddam Hussein and to do all that we can to achieve that', and while telling the House of Commons that '[i]f we can possibly find the means of removing him, we will', the Prime Minister also pointed out that the stated aims of Desert Fox had been deliberately confined to measures that were deemed to be 'achievable' in order to muster international backing for the attacks. The importance of getting 'the maximum possible support in the rest of the world', he explained, was 'one of the reasons why we established a limited set of military objectives'.[14]

Yet despite this carefully constructed rationale, the attacks were widely condemned. Viewed by many as a cynical attempt by President Clinton to divert attention away from his impeachment proceedings over the Monica Lewinsky scandal, and with Britain standing alone within the European Union as the only country to explicitly support the United States, the military campaign put Britain's transatlantic-bridge strategy under growing strain. In addition, the New Labour government also came under heavy fire over the legality of the move, given that the strikes had not received any authorisation from the United Nations. The government's response, however, was that although UN approval would have been desirable, it was not in this event necessary on the grounds that the action was supported by previous UN resolutions. While this view was regarded by legal officials at the Foreign Office as being 'controversial', Blair emphatically asserted that the attacks were 'the right thing to do', and insisted that '[w]hen the international community agrees certain objectives and then fails to implement them, those that can act, must'.[15]

For all this, the air strikes also produced limited results. Despite the insistence of the Ministry of Defence (MoD) that Iraq's WMD capability had been 'set back significantly', and despite claims by Tony Blair that the operations had 'inflicted the kind of military damage we were seeking', US intelligence judged the attacks to have made 'very little impact' on Iraq's ability to reconstitute its CBW programmes. President Clinton, too, later remarked that the United States 'had no way of knowing' exactly what the results of Desert Fox had been, given that the attacks had now shattered any prospect of the UN inspectors being allowed to return to Iraq.[16] As John Morrison, former Deputy Chief of Britain's Defence Intelligence Staff (DIS), put it, New Labour officials were now trying to spin the results of the conflict in a wholly unwarranted way. Intelligence analysts, he claimed, had been put 'under pressure' to affirm that the attacks had been 'a great success', when it was felt within the intelligence community itself that this was not actually the case.[17]

In any event, the controversy over Desert Fox was swiftly followed by the emergence of a new international crisis. This time, however, the epicentre was located in the Balkan peninsula, a region infested with ancient ethnic tensions and riven with new territorial hatreds following the collapse of the Soviet Union and the subsequent disintegration of Yugoslavia during the Balkan war of the early 1990s. The initial Western response to these centrifugal forces, based on the view that there were few geostrategic interests at stake and that intervention would be therefore costly and dangerous, had proved to be wholly counterproductive and had led to a growing sense of public anger at the atrocities that were being allowed to take place on the doorstep of Europe. The tipping point that eventually prompted a substantial Western response was a campaign of ethnic cleansing being pursued by Serbian President Slobodan Milosevic against the Albanian Muslim population of Kosovo, a province whose autonomy had been the subject of a long and bitter dispute. By the late 1990s, with a series of ultimatums to end the hostilities having been allowed to pass unheeded, with public outrage markedly escalating, and with international pressures also starting to gather, Milosevic agreed to take part in peace talks at Rambouillet in France. The diplomatic effort, however, soon collapsed and the violence began to intensify.

In response, with the United States and Britain taking a clear lead, members of NATO embarked on the first military offensive in the organisation's fifty-year history, mounting an intensive bombing campaign designed to force a Serbian withdrawal. Yet again, this led to the deployment of British forces in a war being conducted without the authorisation of the United Nations, and with both China and Russia having made it clear that they would veto any attempt to legitimise the attacks in this way. Moreover, the military operation was also in contravention of the NATO Charter itself, which permitted such actions only as a means of self-defence, and also ran contrary to the advice of Foreign Office lawyers, who maintained that the proclaimed humanitarian motives were insufficient to justify the use of force under international law. Nevertheless, invigorated by the 'success' of Desert Fox, and increasingly keen to press further ahead with an interventionist foreign policy, Tony Blair remained undeterred. Placing himself firmly in the vanguard of those calling for action against Milosevic, Blair asserted that the NATO air strikes were essential in order to prevent a 'humanitarian disaster'. Kosovo, as he put it, was the first 'progressive war', being waged not for naked self-interest, but for the universal values of human rights.[18]

The spread of our values

Yet while this contention held a degree of truth, the motivations behind the military campaign were far more complex. One central factor was a growing need to maintain the credibility of NATO itself, which had been badly damaged by its ineffectual response thus far to the Balkan crisis, and which was facing an increasingly uncertain future in the post-Cold War world. With the prospects of any NATO expansion—and with it hopes of permanently locking ex-Soviet states into the Western orbit of the world system—being similarly undermined, senior officials within the alliance were anxious for a successful campaign in Kosovo in order to help revive its authority and to thereby help re-establish the international vitality of the US–European axis. A second and related factor behind the war was that the prolonged instability in the Balkan frontier was also now seen to pose a growing threat to core Western states themselves, buffeting them with cross-border flows of refugees, narcotics, and organised crime. In addition to this, the wider ramifications of the conflict throughout South-East Europe were a cause of growing concern, with the possibility of disorder spreading to Greece and Turkey, and with the risk of undermining relations with post-communist Russia adding further to the pressure to restore peace in the region.

While the geo-strategic interest behind intervention was now clearly apparent, economic interests, too, were invariably at stake. Most notably, a proposed route for the supply of oil from the Caspian Sea, and with it the prospect of billions of dollars in investment, was now becoming increasingly endangered by the interminably conflicted state of the region. In detailing the importance of the Trans-Balkan pipeline, US Energy Secretary Bill Richardson thus outlined the new-imperialist rationale behind the Kosovo campaign. The military action, he said, was as much 'about America's energy security' as it was 'about preventing strategic inroads by those who don't share our values'. The broader objective, then, was to ensure that newly independent Soviet states became 'reliant on Western commercial and political interests'. The United States, he explained, had 'made a substantial political investment in the Caspian', and it was 'very important to us that both the pipeline map and the politics come out right'.[19]

A further weighty factor behind the decision to take military action against Yugoslavia was, of course, the increasingly outraged voice of Western public opinion calling for some form of action to stop the desolate images of suffering that now streamed daily onto its TV screens. Indeed, the degree of sensitivity towards public opinion with which the war itself was prosecuted was evident from the outset, with officials explicitly ruling out the use of ground forces for fear that NATO might find itself sucked into a quagmire with no discernible means of escape. That this would pose a central dilemma for the NATO operation itself, however, soon became apparent, as the failure to consider ground troops merely served to embolden the Serbs and to intensify the process of ethnic cleansing.[20]

Hopes for a swift conclusion to the war were also damaged by the media coverage of the conflict, as poorly equipped NATO staff ran headlong into a public-relations nightmare regarding large-scale refugee flows and civilian casualties. Matters were made worse by a series of self-inflicted wounds. The most prominent of these, the accidental bombing of a civilian convoy in mid-April, severely undermined the moral claims of the coalition and threatened to split the alliance asunder. In an attempt to neutralise the problem, Alastair Campbell was swiftly dispatched to transplant the panoply of New Labour's media-management techniques to NATO's Media Operations Centre in Brussels. Utilising a variety of methods, including rapid rebuttals, the infamous 'grid' (designed to ensure the effective timing of announcements), and even an 'article factory' to pump out ghost-written pieces signed by allied leaders, Campbell set out to co-ordinate and promote the NATO message, his express aim being 'to try to hold the public's interest on our terms'. As the heat of the propaganda battle rose, Campbell also turned his guns on those elements of the Western media that refused to accept the veracity of the

NATO line, accusing reporters of having an 'unhealthy relationship' with the 'Milosevic lie machine'.[21]

Despite providing a more coherent media projection, and though public opinion in Britain grew in favour of the war as it progressed,[22] Campbell's best efforts were also undermined by a series of public-relations disasters, the worst of which included the destruction of a Belgrade television station and the accidental bombing of a Chinese embassy. With such mistakes highlighting the inadequacies of the bombing campaign, and with many in NATO now moving towards the idea of negotiating a settlement with Milosevic, the prospects of ensuring a Western victory and of bolstering the credibility of the United States and Europe were becoming matters of increasingly serious concern.

In response, Tony Blair began to mount a vigorous political offensive, intensifying the humanitarian rhetoric and putting greater pressure on Bill Clinton to reconsider the use of ground forces. By the latter half of April, the signal coming from the British government was that it might now be possible for NATO to fight its way into Kosovo in the context of a 'semi-permissive environment'. While this aggressive posturing left the Prime Minister looking increasingly isolated and did little for his relations with the US President, who was now being made to look weak and indecisive on the international stage, Blair heightened the brinkmanship still further by launching his new vision for the rules governing the conduct between nations in the twenty-first century. Describing this as the 'Doctrine of International Community', Blair contended that the old tenets of state sovereignty that had been the foundation stone for international relations since the seventeenth-century Treaty of Westphalia were now becoming increasingly defunct in the globalised, post-Cold War era. In this new contextual environment, where internal disorder held the potential for cross-border threats to international peace and security, Blair contended that intervention in a state's internal affairs could no longer be considered a taboo subject for the global family of states, and argued that such a course of action might, on occasion, be required to maintain international order. Beyond this, in the case of Kosovo, was also the question of credibility and the opportunity to send out a signal to other potentially deviant regimes. As Blair maintained:

> One of the reasons why it is now so important to win the conflict is to ensure that others do not make the same mistakes in the future. That in itself will be a major step to ensuring that the next decade and the next century will not be as difficult as the past.

More broadly still, the Prime Minister sought to locate the action in Kosovo within the context of a vision for a wide-ranging reordering of the global political economy. Emphasising the need for economic, financial, and political reform, for closer co-operation on environmental change and third-world debt, and for more transparency to ensure good governance and 'sound' economic policies, Blair maintained that the best means of ensuring stability was to ensure the spread of human rights, freedom, justice, and democracy. The action in Kosovo, then, was the first step towards establishing an entirely new world order. It was, as he explained, a 'just war', since

> our actions are guided by a more subtle blend of mutual self-interest and moral purpose in defending the values we cherish.... If we can establish and spread the values of liberty, the rule of law, human rights and an open society then that is in our national interests too. The spread of our values makes us safer.[23]

As high risk as this strategy was, it also proved to be largely successful in prompting a turnaround by Bill Clinton, who by the following month was now prepared to countenance the use of American ground forces in order to secure a NATO victory. While this established a credible threat that Western armies might soon be used to break the deadlock with Yugoslavia, the diplomatic front also began to advance. At the beginning of June, following a breakthrough in the attempt to persuade Russia to add its opposition to the Serb offensive, Slobodan Milosevic suddenly capitulated. Serbian troops were pulled back, control of Kosovo was passed over to the United Nations, and NATO breathed a heavy sigh of relief.

Gut British instincts

While the events of Desert Fox and Kosovo were instrumental in shaping and entrenching the desire of the New Labour government, and especially that of Tony Blair, to pursue an assertive foreign policy, the question of Iraq also remained a live issue. In May 1999, a joint memo produced by the Foreign and Defence Secretaries, Robin Cook and George Robertson, set out the government's ambitions in this regard. The short-term aim, it noted, was 'to reduce the threat Saddam poses' to the Middle East by 'eliminating his WMD programmes', while in the longer term the ultimate objective was to help bring order to the region by reintegrating 'a territorially intact Iraq as a law abiding member of the international community'. The memo also detailed concerns about the 'disadvantages' of the current policy of containment, claiming that it was expensive, required 'constant diplomatic effort' and 'a significant military presence', and did not 'produce rapid or decisive results'. Officials were also concerned that containment was 'not always easy to justify to public opinion', as had been amply demonstrated by the high level of criticism both of the US and British air strikes as well as of the humanitarian impact of the sanctions regime. However, while bemoaning these difficulties, the paper also concluded that no other viable options were open at the present time, and thus observed that '[h]owever difficult it may be to sustain ... it is not clear what the alternatives would be'. Although any notion of leaving Iraq to its own devices was rejected out of hand as 'an admission of failure' that would leave Saddam Hussein free to pose 'a major threat to regional security and British interests', a policy 'of trying to topple Saddam' was also rejected, albeit not on the grounds that it would be unlawful or unsafe, but on the basis that it 'would command no useful international support'. As such, the considered view was that containment, for all its obvious and unpalatable imperfections, was for the time being deemed to be 'the only usable option for achieving our policy objectives'.[24]

Over the course of the following year, however, it was domestic rather than foreign affairs that exercised the government, faced as it was with a rising tide of disillusion with both the style and the content of the New Labour project. By the spring of 2000 the situation, according to Blair's chief opinion pollster, Philip Gould, had become a matter of 'serious' concern. In a memo to the Prime Minister, Gould warned that there was now a growing sense that the government's strength was starting to 'ebb away', and that its credibility had been undermined 'by a combination of spin, lack of conviction and apparently lack of integrity'. 'Perhaps worst of all', he added, 'the New Labour brand had been badly contaminated' and was now 'the object of constant criticism and, even worse, ridicule'. 'We have', he lamented, 'got our political strategy wrong'. In particular, Gould's assessment of the problem was that the government was seen as being 'soft' on crime, as being insufficiently supportive of family values, and as lacking in patriotic verve. The proposed solution, then, was to adopt a stronger and more coherent approach based on 'a series of uncompromising and single minded positions' across the policy spectrum. In sum, he noted, '[w]e need to reinvent the New Labour brand'.[25]

Blair was in broad agreement with all of this. The government, he concurred, needed to focus more intently on domestic affairs, needed to develop 'a thoroughly worked-out strategy ... with a message which ties it all together', and needed to come up with some 'eye catching initiatives' designed to grab the media headlines and to create the impression that the government was moving forward with a reinvigorated policy drive. However, though anxious to be 'personally associated with as much of this as possible', Blair also bemoaned the fact that the government was apparently being seen as 'insufficiently assertive' on foreign policy and defence issues. Complaining that the action in Kosovo had not 'laid to rest any doubts about our strength in defence', the Prime Minister noted that there was still a perception in the country that the government was 'somehow out of touch with gut British instincts'.[26]

Within a matter of months, a prime opportunity to address this political deficiency with an eye-catching initiative in foreign affairs presented itself. Following an outbreak of renewed disorder in Sierra Leone, where the reinstalled Kabbah presidency was now facing a surge in attacks from anti-government rebels, Blair once more opted for a deployment of British military force. Buttressed by the pre-existing involvement of the United Nations, as well as by Britain's own colonial links and strong bilateral ties with the African country, the Prime Minister dispatched 1,000 troops to help restore order and to help defend the nation's capital, Freetown. In so doing, Blair was carried still further along the road of foreign interventionism. With his enthusiasm for such measures buoyed by the resulting success of the operation, Blair's penchant for more ventures was now becoming clearly evident. As he put it to Clare Short, the International Development Secretary: 'If it were down to me, I'd do Zimbabwe as well'.[27]

Nevertheless, in domestic affairs the government remained bedevilled by crisis. A dramatic series of national fuel protests during September was followed within months by a mass outbreak of foot-and-mouth disease, forcing New Labour officials to postpone their carefully laid plans for a spring general election. Still, having spent the best part of a hundred years trying to secure a full consecutive term in office, a few more weeks spent in anticipation would prove to be a mere bagatelle. In May 2001, just slightly later than expected, New Labour finally secured its historic second term following an equally historic second landslide victory. Yet all was not as it appeared to be. With the Conservative party still in deep disarray, and with no real opposition to speak of, the size of the government's parliamentary dominance belied the underlying mood of the electorate, which remained distinctly underwhelmed by New Labour's performance to date. With less than three-fifths of the British public being sufficiently moved to vote, with turnout falling to its lowest levels since the emergence of mass democracy in 1918, and with just two-fifths of all votes cast actually going to the Labour party, the government's much-coveted prize of re-election had been effectively secured with the support of less than a quarter of Britain's total electorate. Impressive though its huge majority and its political command of the House of Commons may have been, the foundations of the New Labour edifice were remarkably shallow.[28]

In a bid to generate some much-needed public enthusiasm for the new government and to create a sense of purpose and dynamism, the election was followed by what would prove to be a defining Cabinet reshuffle. To a large degree, this was also driven by Blair's desire to strengthen his own personal control over the direction of the government and by a need to create the necessary conditions to enable him to forge ahead with plans to radically reform Britain's public services—the key theme, if there was one, to have emerged from the election campaign. The preferred means of gaining control over the levers of domestic policy, however—a putsch involving the move of Gordon Brown to the Foreign Office and a hiving off of key Treasury functions to Number 10—was ultimately abandoned due to the political dangers of inducing a large and destabilising backbench revolt. Instead, the high point of the reshuffle saw Robin Cook moved from the Foreign Office to become leader of the House of Commons, with Jack Straw, a minister far more amenable to pursuing a policy line fashioned by Number 10, moving in from the Home Office as his replacement. In this instant, the die was effectively cast. As he was unable to dislodge Brown's ubiquitous influence over the domestic sphere, Blair's predilection for foreign affairs would begin to grow ever stronger. Perfectly suited to his own fondness for direct, informal, and personalised decision-making, this penchant would now provide the Prime Minister with an opportunity to glide far above the daily grind of domestic political life, and to act on the highest stage possible with relatively few immediate constraints from Parliament, from the Labour party, or, it would seem, from public opinion.[29]

Pax Americana

While Blair's desire to pursue a more interventionist foreign policy in relation to Iraq had thus far been hampered by a lack of international support, by the turn of the millennium political forces that would soon reshape this balance were mustering in the United States. Emanating from the right of American politics, the particular driving force came from the neo-conservative movement, where prominent figures, including Paul Wolfowitz, Dick Cheney, and Donald Rumsfeld, had long been calling for a more aggressive use of US military power in order to capitalise on its new-found position as the world's sole remaining superpower. These aims were first outlined in 1992 in a document entitled 'Defense Planning Guidance', overseen by Wolfowitz, then the Under-Secretary of Defense in the first Bush administration. Calling for a new US foreign-policy strategy for the post-Cold War era, this argued that America's primary goal should be to ensure its continued dominance by preventing 'the re-emergence of a new rival' and by preventing 'any hostile power from dominating a region whose resources would … be sufficient to generate global power'. In practice, this meant that a key focus would be the Middle East, given the crucial need to ensure continued 'access to vital raw material, primarily Persian Gulf oil'. In sum, the document claimed that the US needed 'to establish and protect a new order' based on 'democratic forms of government and open economic systems', and to dissuade potential competitors 'from challenging our leadership'.[30]

More particularly, many neo-conservatives harboured a deep antipathy towards Iraq and a deep-rooted ambition to correct the grievances remaining from the Gulf War. In 1998 eighteen prominent neo-conservatives, many of whom (including Wolfowitz and Rumsfeld) later went on to become members of the George W. Bush administration, sent an open letter to Bill Clinton complaining that the current policy of containment was 'dangerously inadequate' and calling on the President to pursue a more strident policy of 'removing Saddam Hussein and his regime from power'. Allowing uncertainty in the Gulf to continue unchecked would, they warned, not only endanger US troops and allies, but also put at risk 'a significant portion of the world's supply of oil'.[31]

In September 2000, the neo-conservative worldview was expressed in its most coherent form to date in a report by a right-wing think tank called the Project for the New American Century. In a document entitled 'Rebuilding America's Defenses', this again argued that the US government should adopt a 'grand strategy' designed to preserve America's dominant global position 'as far into the future as possible'. Hailing the 1992 Defense Planning Guidance as a 'blueprint for maintaining US pre-eminence' and for 'shaping the international security order in line with American principles and interests', the document went on to outline several key aims. These included the need to secure and expand the 'zones of democratic peace', to ensure 'a favourable order in vital regions' (primarily Europe, East Asia, and the Middle East), and 'to extend the current Pax Americana'. Indeed, such expansionism was itself to form an integral part of this imperialist framework. Given that any sign of withdrawal would undermine America's superpower credentials, erode the credibility of its will to act, and thus embolden its enemies, the paper called for a sufficiently large increase in American military spending to enable it to fight and win 'multiple large-scale wars' simultaneously. As part of this, and observing that the United States had 'for decades sought to play a more permanent role in Gulf regional security', the paper also highlighted the need for immediate intervention in Iraq in order to extend American influence in the Middle East. Thus:

> While the unresolved conflict with Iraq provides the immediate justification, the need for a substantial American force presence in the Gulf transcends the issue of the regime of Saddam Hussein.[32]

Two months later, the neo-conservative Republican candidate, George W. Bush, won the most tightly contested, fiercely fought, and controversial US presidential election in history. Despite losing the popular vote to his Democratic rival, Al Gore, Bush secured his eventual victory following weeks of legal wrangling, and following a 5–4 verdict in the Supreme Court that swung on the casting vote of a Republican judge. Any thoughts that the manner of their victory would lead to a moderate policy approach, however, were soon dispelled as the neo-conservatives quickly set about installing their new-imperialist strategy. With the more virulently hawkish tendencies within the administration initially lacking a sufficient rationale and justification for the pursuit of expansionary measures, the Bush regime primarily sought to exercise US power in a passive-aggressive fashion, through a systematic disengagement from multilateral institutions and agreements. The 1997 Kyoto Treaty aimed at cutting greenhouse gas emissions was rejected on the grounds that it would damage the US economy; the 1972 Anti-Ballistic Missile Treaty was discarded in favour of a National Missile Defence Program on the grounds that it was anachronistic in the circumstances of the post-Cold War world; the provisions of the 1972 global convention on biological weapons were similarly disposed of; and the ratification of the Comprehensive Test Ban Treaty was refused, as was the recognised authority of a proposed International Court.[33]

While this disengagement sent out a clear signal as to the self-interested intentions of the new US government, within a matter of months the imperatives for an even more aggressive approach began to sharpen considerably. With the underlying structural weaknesses of the US economy opening up into a steep recession, with a severe deterioration in America's financial position transforming it into the largest debtor nation of all time, and with rising international competition, especially from newly industrialising nations such as India and China, now posing a serious threat to US prosperity and internal social cohesion, the conditions were ripe for a more vigorous deployment of American power in order to safeguard domestic economic growth and political stability.[34]

For Tony Blair, the election of George W. Bush provided a prime opportunity to reaffirm his commitment to the transatlantic relationship. In February 2001, the Prime Minister travelled to the United States for an inaugural meeting with the US President at Camp David. At the ensuing press conference, held just days after a renewed spate of US and British attacks in the Iraqi no-fly zones, Bush reaffirmed Britain's position as America's 'strongest friend and closest ally', and the two leaders both reasserted their joint commitment to address the thorny question of Iraq. The message from Blair was one of their 'absolute determination' to ensure that the menace of Saddam was kept contained, coupled with warnings that the weapons of mass destruction issue was now 'a real threat', and that Iraq would seek to develop WMD 'given the chance'. In a slightly less veiled response, Bush himself declared that the sanctions regime was 'not very effective', and warned of 'appropriate action' if Iraq was caught 'developing WMD'.[35]

This assessment of the potentiality rather than the actuality of the threat posed by Iraq's weapons of mass destruction concurred with the assessment of the British intelligence agencies. By the summer of 2001, the view of the JIC was that while Iraq may have been attempting to reconstitute a nuclear weapons programme, it would not be able to construct an actual nuclear weapon in less than five years (even assuming that it could get hold of the required material) and that while it had 'increased the pace and scope' of its missile research and development programmes, it was 'probably' in possession of only a handful of ageing Scud-derived missiles with 'little accuracy'. While the JIC also felt it to be 'likely' that Iraq was still trying to make CBW and that there were 'grounds for concern', officials were also sure to point out that the intelligence picture on Iraq's WMD was 'limited', 'patchy', and 'unclear'.[36] A similar picture was also being presented by the US intelligence agencies, who judged that while Iraq 'might' be in possession of various chemical and biological stockpiles, and while it was thought to be continuing to work on producing CBW, it did not, as yet, have any weaponised material.[37]

49

A moment to seize

The events of 11 September 2001 brutally exposed the fomenting threat posed to core Western states by unstable conditions within the frontier zones of the global political economy. In particular, the attacks were seen to highlight the dangers of a conjunction between rogue states, an international proliferation of WMD, and extreme (primarily Islamic) terrorist organisations. Congruent with this analysis, the Bush administration now set course for a more assertive imperialist strategy as a means of dealing with these issues. This took the form of an American-led 'war on terror', the apparent objective of which was to ensure the complete destruction of international terrorism and to promote the values of 'freedom' and 'democracy' as the harbingers of international stability, security, prosperity, and justice. The anodyne nature of this discourse was also far from accidental. By enabling disparate nations from all corners of the earth to subscribe to the project in support of the US without compromising their own domestic political integrity, the vacuity of the 'war on terror' would successfully allow the neo-conservatives to pursue their long-held ambitions for a new world order under the ideological banner of international unity.

That the war on terror would not be confined to al-Qaeda, the perpetrators of the 9/11 attacks who were presently being harboured by the Taleban regime in Afghanistan, was clear from the outset. Quickly concluding that the attacks provided both the opportunity as well as the justification for the pursuit of a more aggressive foreign policy, hawkish elements in Washington began to press for a more vigorous and expansionary response. Donald Rumsfeld, the US Secretary of Defense, enthused that the attacks would now enable the United States to go far beyond al-Qaeda and, in particular, that it would allow it to secure the goal of regime change in Iraq. The aim, as he put it, should be to 'hit Saddam Hussein at the same time', to '[g]o massive. Sweep it all up. Things related and not'. Or, as Condoleeza Rice, the President's National Security Advisor, exhorted, the US needed to 'capitalise on these opportunities'. Indeed, within twenty-four hours of 9/11, the President himself was exhorting counter-terrorism officials to drag up 'any shred' of evidence that might be used to link Saddam to the attacks.[38]

The view that the events of 9/11 provided a unique opportunity to refashion the global order was one that was also shared by Tony Blair. Instantly recognising that the pursuit of a more interventionist foreign policy by the United States would offer a means of strengthening British influence on the global stage, the Prime Minister argued that the terrorist attacks were a clear demonstration that the 'good life of the West' was now under threat from 'chaos and strife' in other regions of the world, and that a policy of active engagement was now 'the only serious foreign policy on offer'. September 11, he proclaimed, had 'opened the world up'. In an attempt to galvanise public support behind the war on terror, the Prime Minister also sought to present the campaign as part of a broader international agenda encompassing the Arab–Israeli conflict, global poverty, and climate change.[39] Fervently gripped by what would become an increasingly messianic zeal, Blair told the Labour party conference in October that the war was fundamentally a global struggle for social justice, designed to bring the 'values of democracy and freedom to people around the world'. Thus:

> [t]he starving, the wretched, the dispossessed, the ignorant, those living in want and squalor from the deserts of North Africa to the slums of Gaza, to the mountain ranges of Afghanistan: they too are our cause. This is a moment to seize. The kaleidoscope has been shaken. The pieces are in flux. Soon they will settle again. Before they do, let us re-order the world around us.[40]

In this context, an attack on al-Qaeda would thus be the mere opening act of a much longer saga. 'The first phase', the Prime Minister augured, 'is the action in Afghanistan. The next phase is against international terrorism in all its forms'.[41] Importantly, Blair also recognised that a widening of the conflict would open the way for dealing with the ongoing issue of Iraq, declaring that it was now time 'for the Saddam-induced suffering of the Iraqi people to be ended'.[42] Although it was impossible to see how this was to be achieved without actually removing Saddam Hussein from power, and although Iraq itself was still believed to pose a potential, rather than an actual, threat to peace and security (with Blair telling one newspaper, for instance, that Iraq was as yet 'still trying to acquire' a WMD capability),[43] the Prime Minister remained adamant that tougher measures were needed. As he would later profess, were the United States not now seeking to adopt a harder line against Iraq, then he would 'certainly have been pressing them to take action', since they were 'the only country with the overwhelming firepower to do this'.[44]

It was also clear from the outset, however, that it would not be possible to achieve any wholesale reordering of the global political and economic landscape through extensive and direct intervention. Given the broad and diffuse nature of the apparent threat to Western civilisation, the adoption of an overtly imperialist strategy designed to directly quell possible intransigents would not only be unwieldy, expensive, and dangerous, but would also help to solidify anti-Western (and especially anti-American) sentiments around the world. As such, the US instead sought to avoid the need for large-scale intervention by credibly establishing its willingness to pursue just such a course of action should it be required. By sending out a strong signal to would-be transgressors that any attempt to undermine or to challenge American geo-strategic interests would be severely punished, the US would be able to engage in a restructuring of the global political and economic order without the need for any 'old-style' imperialist entanglements.

The success of this new imperialist strategy thus hinged on establishing a credible willingness to use force. While the impending invasion of Afghanistan would prove to be useful in this respect, the unleashing of overwhelming military power against one of the poorest and most weakly armed countries on earth would not necessarily provide a convincing display of resolve. For this, Iraq would serve a far more useful purpose. From among the variety of factors now conspiring to drive US foreign policy—including Iraq's geographical location atop the world's second-largest supply of oil (control of which would enable the United States to reduce its dependency on Saudi Arabia, to safeguard the dollar as the world's chief reserve currency, and hence to sustain large current account deficits without harsh domestic adjustments)[45]—a discernible advantage of imposing regime change in Iraq was that this would also provide a more effective means of establishing US credibility, and hence of reordering the Middle East and the wider world, than would an attack on Afghanistan. As Bush declared, the installation of democracy in Afghanistan and Iraq would 'show the power of freedom to transform that vital region' and would provide the 'inspiration for reforms throughout the Muslim world'.[46] Or, as Paul Wolfowitz (the US Deputy Defense Secretary) put it, a central advantage of attacking Iraq was that it was sufficiently weak to guarantee a swift military victory, and sufficiently difficult to establish US credibility. It was, he explained, eminently 'do-able'.[47] This being the case, while keen to maintain a tight focus on the war on terror for fear that a rapid escalation would undermine international support, and hence external legitimacy, for the campaign, the President remained adamant that the theatre of operations would nevertheless soon need to be widened. 'We won't do Iraq now', he remarked, '[b]ut eventually we'll have to return to that question'.[48]

Concluding remarks

The contextual framework within which the question of Iraq developed as a political issue in Britain during the late 1990s was based on a trio of interrelated themes: the transformation of Iraq into an international pariah, the adoption of an assertive foreign policy by the New Labour government, and the ascent to power of the neo-conservative Bush regime in the United States. This framework was also fundamentally conditioned by the dominant norms and values underpinning the structures of the British political system. Having facilitated the rise of New Labour as a highly centralised, hierarchical, and elitist political organisation, the con-stitutional architecture of the British state served to amplify these effects in office by imposing relatively few barriers on the use of executive power. In terms of foreign policy, the inculcation of these behavioural norms and values was expressed in the adoption of a strong and interventionist approach, utilising the broader framework of a transatlantic-bridge strat-egy as a means of elevating and projecting British power across the world stage. Falling increasingly under the direct personal control of the Prime Minister, this approach was further entrenched by the campaigns involv-ing Iraq, Kosovo, and Sierra Leone, all of which were seen to demonstrate the virtues of strong and decisive leadership, and all of which certainly demonstrated the high degree of latitude afforded the British premier in foreign affairs.

Importantly, New Labour's foreign-policy strategy also envisaged the pursuit of regime change in Iraq. With Iraq seen as a primary, if an as yet potential, node of instability within the global political economy, a policy of regime change would help to entrench a world order constructed around Western interests by enhancing the credibility of the main Western powers, and by thus sending out a warning signal to other would-be trans-gressors that any attempt to undermine these interests would not be tol-erated. While this centrally determined policy preference was initially ruled out by a variety of political and legal difficulties, the rise of the neo-con-servative Bush administration in the United States, coupled with the events of 9/11, led to a dramatic loosening of these constraints. By agree-ing to support the new-imperialist strategy now being pursued by Washington, Blair was presented with a golden opportunity to help refash-ion the world order and to remove Saddam Hussein. It was one he was not about to pass up.

4

The March to War

The atrocities of 9/11 provided the Bush administration with the pretext to unleash a militarily enforced policy of regime change in Iraq. Key among a variety of motives, the overthrow of Saddam Hussein would provide a useful means of establishing US credibility in the war on terror, and would thereby form an integral part of its new-imperialist strategy designed to expand American political and economic influence across the globe. Importantly, these developments in the United States also enabled senior figures within the New Labour government to pursue their own ambitions of global reordering. Crucially, this too involved a policy of regime change in Iraq. This led to the adoption of a strategy designed to secure legal and political cover for such a move by highlighting the apparent dangers of Iraq's WMD, by focusing on the need for new UN weapons inspections, and by engaging in a concerted propaganda campaign designed to sway domestic and international opinion in favour of stiffer measures. The specific way in which this strategy was constructed also laid bare the highly secretive and centralised nature of decision-making within the New Labour government, which was effectively controlled by a tightly knit group based around Number 10: neither the Cabinet nor Parliament were included in the process of formulating the Iraq policy, and neither were they aware of its underlying developments.

The least worst option

While the attempt to construct an international coalition for the war on terror placed Tony Blair at the heart of world affairs, the drive towards global multilateralism was matched by an increasing degree of unilateralism at home. With Parliament in recess and with the Cabinet disbanded, the government's response to the 11 September crisis was essentially deter-mined by an informal coterie consisting of Blair and his inner court of per-sonal advisors. Chief among these were Foreign Secretary Jack Straw, Alastair Campbell (now the government's Director of Communications and Strategy), David Manning (Blair's foreign-policy advisor), and Jonathon Powell (the Prime Minister's Chief of Staff), as well as John Scarlett (head of the JIC) and Sir Richard Dearlove (Chief of the Secret Intelligence Service, MI6). The full Cabinet itself convened just once in the initial three weeks after 9/11, and this, too, was a mere briefing exercise rather than a collective discussion about the appropriate course of action to take.[1] Nevertheless, this willingness to set procedural conventions aside in favour of looser and more malleable arrangements was justified by the Prime Minister on the grounds that such flexibility was essential in order to enable him to take direct personal control of events during a crisis. As he explained,

> when you are in a situation like that you have got to put aside the normal bureaucracy and thinking. If you are constrained by that, forget it, you will never get on top of it at all and you have got to be prepared to knock the rules out of the way in order to get the thing done.[2]

In this vein, the fight against global terrorism also provided a useful pretext for strengthening the internal powers of the state itself. In a hastily contrived move, the Anti-Terrorism, Crime and Security Act created a range of new measures, including the ability of the Home Secretary to indefinitely detain a foreign national without charge should he or she be designated a 'suspected international terrorist'. This derogated from Article 5 of the European Convention on Human Rights, was widely con-demned by human-rights and civil-liberties groups, and was subsequently found to be illegal by the High Court in December 2004.[3] The onset of the war on terror also brought out the worst of New Labour's entrenched desire to spin and control the flow of politically sensitive information. Starkly exposed in the subterranean remarks of Jo Moore, a government special advisor who suggested to ministers that 9/11 was 'a good day to bury bad news', the government's emphasis on media management was manifest in a somewhat less cynical fashion during early October, when a largely open-sourced information dossier on al-Qaeda was produced. This was designed to coincide with an emergency session of Parliament, which was now recalled by the Prime Minister as part of the drive to secure public support for military action against Afghanistan.[4]

Managing the flow of information was also central to the government's handling of the military campaign itself. The US-led invasion started on 7 October with a sustained aerial bombardment, and Parliament was again restricted to a vote on the adjournment with military engagements already under way. The invasion soon gave rise to mounting public concerns in Britain about the potential for a humanitarian crisis, and to growing fears that it might increase the risk of terrorist attacks. As public opinion began to turn in favour of a pause in the bombing, the government went on the offensive. Key to this domestic assault was the establishment of a Coalition Information Centre, a media-handling and monitoring unit based in Islamabad, Washington, and London that was designed to help present the war in the most favourable light for the government. In particular, the pressure fell heavily on the BBC. At one point, Alastair Campbell fired off a sixteen-page litany of complaint to Richard Sambrook, the BBC's Head of News, severely criticising its coverage of the war. Accusing the organisation of broadcasting a 'catalogue of lies', the government's Director of Communications and Strategy drew special attention to the output of the BBC reporters Andrew Gilligan and Rageh Omar, deriding it as 'Taleban propaganda'. Sambrook was also apparently warned that if the BBC did not pull all of its reporters out of Afghanistan, the government would 'throw everything at you'.[5] In the event, however, the rapid obliteration of the Taleban and the effective dispersal of al-Qaeda produced a swift end to the preliminary conflict and ensured that such threats were not put to the test. Although the BBC would be back in the government's sights before long, for now attention began to turn to other matters.

With victory in Afghanistan a cast-iron certainty, from mid-November the chief hawks in Washington started to pursue their policy of regime change in Iraq with more vigour. The existing plans for a military invasion began to be secretly updated, covert CIA operations to depose or kill Saddam Hussein were intensified, and Hans Blix, the head of the UN's new weapons inspectorate, UNMOVIC,[6] was informed by US officials that while the war in Afghanistan had delivered a 'useful demonstrative effect' to the rest of the world, the expectation was that Saddam Hussein would never voluntarily comply with his obligations to disarm.[7] At the same time, senior figures in the Bush administration now began to construct the public case for action in order to drum up support for the policy. Despite uncertainties within the US intelligence community, Donald Rumsfeld asserted that the government had 'bulletproof' evidence linking

Iraq to al-Qaeda (though he would later confess that there was no 'strong, hard evidence that links the two'),[8] while Colin Powell, the US Secretary of State and the hitherto leading moderate voice within the administration, now maintained that the United States had been 'concerned' about Iraq's development of WMD and its sponsorship of terrorism 'for a long time', and warned that the US government was now considering 'a variety of options' to secure its objective of regime change.[9] This stood in stark contrast to his claim just eight months earlier that Iraq did not have 'any significant capability with respect to weapons of mass destruction'.[10] This hardened stance was also signalled by the President himself. In his annual State of the Union Address, Bush denounced Iraq, Iran, and North Korea as constituting an 'axis of evil' that was supportive of terrorist organisations and that was determined to acquire WMD with which to threaten the United States and its allies. To deal with such dangers, the President declared that the US government was now prepared to act pre-emptively and would, if necessary, take unilateral action against any emerging or potential threats. The war on terror, he warned, was 'only beginning'.[11]

But the claims emanating from the Bush administration did not match the intelligence reports being received by the British government. By mid-November 2001 the JIC had already concluded that there was 'no evidence' of any 'practical co-operation' between al-Qaeda and Iraq, and that any future co-operation was 'unlikely because of mutual distrust'.[12] The JIC's assessment of Iraq's WMD capacity was equally negative. Throughout the early months of 2002, it noted that the intelligence on the subject was 'poor', and that it was founded on 'sporadic and patchy' information. At most, the JIC considered Iraq to possess no more than twenty medium-range ballistic missiles (with development programmes for a proscribed longer-range version being 'unlikely' to present any danger before 2007 if sanctions remained in place), that it 'may' have retained some stocks of chemical and biological agents, and that while it had the ability to produce 'significant quantities' within weeks and months respectively, there was 'very little evidence' to suggest that any chemical, biological, or nuclear weapons programmes were currently being pursued. Moreover, the JIC was also of the view that Saddam would only be likely to use any WMD 'if his regime were threatened', and warned that greater dangers were being posed by the proliferation of weapons from other sources, such as North Korea and Iran.[13]

Nevertheless, senior figures in the New Labour government were also now hardening in their desire to secure regime change in Iraq. In the spring of 2002 a top-secret options paper compiled by the Cabinet Office Overseas and Defence Secretariat outlined the framework within which the government's policy was now developing. It argued that while the strategy of containment had 'severely restricted' Iraq's ballistic missile programme, had 'hindered' its chemical and biological programmes, and had 'effectively frozen' its nuclear programme, the attempt to keep Iraq under control was now breaking down. As such, while there was deemed to be 'no greater threat now than in recent years that Saddam will use WMD', the government's long-standing objective of reintegrating Iraq into the global political economy was now thought to necessitate a new approach, and this would inevitably require a change of regime. 'Implicitly', the paper argued, 'this cannot happen with Saddam Hussein in power', and the only 'certain means' of removing him and his elite was 'to invade and impose a new government'.[14]

Such a conclusion left the British government with limited options. Given that regime change had 'no basis in international law', and given that an invasion would therefore be 'legally very difficult' in the absence of a clear link between Iraq and international terrorism, the paper stated that war could only be justified if Iraq was found to be in breach of UN Resolution 687 (passed at the end of the Gulf War), on the grounds that this would revive the legal authority to use force. While this line of argument was contested by Foreign Office legal advisors, who claimed that it would be 'unlikely to receive any support' from the international community,[15] the options paper itself also noted that going to war to enforce a UN resolution would require the express authorisation of the Security Council, and that this would only be obtained if Iraq refused to readmit (or subsequently expelled) UN weapons inspectors, or if 'incontrovertible' proof of 'large-scale' WMD activity could be presented. Obtaining such a 'legal justification for large scale military action', however, was deemed to be an unlikely proposition, given that the present state of the intelligence on Iraq's WMD was 'insufficiently robust to meet this criterion'. The paper thus concluded that the recommended strategy for dealing with these difficulties should be to maintain the policy of containment as 'the least worst option', while at the same time adopting 'a staged approach' based around 'establishing international support, building up pressure on Saddam, and developing military plans'. The UN inspections process, it observed, would also need to be restarted, backed by 'the risk of military action', and while officials were cautioned to avoid 'overtly espousing regime change', it was also noted that a means of 'sensitising the public' would have to be devised—namely 'a media campaign to warn of the dangers that Saddam poses and to prepare public opinion both in the UK and abroad'. The 'optimal times' for military action, it was presciently observed, were in the spring of 2003.[16]

Very carefully done

While Blair was now aiming to allay public fears that Iraq was being lined up as the next target in the war on terror by continuing to insist that 'no decisions have been taken',[17] leaked documents detailing high-level talks between British and US officials at this time provide evidence of a much firmer disposition. On 14 March, Sir David Manning dispatched a memo to the Prime Minister outlining his discussions with Condoleeza Rice. This noted both Blair's keenness to be involved with the American-led policy and the domestic difficulties that would be involved in this course of action. Thus, Manning wrote:

> I said that you would not budge in your support for regime change but you had to manage a press, a Parliament and a public opinion that was very different than anything in the States. And you would not budge on your insistence that, if we pursued regime change, it must be very carefully done and produce the right result.

Indeed, the need for such caution was clearly evident. As Manning warned, the Bush administration was underestimating the difficulties involved in securing regime change, and was not giving sufficient forethought to the postwar situation. The 'big questions', such as 'how to persuade international opinion that military action against Iraq is necessary and justified' and 'what happens on the morning after', were, it was noted, yet to be answered. Indicating a possible route through these difficulties, however, Manning suggested that Blair should direct his influence in Washington towards ensuring a greater focus on postwar planning, and that he should also seek to deal with Iraq by using the pressure of UN weapons inspections, since any refusal from Saddam about accepting unfettered access 'would be a powerful argument' in favour of stronger measures.[18]

Four days later a similar memo was received from Sir Christopher Meyer, the British ambassador to the United States. Detailing his discussions with Paul Wolfowitz, Meyer pointed out that the idea of regime change would be 'a tough sell' and warned that Blair would need 'cover' for any military action. In terms of the political manoeuvring required,

Meyer highlighted the 'critical importance' of the Middle East peace process 'as an integral part of the anti-Saddam strategy', emphasised that the risk of WMD would also be 'crucial to the public case', and, like Manning, suggested that the Prime Minister should seek 'to wrongfoot Saddam on the inspectors and the UN Security Council resolutions'. In sum, the view being presented to the Americans was that: 'We backed regime change, but the plan had to be clever and failure was not an option'.[19]

The difficulties of pursuing such a policy were also highlighted by Peter Ricketts, the Political Director of the Foreign Office. Outlining his concerns to Jack Straw on 22 March, Ricketts pointed out that there were as yet 'no clear and compelling objectives' for military action, and that there would be 'real problems' in portraying Iraq as a current threat, since while its WMD programmes were 'extremely worrying', even the best of surveys 'will not show much advance in recent years'. '[W]hat has changed', he observed, 'is not the pace of Saddam Hussein's WMD programmes, but our tolerance of them post-11 September.' Also recommending that the political strategy should be to seek the readmission of UN inspectors on the grounds that any obfuscation by Saddam would provide 'a stronger ground for switching to other methods', Ricketts nevertheless presented the government's dilemma in stark terms. As he put it:

> To get public and Parliamentary support for military options we have to be convincing that the threat is so serious/imminent that it is worth sending our troops to die for.[20]

These concerns were subsequently echoed by the Foreign Secretary himself. In a memo to the Prime Minister three days later, Straw too urged the need for caution, warning Blair that there was 'a long way to go' before Labour MPs would be convinced about the need for action, and pointing out that the 'risks are high, both for you and the Government'. Restating the line that it was not 'the threat from Iraq' but the 'tolerance of the international community', especially the US, that had changed since 9/11, Straw further emphasised the need for formal cover, warning that British action would need to be 'narrated with reference to the international rule of law' and stressing that the UN process would thus be needed 'in terms of public explanation, and in terms of legal sanction for any subsequent military action'. Furthermore, while arguing that Iraq's breach of UN resolutions should form 'the core of a political strategy', the Foreign Secretary also warned of several 'potential elephant traps'. The first of these was the issue of regime change itself. Since this was illegal under international law, Straw cautioned that 'it could form part of the method of any strategy, but not a goal', and pointed out that while it could usefully be argued that regime change was an essential means of removing the threat of WMD, the latter objective itself had to be the stated end. The rationale for such action, too, he added, would also need strengthening. On the 'big question', namely 'what will this action achieve?', the Foreign Secretary warned that at the moment, '[t]here seems to be a larger hole in this than anything'.[21]

In early April, the Prime Minister convened with Bush for a summit at the President's ranch in Crawford, Texas. According to a leaked Cabinet Office briefing paper, during the course of these discussions Blair followed the line presented by his advisors, agreeing 'that the UK would support military action to bring about regime change, provided that certain conditions were met'. Chief among these were that efforts should be made to reinvigorate the Middle East peace process, and that the Iraq issue should be addressed through the United Nations as a means of establishing legal cover and of helping to raise domestic and international support for the use of military force.[22] Desirous of ensuring a degree of international agreement in order to help bolster US public opinion and to avoid a loss of international support for what now appeared to be an increasingly faltering war on terror, the President readily agreed to acquiesce in this strategy despite fears within the administration (most notably from Rumsfeld and Vice-President Cheney) that it would shackle the United States to a multilateral deadweight. At the ensuing press conference, however, Bush struck a less mollifying posture, declaring that 'the policy of my government is the removal of Saddam', and that 'all options are on the table'. Though anxious to portray a more cautious approach for fear of stepping outside his currently proscribed legal and political boundaries, the Prime Minister was also keen to press home the case. Professing to 'know' that Iraq had been 'developing' WMD, and that this constituted a clear threat to international security, Blair too warned that 'all the options are open' for dealing with the issue.[23]

Getting rid of Saddam

That such assertions stood in contrast to the intelligence assessments of the JIC, which had not stated with any certainty at all that Iraq was developing WMD, was apparently of little concern. Indeed, such was the enthusiasm for effecting a regime change in Iraq that senior officials on both sides of the Atlantic were now increasingly willing to be convinced about the reality of the Iraqi threat regardless of the actual intelligence that was on offer. Paradoxically, such self-deception was also enhanced by the intensely secretive nature of the Iraqi regime itself, with the lack of any clear and firm intelligence lending further credence to the view that the true scale of Iraq's WMD capacity was being concealed, and that an unseen yet deadly peril was being amassed against them. As such, since the available intelligence was not thought to be an adequate reflection of the real situation, the exaggeration of this material was now felt to be both legitimate and a necessary course of action to take. Needless to say, the task of persuading domestic and international opinion as to the validity of this viewpoint, and hence of the need for more forceful measures, would require something more than assertions of faith and speculation.[24]

As manoeuvres to prepare public and political opinion began to get under way, such claims were subsequently repeated by Blair, albeit somewhat inconsistently, throughout the spring. In some of the more notable examples of this, the Prime Minister told the House of Commons that Iraq was 'developing' WMD, which posed a threat 'not just to the region, but to the wider world'; told journalists that Iraq had actually 'acquired' WMD and that the threat was 'not in doubt at all'; and told the American television channel NBC that Iraq was in possession of 'major amounts of chemical and biological weapons'. Furthermore, despite proclaiming that the right way to deal with these issues was through the United Nations, the Prime Minister also played down the prospects of arriving at a peaceful conclusion, asserting that he did not believe that sufficient co-operation would ever be obtained. As he put it: 'there are some regimes, like Saddam's in Iraq, where you are never going to be able to come to an arrangement or a partnership'.[25]

The day after the Crawford summit, Blair's circumspective guard dropped still further. Outlining his vision of the future world order in a speech at the George Bush Senior Presidential Library, the Prime Minister called for an entirely new system of 'interlocking alliances' between the world's major powers (the centre of which was to be the British and US axis), and argued strongly in favour of utilising a more active foreign policy as a means of dealing with the dangers of global instability. Signalling, too, that this should not be constrained by the existing systems of laws and conventions governing interstate relations, Blair asserted his belief in the legitimate use of military force as a defence against terrorism and WMD, maintaining that 'if necessary and justified', such actions 'should involve regime change'.[26] That this formulation offered a framework for pursuing a harder line against Iraq was made abundantly clear the following month, with the Prime Minister detailing his views on the situation to BBC's *Newsnight* programme. As he put it,

> I certainly believe that getting rid of Saddam would be highly desirable and I certainly endorse the policy of doing everything we can to get rid of Saddam Hussein if at all possible.[27]

However, while the government's Iraq policy was now developing at a pace, the decision-making process itself was not being conducted in a clearly structured and collective manner. Rather, in traditional New Labour style, this was essentially driven by an informal, secretive, and highly centralised cabal clustered around Number 10. Although the question of Iraq was discussed in Cabinet more than any other topic from spring to autumn, and while it was covered no less than two dozen times in the nine months prior to the start of the war, such discussions amounted to little more than oral briefings by the Foreign Secretary, the Defence Secretary, and the Prime Minister, and were described by Clare Short as a mere series of 'updates' on the situation rather than a rigorous process of collective engagement.[28] While small groupings of ministers were briefed on the outlines of the intelligence by John Scarlett, the Cabinet itself did not engage in any substantive discussion either of the underlying risks or of the various alternative diplomatic and military options available, did not discuss the merits or otherwise of the intelligence material in any detail, and was not privy to any of the papers and discussions that had been informing the government's approach.[29]

Moreover, while the Cabinet's main circuitry for dealing with foreign-policy issues, the Defence and Overseas Policy Committee (DOP), did not convene at all from June, a series of around twenty-five informal meetings attended by a small number of key ministers, officials, and military staff now formed the primary organisational framework in which the policy evolved.[30] This centralisation was further compounded by a restructuring of the Cabinet Office, with responsibility for intelligence and security matters now being passed over to David Omand, the newly created Security and Intelligence Co-ordinator. By establishing a direct link between the Prime Minister and the JIC, which had previously reported to the Cabinet Secretary, the result, as Lord Butler would later point out, was to further sideline the Cabinet in intelligence matters and 'to concentrate detailed knowledge and effective decision-making in fewer minds at the top'.[31]

All this, however, was crucially facilitated by the uncodified structures and processes at the core of the British political system. With only the norms of convention and the dictates of political expediency to constrain their activities, Blair and his courtiers found little to prevent them from developing and pursuing the Iraq policy as they wished, relatively free from external hindrance. Indeed, such was the wide degree of latitude and free reign now afforded by Britain's constitutional architecture, that, unlike those of the DOP, the *ad hoc* and informal meetings on the Iraq policy were not even officially recorded. This led the Cabinet Secretary Sir Andrew Turnbull himself to remark that, '[t]here is surprisingly little which codifies when a meeting is minuted and when it is not'. Moreover, while Turnbull sought to justify this by arguing that the ability of ministers 'to chew the fat' without fear of their views being recorded was an essential part of good government, the lack of detailed and formal minutes also undermined the ability of those outside the process to ascertain where responsibility for decision-making lay, and thus removed one of the key mechanisms for scrutinising the executive and for holding its members to account.[32]

In addition to this, the Cabinet itself remained distinctly unwilling to confront the Prime Minister over the direction of the Iraq policy. While a number of concerns were raised at one notable meeting in mid-March (at which disquiet was emolliated by Blair's emphasis on the UN process), the general picture, as Robin Cook pointed out, was that ministers 'could not have hoped for fuller opportunities to discuss Iraq', but had patently failed to exercise their constitutional responsibility by refusing to 'express anxiety about the drift to military action' or to engage in any 'great debate' on the matter.[33] In sum, Cabinet decision-making on Iraq took the form of 'a question and answer session' in which Blair behaved as if he were addressing 'a party branch' rather than the 'supreme body of collective government'.[34] Or, as one minister put it, the situation represented nothing less than 'a complete breakdown of the normal arrangements for the British government system', to the extent that the Cabinet had now 'ceased to function'.[35]

Such concerns about the centralised nature of the government's policy-making on Iraq, however, were also disposed of in a typically brusque manner. Insisting that ministers had been given plenty of opportunity to discuss the matter, Blair later maintained that the Cabinet system was very much 'alive and well', and that New Labour was 'a government that involves people fully'.[36] Jack Straw, on the other hand, argued that some of the discussions 'had to be very tightly held' given the political sensitivities surrounding the issue. 'There has always been an entourage in Number 10', he pointed out, 'and people need to chill out about that'.[37]

A realistic political strategy

While presenting the Prime Minister with a much-coveted opportunity to pursue a more interventionist line in the global arena, the outbreak of the war on terror proved to be a double-edged sword. Though Blair continued to emphasise the need to maintain strong relations with both Europe and America, by the summer the policy of tying the government to the neo-conservative mast was starting to put the transatlantic-bridge strategy under increasing strain. The key reason for this was a growing divergence between the geo-strategic perceptions of the United States and those of core Western European nations. While more than four-fifths of Americans now considered the development of WMD by Iraq to be a serious danger, fewer than three-fifths of Europeans concurred, and while more than nine-tenths of Americans felt that international terrorism was a threat to vital interests, this view was shared by fewer than two-thirds of Europeans.[38] More precariously, Blair's unwavering support for the war on terror was also starting to put his domestic political position under mounting pressure. More than half the respondents in a YouGov survey stated their opposition to any military action against Iraq, almost half claimed that they did not trust the Prime Minister, and two-thirds felt that he was acting as Bush's 'poodle'. More worryingly still, over half thought that Blair should resign before or shortly after the next general election.[39]

Despite the difficulties caused by alienating both European and domestic opinion, the Prime Minister remained convinced about the efficacy of remaining as close as possible to the United States. In Blair's view, although a US invasion of Iraq would now happen 'whatever anyone else said or did', and although public opinion in Britain, Europe, and the rest of the world would not support such action without the express authorisation of the United Nations, leaving America to pursue a unilateral course of action 'would be more damaging to long-term world peace and security' than any actions that it might take as part of a coalition. Put simply, the closer the British government stood to the United States, the greater would be its capacity to influence the way Washington set about reordering the global political economy.[40]

With the national interest thus determined, the fact that there was likely to be strong domestic opposition to the pursuit of regime change in Iraq was thereby dismissed as a legitimate reason for pursuing an alternative course of action. Nevertheless, while the views of the British public would not, in the event, be allowed to derail the government's ultimate objectives, officials remained sharply aware that it would be far less risky and far more practical if domestic opinion could be persuaded to acquiesce in the venture. To this end, the New Labour spin machine was now vigorously pressed into action. Ironically, one of its first aims was to dispel the prevailing image of the government as being obsessed with media management and control-freakery. To achieve this, it was duly announced that Blair could now be directly questioned on a biannual basis by the House of Commons Liaison Committee, a move that was presented as a triumph of democratic accountability, openness, and transparency. The true purpose, however, was to provide the Prime Minister with a platform for disseminating New Labour's political message and for dispelling the government's image as being obsessed with spin at the expense of substance. Indeed, as Blair himself explained during his very first appearance before the committee, the arrangement would help the government to deal with the 'relentless 24 hour media gaze', and would help to 'make sure that people understand better what we are about'. In short, it would provide the government with 'a way of overcoming what [are] perceived ... as issues to do simply with news management'.[41]

Further belying the committee's appearance as a democratising reform, Blair also took the opportunity to reassert his credentials as a firm leader, telling its members that he would 'make no apology for having a strong centre', and insisting that the need for resolute and decisive action was now more 'essential' than ever, given 'the totally changed foreign policy and security situation'. To affirm the centralising message still further, the Prime Minister repeatedly refused to commit to allowing a substantive parliamentary vote on any decision to go to war with Iraq, stating merely that the House of Commons would 'have the fullest opportunity to debate the matter and express its view'. More concrete assurances, however, were not forthcoming, with Blair insisting that he would not be pinned down 'to any specific form of consultation'.[42]

The Prime Minister remained similarly non-committal about the need to gain the sanction of the United Nations before taking any action.

Informing ministerial colleagues that the government 'should not tie our-selves down to doing nothing unless the UN authorised it', Blair dealt a similarly curt response to questions concerning the legality of any conflict, telling the Cabinet that '[t]he time to debate the legal base for our action should be when we take that action'.[43] This stymieing of debate, however, was hardly surprising given the less-than-encouraging nature of the legal advice that had been thus far received from the Attorney-General, Lord Goldsmith. As it presently stood, Goldsmith's assessment (concurring with the prevailing view at the Foreign Office) was that self-defence and humanitarian intervention were not justifiable reasons for military action, and that the use of force could only be authorised with an entirely new UN resolution.[44]

The government's strategy for dealing with the Iraq issue was further consolidated in July during a high-level policy discussion at Downing Street. The central purpose of this meeting, as outlined in the accom-panying briefing paper, was to develop 'a realistic political strategy' centred around the United Nations, the issue of WMD, and a concerted 'informa-tion campaign' designed to persuade domestic and international opinion of the veracity of the case against Iraq. In other words, the overarching aim was to 'create the conditions in which we could legally support military action'. The key to this, it was observed, would be to focus attention on the weapons issue. By highlighting the apparent dangers of Iraq's WMD, officials recognised that this would offer an indirect means of deposing Saddam Hussein, since while it was acknowledged that regime change *per se* was 'not a proper basis for military action under international law', it was nevertheless now considered to be 'a necessary condition for control-ling Iraqi WMD'. In a strategic sense, then, focusing on the removal of Iraq's WMD would inevitably require and would thus lead to the removal of Saddam Hussein, while diverting attention onto safer political and legal territory. On this basis, officials were informed that the only viable route to take was a process of renewed UN inspections, which could be effec-tively designed to ensnare the Iraqi dictator. 'It is just possible', the paper maintained, 'that an ultimatum could be cast in terms which Saddam would reject ... and which would not be regarded as unreasonable by the international community'.[45]

At the meeting itself, details of which were designated as 'extremely sensitive' and to be divulged only to those with a genuine 'need to know', senior members of Number 10's Iraq coterie worked out their strategy in more detail. The meeting began with a summary of the intelligence on

Iraq. John Scarlett emphasised the 'tough' nature of Saddam's regime and reiterated that the only way to overthrow it 'was likely to be by massive military action', while Richard Dearlove informed the gathering of his understanding, based on discussions in Washington, that the Bush administration now regarded military action as 'inevitable', that the justification for this was going to be 'the conjunction of terrorism and WMD', and that 'the intelligence and facts were being fixed around the policy'. Dearlove also warned that while the Americans would have 'no patience with the UN route', British involvement in helping to secure regime change was nevertheless considered to be 'essential'.[46]

Though agreeing that a US invasion of Iraq was now unavoidable, Jack Straw was keen to repeat his earlier warning that the case against Iraq was 'thin', given that 'Saddam was not threatening his neighbours, and his WMD capability was less than that of Libya, North Korea or Iran'. On this basis, the Foreign Secretary thus argued that the government's strategy should be to devise a plan to present Saddam with an ultimatum for re-admitting the UN weapons inspectors, though he added that this would need to be done 'discreetly' in order to circumvent any US resistance to proceeding via the United Nations. Although agreeing with this approach, the Attorney-General expressed grave doubts as to whether it would be practicably possible. Warning that 'the desire for regime change was not a legal basis for military action', the government's chief legal advisor stated that the use of force could only be justified on the grounds of self-defence, humanitarian intervention, or UN authorisation, and that while the first two routes 'could not be the base in this case', relying on previous UN resolutions to provide the requisite authority would, at the present time, also prove to be 'difficult'.

The expressed view of the Prime Minister was also in accord with the need for a UN-based approach designed to entrap Saddam Hussein and to provide a legal justification for military action. As he explained, 'it would make a big difference politically and legally if Saddam refused to allow in the UN inspectors', and that '[i]f the political context were right, people would support regime change'. In Blair's mind, therefore, '[T]he two key issues were whether the military plan worked and whether we had the political strategy to give the military plan the space to work'. Following a final word of caution from the Defence Secretary, Geoff Hoon, who pointed out that the Prime Minister 'would need to decide this early' if British troops were to participate with the United States, the meeting concluded on the working assumption 'that the UK would take part in any military action'. Jack Straw was charged with the task of discreetly putting together a UN ultimatum, Scarlett was commissioned to 'send the Prime Minister a full intelligence update', and Goldsmith was dispatched to 'consider legal advice' with officials at the Foreign Office and the Ministry of Defence.[47]

A case for war

All this, however, was a mere prelude to the government's major weapon in the propaganda war, which was to be the production of an intelligence-based dossier outlining in detail the threat posed by Iraq's WMD. This process had been initiated earlier in the year with the production of a dossier on WMD proliferation in general, and had been followed by a dossier focusing explicitly on the situation in Iraq.[48] Publication of the latter document, however, had thus far been delayed, ostensibly, according to Blair, because it 'would inflame the situation too much' given the growing media speculation over the prospect of military action. A more pertinent reason, though, was that the dossier had lacked the necessary gravitas for convincing domestic opinion of the need to adopt a harder line against Iraq. Peter Ricketts, for instance, noted that publication was delayed so that the government could 'build up a fuller picture', while John Scarlett revealed that publication had been held back due to a lack of evidence, observing that the dossier lacked sufficient 'detail and information to explain the assessment judgments which were in it'. A further, more mundane reason was also flagged up by Alastair Campbell, who noted simply that the dossier was 'not terribly good'.[49]

The final dossier on Iraq's WMD was published in September and was presented as providing yet further evidence of the government's open and transparent nature, as well as its responsiveness to public opinion. The process of putting the intelligence out, Blair explained, had been driven by a combination of the 'tremendous amount of information and evidence' flowing across his desk on Iraq's WMD and, in a reversal of his prior concerns about inflaming public fears, by 'a renewed sense of urgency' about the way in which the issue was being 'publicly debated'. The purpose of the dossier, he maintained, was simply 'to respond to the call to disclose the intelligence that we knew'. Comments by Jack Straw, however, indicated a rather different set of concerns, namely that public opinion was not moving in the right direction for the government. As he put it:

if we were going to be able to make out a case for war against Iraq, we were
going to have to publish the material ... otherwise we would have just faced
day in and day out a constant complaint that we had no basis, that we had no
proper reason.[50]

Indeed, that the whole question of Iraq was now featuring prominently on
the national political agenda was due in no small part to the continuing
assertions of the Prime Minister himself concerning the need for stronger
action. Blair still refused to commit wholeheartedly to the path of the
United Nations, and observed merely that it would be 'better to have the
international community with us', but his underlying objective of regime
change continued intermittently to break the surface during his public
pronouncements on the matter. Outlining his thoughts at the beginning
of September, for instance, the Prime Minister described the situation
concerning Iraq as one in which

either the regime starts to function in an entirely different way—and there
hasn't been much sign of that—or the regime has to change. Now that is the
choice, very simply.[51]

At around the same time, production of the final dossier also began in
earnest. On 5 September, an informal, *ad hoc* gathering of intelligence
officers and government officials met to discuss 'presentational' aspects
relating to the project. Chaired by Alastair Campbell, whose own view was
that the existing dossier would need a 'substantial rewrite' to make it suitable for public consumption, the meeting charged John Scarlett (infa-
mously described by Campbell as a 'mate') with the task of drawing up an
entirely new version. Though insisting that it was 'fundamentally' important for the credibility of the dossier that it be seen as the work of the JIC,
Campbell was also aware that the dossier needed 'to be revelatory'. As he
put it, 'we needed to show it was new and informative and part of a bigger
case'.[52]

The intelligence picture on Iraq, however, had changed relatively little
during the course of the summer. In August the JIC noted that there had
been 'little intelligence' on Iraq's WMD since 1998, maintained that
Saddam Hussein would face difficulties in using such weapons due to
questions over 'the loyalty of his commanders' and the availability of
sufficient material, and restated its view that the pre-emptive use of WMD
by Iraq was unlikely since this would provide 'a justification for US
action'.[53] While new intelligence received at the end of the month
indicated that Iraq could possibly launch a chemical or biological weapons

attack within an average time-scale of between twenty and forty-five minutes, this information also remained vague and was far from certain.[54] Further still, as late as 9 September, the JIC's assessment was that although Iraq had weapons of mass destruction, the capacity to produce more, and the ability to fire them within three-quarters of an hour, nonetheless the intelligence remained 'limited', and many of the claims derived therefrom were thus 'necessarily based on judgement and assessments'. In addition to this, and somewhat contradictorily, the JIC pointed out that Iraq had 'probably dispersed' its WMD, thereby degrading its capacity to use them with any degree of rapidity, and again reiterated that Iraq was 'unlikely' to use such weapons 'prior to any attack' since this would provide the trigger for an American-led invasion. Thus, the view of the government's own intelligence providers was 'that the political cost of using CBW weapons would outweigh the military advantages and that Saddam would probably not use CBW pre-emptively'.[55]

The day after receiving this assessment, however, Blair outlined the case for action in a speech to the TUC conference. Arguing that containment had only worked 'up to a point', and that Iraq was now spending around $3 billion of illicit funds a year on WMD programmes, the Prime Minister reasserted the need to deal with the threat from Iraq now, insisting that while it 'may not erupt and engulf us this month, perhaps not even this year or the next ... it will at some point'. The British people, he urged, should 'listen to the case I will be developing over the coming weeks and reflect on it'.[56]

A major problem

Set against this panoply of official proclamations concerning the threat from Iraq's WMD, on 10 September Scarlett produced his first draft version of the dossier. Belying the lack of any substantially new intelligence material, this now espoused a more forceful line than any of the JIC's previous reports. While the dossier repeated the JIC's assessment that Iraq possessed WMD, was able to produce more, could fire them within 45 minutes, and was pursuing nuclear weapons, it contained none of the qualifications and caveats about the nature of the intelligence, and made no mention of the committee's view that a pre-emptive attack by Iraq was unlikely.[57]

While the new draft dossier created a qualitatively different impression about Iraq's WMD capabilities and intentions than had previously been the case, New Labour apparatchiks continued to harbour deep concerns about its suitability as a tool of public persuasion. Phillip Bassett, a senior special advisor working for Campbell, noted for instance that the dossier needed 'more weight' and that the government was 'in a lot of trouble' as it presently stood; the Prime Minister's official spokesman, Godric Smith, maintained that it was 'a bit of a muddle', and his counterpart, Tom Kelly, argued that it did not do enough to 'differentiate between capacity and intent' and required a 'more direct argument on why containment is breaking down'.[58] Concerned that much of the evidence in the dossier was also 'largely circumstantial', Daniel Pruce, a government press officer, maintained that some 'drafting changes' would be useful in order to 'convey the impression' that Iraq had been actively pursuing WMD, and suggested using 'copies of original documentation, if necessary with parts blanked out, to add to the feeling that we are presenting real evidence'.[59]

Jack Straw and Geoff Hoon were also critical of the dossier. The former advised that it needed 'a killer paragraph' on Iraq's defiance of the United Nations, while the Defence Secretary later explained that 'in a political sense' the draft version was 'insufficiently dramatic to make our case as strongly as I would have liked'. Although Alastair Campbell later dismissed such comments as nothing more than 'office chatter', the government's Director of Communications himself was now placed in charge of a team to supervise the dossier 'from a presentational point of view' and to make 'recommendations and suggestions' to Scarlett about ways in which it could be improved. With the publication of the dossier also designed to coincide with the production of similar material in the United States, Campbell further noted that the document needed to be one 'that complements rather than conflicts' with the assessments of the US government.[60]

With New Labour's chief spinmeister in place, the search for useful information to go in the dossier was now intensified. On 11 September a circular e-mail issued those involved in its production with 'a last(!) call for any items of intelligence that agencies think can and should be included', and reminded participants that Number 10 wanted the dossier 'to be as strong as possible'. According to John Morrison, this was a clear sign that the government was now 'scraping the bottom of the barrel' in its bid to strengthen the case against Iraq. Or, as Dr David Kelly, the government scientist whose suicide would later lead to the establishment of the Hutton Inquiry, concurred, the officials involved 'were desperate for information'.[61] Nevertheless, within a week Scarlett had produced an even more assertive draft of the dossier. While this carried a somewhat weaker claim on the speed at which Iraq could fire its WMD (now record-ing that intelligence 'suggested' that Iraq 'may' be able to deploy them within 45 minutes), the new version also maintained that Iraq's posses-sion of WMD had now been 'established beyond doubt'.[62]

By this time the process of constructing the dossier was also proving to be a source of distinct unease within the intelligence community. One unnamed official recorded that the dossier had a 'lot of spin on it', while others, according to David Kelly, were concerned about the way in which comments on earlier drafts had 'largely not been reflected in the later drafts', and were alarmed at the way in which 'people at the top of the ladder didn't want to hear some of the things' that were being said.[63] Dr Bryan Jones, the head of the nuclear, chemical, and biological warfare division of the Defence Intelligence Staff (DIS), also complained that the claims being made about Iraq's possession of WMD were 'far too strong', that the 45-minute claim was 'nebulous' and 'vague', and that the intelli-gence services 'did not have a high degree of confidence' in the evidence concerning Iraq's WMD. Blair's claim to 'know' that they were in posses-sion of such weapons, he maintained, 'was simply not true'. As Morrison put it, the Prime Minister's promulgations were being greeted throughout Whitehall with a 'collective raspberry'.[64]

Such misgivings, though, were summarily dismissed by senior officials. Geoff Hoon later claimed that the concerns related merely to 'technical amendments', Scarlett maintained that they were entirely normal and were only of 'a working level', while Blair proposed that the linguistic nuances used to present the government's claims about Iraq's WMD were of 'hardly earth shattering significance'.[65] More important still, on 20 September Bryan Jones was informed by his line manager that 'other intelligence' which effectively neutralised his concerns had now come to light, but that his team would not be permitted to see it due to its highly sensitive nature. This referred to a recent and surprise arrival of new information which, despite coming from an untested source within the Iraqi military, and despite arriving via an Iraqi army chief with links to an exile group, was now being seen to offer conclusive proof about the veracity of the 45-minute claim. Jones was assured, however, that the evidence had been thoroughly assessed by Richard Dearlove and his deputy, Martin Howard (despite their apparent lack of high-level experience in CBW analysis), and that the intelligence had been judged to be satisfactory. On this basis, Jones was told that no further complaints were now to be submitted.[66]

For all these concerns, though, the dossier was still deemed to be insufficiently persuasive. In particular, government officials felt that it did not make a strong enough case for taking action against Iraq, since it did not provide any evidence to show that Saddam Hussein posed an immediate danger. As Jonathon Powell remarked, the problem with the dossier was that it 'does nothing to demonstrate a threat, let alone an imminent attack from Saddam', and that 'it shows he has the means but it does not demonstrate he has the motive to attack his neighbours let alone the west'. 'The threat argument', he warned, 'will be a major problem'.[67]

Likewise, both Blair and Campbell were also of the opinion that the latest version of the dossier still needed 'a little rewriting'. In particular, concerns were raised about the way in which 'the nuclear issue' was being presented, while the Prime Minister also wanted 'more pictures' and 'more on human rights' in order to drive home the nature of the Iraqi regime. With a view to strengthening the dossier, Campbell subsequently presented Scarlett with a list of suggested revisions. Among these, it was noted that the executive summary 'would be stronger' if it emphasised that Iraq had 'made real progress' on WMD despite the policy of containment, that the dossier as a whole would be improved if it could be stated that Iraq had actually 'secured', rather than sought, uranium from Africa for possible use in a nuclear-weapons programme, and that the dossier 'would be stronger' if it could be 'more explicit' about the details of the intelligence reports given to the Prime Minister.[68] Although Campbell later claimed that this was 'not actually making a suggestion' but was simply 'making an observation', Scarlett's view was that the recommendations were of a more pressing nature. Campbell, he believed, was 'making requests, really, for changes', and was asking if 'on the basis of the intelligence could it be strengthened?'[69]

The following day Scarlett informed Campbell that 'in most cases' his advice had now been incorporated into the dossier, and that the language had 'been tightened' in line with his proposals at the expense of the more 'cautious' suggestions being made by various members of the DIS. With these changes in place, the JIC met on 18 September to formally discuss the dossier for the last time, and a final draft version was circulated to its members the next morning.[70] At the same time, however, Jonathon Powell was raising further concerns in an e-mail to Campbell and Scarlett. Reminding Campbell of the need to consider the kind of headline they wished to see in the London *Evening Standard* following the publication of the dossier, Powell then recommended a further change in its content. According to the Prime Minister's Chief of Staff, the dossier's current description of Saddam's willingness to use WMD 'if he believes his regime is under threat' was 'a bit of a problem', since it would support the argument that there was in fact no current WMD threat and that 'we will only create one if we attack him'. As such, Powell's suggestion that Scarlett should 'redraft' the relevant paragraph was subsequently taken up, and by the time the final version of the dossier had been produced the next day, unbeknownst to other members of the JIC, the offending text had been duly struck out. For good measure, a concluding section admitting that the government's knowledge of the Iraq situation was 'partial' and that Saddam would only use WMD 'to protect his power and eventually to project it when he feels strong enough to do so' was also dropped. The title of the dossier, too, was changed from 'Iraq's Programme for Weapons of Mass Destruction' to the more assertive 'Iraq's Weapons of Mass Destruction'. Thus concluded, the document was now signed off by Scarlett and its ownership passed over to Number 10.[71]

A very worthwhile objective

On 24 September the government's dossier was finally published. This claimed that Iraq's possession of WMD had been 'established beyond doubt', that these 'could be activated within 45 minutes' (a point that was repeated no less than four times), and that Iraq had 'existing and active military plans' for their use. The dossier also maintained that Iraq was potentially just one or two years away from producing a nuclear weapon, that it had tried to obtain a significant amount of uranium from Africa for this purpose, and that it was concealing its ballistic missiles while actively developing longer-range versions capable of hitting British military bases in South-East Europe. Moreover, despite lacking any supporting evidence, the dossier also asserted that Iraq placed 'great importance' on the possession of WMD and warned that Saddam Hussein 'does not regard them only as weapons of last resort'. The threat, it claimed, was 'serious and current'.[72]

On the same day, these claims were repeated by Blair in the House of Commons. Blair having resisted pressure for a recall of Parliament throughout the summer, and with it the prospect of a sustained period of potentially difficult questioning, the decision to hold an emergency session now enabled New Labour's elite executive to promote its case against Iraq to the fullest.[73] In the ensuing debate, the Prime Minister told the House that the intelligence picture contained in the dossier was 'extensive, detailed and authoritative', that Iraq's WMD programme was shown to be 'active, detailed and growing', and that the policy of containment was clearly no longer working. Citing the defection of Hussein Kamel in 1995, Blair also drew attention to Iraq's pathological efforts at concealment and warned that any failure to act would now undermine the credibility of the 'international community' at the risk of global instability. There was, he warned, no way in which Saddam 'could begin a conflict using such weapons and the conflict not engulf the whole world'. The 'history and the present threat' he posed were both very real.[74]

Such apocalyptic visions, however, did not quite convey the full picture. Rather, the variety of statements now being made by government figures, both in the dossier and publicly, represented a stretching and spinning of the intelligence in such a way as to exaggerate the threat posed by Iraq's WMD. Claims that Iraq's weapons programmes were 'growing', for example, were contradicted by the secret spring memos, which noted that the government's calls for stronger action had derived not from any acceleration in Iraq's WMD activity but from the greater sensitivity to potential security threats in the wake of 9/11. The claim that the intelligence was 'authoritative' was also contradicted by the fact that the vast majority of evidence had been derived from a small handful of sources (with around two-thirds of MI6 reports deriving from just two main human inputs), later prompting Lord Butler to comment on 'the relative thinness of the intelligence base'. And Blair himself was well aware of these limitations, having received a personal briefing on the intelligence from Dearlove (in contravention of the normal protocol for channelling such information to the Prime Minister through the JIC), in which he had been informed that the source of the 45-minute claim was 'unproven', and that the case itself remained 'developmental'.[75] Further still, statements referring to the initiation of conflict by Iraq were also in contrast to the JIC's stated view that Saddam had no plans to use WMD prior to an attack from outside, while the claim that such weapons could be fired within 45 minutes was contradicted by parallel claims being made about Iraq's renewed concealment efforts. In this regard, citing the case of Hussein Kamel as evidence of Iraq's inherently deceitful nature was also somewhat disingenuous, since officials failed to mention his associated claim that Iraq had actually destroyed all of its WMD after the Gulf War. Moreover, the fact that no one was able to raise this point with the government was not surprising, since the transcripts of Kamel's interviews were themselves only revealed following a leak early in 2003.[76]

In addition to this, the dossier itself was also guilty of omission. None of the qualifications, caveats and uncertainties highlighted by the JIC in its intelligence assessments were incorporated into the final version, which instead presented the material as being definitive and incontrovertible. Although history now records that virtually all the claims made by the dossier concerning Iraq's WMD proved to be spectacularly wrong, two claims in particular have come to symbolise the affair. The first of these was the 'uranium-from-Africa' claim. Cited by the government as evidence of Iraq's ongoing nuclear-weapons programme, this was later shown by the IAEA to have been based on forged documentation, and while the British government has continued to insist that it was using other, more credible intelligence, the evidence for this has yet to be produced.[77]

The second, and more infamous, claim was the '45-minute' warning. As one of the few pieces of new information to be included in the dossier, this not only formed one of its most prominent and eye-catching disclosures (described by Charles Duelfer, the soon-to-be head of the Iraq Survey Group, as the 'most striking intelligence' in the dossier),[78] but was also central in creating the impression that Iraq posed a 'serious and current' danger. It also proved to be highly misleading. The late-arriving and highly sensitive intelligence apparently justifying the inclusion of the claim— information so sensitive that it could not be seen by the relevant analysts— was later withdrawn by the intelligence services in July 2003 on the grounds of its unreliability, while the inclusion of the claim in the dossier itself was strongly criticised for its vague nature by the Foreign Affairs Committee, the Intelligence and Security Committee, as well as the Butler Report. Worse still, it later transpired that analysts also believed the '45-minute' intelligence itself referred to battlefield munitions rather than to full-scale WMD, a distinction which Blair purported to have been unaware of prior to launching the conflict, though one with which a range of officials, including Jack Straw, Geoff Hoon, Alastair Campbell, Robin Cook, Richard Dearlove, and John Scarlett, were all fully acquainted. Moreover, while the JIC chairman himself later told the Hutton Inquiry that the intelligence 'related to munitions, which we had interpreted to mean battlefield mortar shells or small calibre weaponry, quite different from missiles', Campbell denied that the 45-minute line was one that the Prime Minister was trying to 'oversell', and the Defence Secretary dismissed the whole thing as 'not a significant issue'.[79]

These disclosures would seem to lead inexorably to one of two possible conclusions. The first is that the Prime Minister wilfully and knowingly misled Parliament and the British public by fostering the impression that

Iraq was capable of launching a full-scale WMD attack within three-quarters of an hour in order to hype the sense of danger and to rally support for the Iraq policy. The second is that the Prime Minister genuinely did not think to inquire into, and likewise nobody thought to inform him about, the specific nature of the intelligence. And this despite the apparent seriousness of the Iraqi threat, despite the close interchanges between senior New Labour and intelligence officials, and despite the government's entrenched obsession with carefully regulating the flow of politically sensitive information. In either case, it is a damning indictment of the British democratic system that none of the main actors involved received even the mildest of rebukes for their conduct.

That such a situation was able to occur at all, however, was not simply due to the personal desire of government officials to produce a strong and convincing dossier, but was crucially facilitated by the underlying structure of the British political system, and by its lack of firm constitutional safeguards and mechanisms concerning relations between the executive and the intelligence agencies. Reliant on uncodified norms and conventions of propriety as insurance against improper conduct, the relationship is characterised by a high level of secrecy and by a palpable absence of scrutiny and accountability. This covert nature is nowhere better exemplified than it is by the Intelligence and Security Committee (ISC), which forms the primary body for examining the expenditure, administration, and policy of the security services. Appointed by, and answerable to the Prime Minister, who may also choose to withhold sections of ISC reports from publication, the committee operates behind closed doors and is tightly bound by the provisions of the Official Secrets Act. As the ISC itself points out, its operations are carried out within a 'ring of secrecy'.[80]

Within this malleable recess of the British constitution, the process of constructing the dossier thus led to a weakening and blurring of the traditionally delineated boundaries between the political sphere and the intelligence arm of the state. The result was that the government, in its desire to make a political case against Iraq, was able to distort the objective presentation of intelligence material. While the Prime Minister insisted that the government had 'described the intelligence in a way that was perfectly justified', the Butler Report later concluded that the close involvement of the JIC with the production of the dossier had put its members under 'strain', had made it more difficult for them 'to maintain their normal standards of neutral and objective assessment', and had led to the creation of a dossier giving the impression 'that there was fuller and

firmer intelligence behind the judgements than was the case'. The publication of the dossier in the name of the JIC, it thus concluded, had
ensured that 'more weight was placed on the intelligence than it could
bear'.[81] Indeed, even the notoriously deferential Hutton Report later
acknowledged that Scarlett and the JIC could have been 'subconsciously
influenced' by Blair's desire to have a dossier that 'was as strong as possible', and could have subsequently made its wording 'somewhat stronger'
than that contained in a normal JIC report. Or, as the head of the JIC
himself put it, the dossier project was 'a very worthwhile objective'.[82]

Concluding remarks

The traditions of elite executive government proved to be very much alive
and well in Britain during 2002. Throughout this time, the centralised and
closed nature of the policy-making process, the relatively weak ability of
Parliament to scrutinise the actions of the central executive, and the discernibly low level of public accountability that therefore arises were all in
abundant display. At each and every turn the structural underpinnings of
the British state, based on the principles of centralisation, hierarchy, and
elitism, facilitated a relatively high degree of free reign for senior members
of the executive and formed the strategic context in which the Iraq policy
was both formulated and developed.

All this was clearly evident from the outset. The government's initial
response to the 11 September 2001 attacks, involving the launch of a war
on terror and an invasion of Afghanistan, was driven in an informal and *ad
hoc* fashion by a coterie based around the Prime Minister and his inner
court of advisors. With no formal mechanisms for ensuring a process of
collective decision-making, with no policy input either from the Cabinet
or from Parliament, and with no constitutional impediments to elite executive action, Blair's inner circle was effectively free to determine that
Britain's national interest now required a militaristic solution to the 9/11
crisis. This was followed by the secretive development of the Iraq policy
itself. During the spring and summer of 2002, senior members of the New
Labour government unilaterally agreed to support a US-led policy of
regime change in Iraq and began to implement a strategy for achieving this
goal based around Iraq's alleged possession of WMD, a renewed process
of UN weapons inspections, and a concerted propaganda campaign
designed to convince domestic and international opinion of the need for
tougher measures. However, at no point during this time was the Cabinet

informed of the qualitative shift in policy away from containment, at no point were ministers involved in any semblance of collective decision-making on the issue, and at no point were they shown the actual intelligence on Iraq's WMD, which remained perceptibly weaker than the assertive claims that were now being made by the Prime Minister.

The elitist and tightly controlled nature of the Iraq policy was further demonstrated in the construction of the September dossier. Designed to emphasise the threat posed by Iraq's WMD, the main weapon in the government's propaganda campaign also revealed the informal and *ad hoc* nature of New Labour's decision-making processes and exposed the unduly close and malleable nature of relations between senior figures in the political and the intelligence spheres of the British state. Moreover, the events surrounding the September dossier also highlighted the ability of the executive to control the flow of politically sensitive information. With little access to alternative facts, the Cabinet, Parliament, and the wider public were all forced to rely on the government's presentation of intelligence material as their key source of information, despite the fact that this had been significantly distorted to suit the purposes of the prime ministerial court.

5

Engulfed

From the autumn of 2002 the government's attempt to gain political and legal cover for a militarily enforced policy of regime change in Iraq began to intensify. At the centre of this was an attempt to deal with the question of Iraq through a new process of UN weapons inspections, which officials believed would spring a trap on Saddam Hussein and legitimise the use of armed force. Although the inspections process was eventually restarted under the terms of Resolution 1441, however, the ongoing failure to uncover any weapons of mass destruction led to growing tensions in the Security Council between an increasingly impatient US–British axis and a Franco-German– led majority favouring a continuation of diplomacy. With domestic opinion also yet to be persuaded about the urgency of the situation, the government's programme of spin and propaganda was again stepped up. This included the production of another dossier outlining Iraq's intransigence, heightened warnings about the threat posed by its WMD capability, a growing emphasis on the humanitarian imperatives for military action, and a deliberate misrepresentation of the views of the French government, which was now presented as being determined to thwart any attempt to deal with the Iraqi danger through consensual means. Although the general public remained far from convinced by all of this, the government's political strategy, buttressed by a controversial last-minute strengthening of the Attorney-General's legal advice on the use of force, proved to be successful in persuading Parliament to endorse the decision to go to war.

One way or another

Even with the government's spin machine on full throttle, the 'information campaign' based on the September dossier proved, on the whole, to be a failure. Despite an immediate flurry of headlines—the most prominent of which belonged to the London *Evening Standard*, which warned that Britain was '45 minutes from attack', and to the *Sun*, which led the charge with 'He's Got 'Em, Let's Get Him'—the dossier itself was widely criticised for providing little new information, and despite Alastair Campbell's claim that 'the coverage went very well right around the world', the state of public opinion remained unfavourable towards the government. Around half of the British electorate reported themselves to have been unconvinced by the dossier of the need for military action, 70% remained opposed to the prospect of going to war without the express sanction of the United Nations, and a clear majority now felt that Tony Blair was acting as a 'poodle' for the US President.[1]

Yet the Prime Minister himself remained unmoved. Believing that public opinion would fall in behind the government once any military action got under way, Blair sought to turn his growing divergence from public opinion into a governing virtue, by portraying himself as a strong and principled leader prepared to forgo his own popularity in defence of the 'national interest'. At the Labour party conference in October, Blair warned that he had 'lost [his] love of popularity for its own sake', and proclaimed that he would not desist in the pursuit of a tough and painful course of action if it was the right thing to do. As he put it, 'the radical decision is usually the right one; the right decision is usually the hardest one; and the hardest decisions are often the least popular at the time'.[2]

The spinning of intelligence in the attempt to secure public support for action against Iraq was mirrored by similar developments in the United States. A stream of public statements from senior figures in the Bush administration detailing Saddam Hussein's possession of WMD, his continuing attempts to develop nuclear weapons, and his establishing of further links with al-Qaeda were also accompanied by the production of an intelligence-based dossier. Like its British counterpart, this was a source of later controversy, not least for its failure to include any of the caveats and uncertainties that had informed the intelligence on which it was based. While this intelligence had warned that knowledge of Iraq's weapons capacity was limited, that the CIA had 'low confidence' in its 'ability to assess when Saddam would use WMD', and that Saddam 'might' link up with al-Qaeda, but only if he was 'sufficiently desperate', the dossier itself presented the case against Iraq as if it were a cast-iron certainty.[3] In contrast to their British counterparts, however, US officials were by now far less vexed about the need to erect a watertight political and legal justification for war. Indeed, that it was the issue of WMD that was being advanced

by Washington as its primary motive for action was due more to bureau-
cratic and presentational concerns. As Paul Wolfowitz later revealed, the
situation within the Bush administration was such that of all the factors
involved in the decision to wage war, the issue of WMD was 'the one
reason everyone could agree on'.[4]

Against this background, on 12 September George W. Bush called for
the readmission of weapons inspectors into Iraq, telling the UN General
Assembly that the US would work to acquire 'the necessary resolutions' to
ensure disarmament. This did not mean, though, that the United States
was now committed to resolving the Iraq issue by multilateral means.
Indeed, the President also made it clear that the United Nations now risked
becoming 'irrelevant' if it did not insist on the implementation of its resolutions, and warned that action in one form or another was now 'unavoidable'.[5] That the outcome of such action would be equally unavoidable was
also becoming increasingly evident. Outlining the situation to the US
Congress, Bush explained that the long-standing policy of regime change
was now being pursued 'even more so in light of 9/11', while at the same
time the publication of the latest National Security Strategy further
detailed the new-imperialist landscape presently being traversed by the
White House. Stating that the Bush administration would take whatever
steps were necessary to advance America's national interests, the Strategy
called for the expansion of 'democracy, development, free markets, and free
trade to every corner of the world' and for a significant increase in US
military bases abroad, and it warned that the United States would 'not
hesitate to act alone' in the pursuit of this agenda. As if to emphasise the
point, senior government figures were also set on publicly denigrating the
entire UN process. As Vice-President Dick Cheney put it, the return of
weapons inspectors 'would provide no assurance whatsoever' about Iraqi
compliance, but would simply 'provide false comfort' that Saddam was
'back in his box'.[6]

In these less-than-propitious circumstances, on 16 September Iraq
accepted the unconditional return of the inspectors, and the process of
haggling over a new UN resolution began. The initial US position, calling
for a full declaration of Iraqi weapons stocks, for any fabrications or omissions to constitute a material breach, and for this in turn to authorise the
use of 'all necessary means' to enforce disarmament, was unsurprisingly
rejected by France and Russia on the grounds that it would provide an
automatic trigger for war. Instead, an alternative two-stage process was
proposed, starting with a resolution to authorise the return of UN

inspectors. Any breaches of this resolution would then be referred back to the Security Council for its consideration, leading, if necessary, to a second resolution authorising the use of military action. After tortuous negotiations, an eventual compromise was reached, leading to the unanimous adoption of UN Resolution 1441 on 8 November. This demanded that Iraq comply with its obligations to disarm fully, immediately, and unconditionally, and warned that it would face 'serious consequences' if it did not. As part of this process, Iraq was also required to produce a dossier listing its full weapons stock within thirty days, and was warned that any false statements or omissions, coupled with a failure to co-operate fully with the weapons inspectors, would constitute a material breach of its obligations. In such an event, the Security Council would then convene immediately 'in order to consider the situation'.

While this final form of words enabled an agreement to be reached by avoiding both an automatic trigger for war (anathema to France and Russia) and the explicit need for a second resolution (anathema to the United States and Britain), it also meant that the final text of the resolution was dangerously vague and open to divergent interpretations. Although most members of the Security Council had consented to Resolution 1441 on the clear understanding that it did not provide an automatic basis for military action, the US government nevertheless insisted that the phrase 'serious consequences' provided just such an authorisation. The British government, too, were in a similar minority, arguing that a second resolution was desirable but not absolutely essential to justify the use of military force, since Resolution 1441 required only that the Security Council meet to 'consider', rather than 'decide' on, any appropriate action following a material breach.[7]

While London and Washington continued to insist that war was not inevitable, and that the overall goal was to uphold UN resolutions on WMD rather than regime change, as had been well noted in the spring discussions the inspections process itself would now effectively spring a trap on Saddam Hussein by making it virtually impossible for Iraq to prove that it did not possess any weapons of mass destruction. On the one hand, if no WMD were found then this would lend credence to the US and British claims that Iraq was concealing its weapons, thereby justifying action on the grounds that it was continuing to deceive and obstruct the UN in clear breach of Resolution 1441. If, on the other hand, the inspections process discovered that Iraq did in fact possess such weapons, then Saddam would be shown to be in clear breach of previous UN resolutions, would be unmasked as a clear and present danger to the international community, and would thus face military action in order to enforce disarmament. For Blair, the matter was clear. '[I]f what they find amounts to a breach of the UN mandate', he explained, 'then Saddam will be disarmed by force.'[8] Or as Scott Ritter, a former member of UNSCOM and an arch-critic of the war, put it: 'The standards of verification ... were impossible for Iraq to meet ... the inspections process was pre-programmed to fail'.[9]

The price of influence

The government also remained less than committed to the prospect of allowing a substantive parliamentary vote on military action prior to the commencement of any hostilities. On 25 November 2002, the Foreign Secretary told the House of Commons during a debate on Resolution 1441 that although the government itself would 'have no difficulty' with this course of action, and while he personally hoped that any vote could be held 'before any military engagement', the practical circumstances of the situation might unfortunately dictate otherwise. Given that 'the safety of our forces requires an element of surprise', he explained, it would be 'utterly irresponsible' to hold a vote signalling Britain's intentions in advance.[10] Indeed, an amendment by the Liberal Democrats opposing war unless it was sanctioned explicitly by both the United Nations and Parliament was heavily defeated. Yet with restive backbench MPs supporting the government on the proviso that the issue would be dealt with through the United Nations, and with the state of public opinion still deemed to be unstable, the government also sought to bolster its position by producing another dossier on Iraq a week later, this time focusing on its human-rights abuses instead of its military capabilities. As with the September dossier, however, this also failed to swing domestic opinion, which remained distinctly sceptical about the motivations behind the publication. So too did the human-rights group Amnesty, which slammed the dossier for being 'opportunistic and selective'.[11]

On 7 December 2002, Iraq produced its own weapons dossier as required under the terms of Resolution 1441. Despite some new information on missile and biological developments, the 12,000-page document was for the most part a recycling of Iraq's previous declarations to the United Nations. The result was to divide the Security Council. While British and US officials claimed that Iraq was in material breach for gaps and evasions, both France and Russia insisted that it was far too early to reach any conclusions that would lead to war. Hans Blix, despite agreeing that the Iraqi declaration was technically a breach, also pointed out that it was not evidence that Iraq actually possessed weapons of mass destruction. To help establish a clearer picture, Blix suggested that it might help the inspectors if Britain and the United States could provide them with some of their own intelligence on the subject. In assenting to this request, however, Washington was careful to point out that it was by no means giving a green light to unlimited inspections. In a warning to Blix, Bush and Cheney insisted that should the process start to drag on, the US was primed and 'ready to discredit inspections' in favour of a more direct and forceful means of disarmament.[12]

Thus the new year began amid a gathering storm. Attempts to resurrect the Middle East peace process were drowning under a rising tide of violence, North Korea was beginning to restart its nuclear programme, India and Pakistan were teetering on the edge of a potentially nuclear conflict over the disputed region of Kashmir, and the shadow of global terrorism continued to loom across the world stage. Relations between the United States and Europe were also becoming increasingly frayed over the question of Iraq, the progressive build-up of military power in the Gulf was offering little dissuasion from the view that war was on the way, and global opposition to the prospect was continuing to mount. In Britain, political difficulties were also continuing to grow. Tony Blair's approval ratings were now at half the levels reached in the heady wake of 11 September 2001, and while less than a sixth of the British public now purported to be in favour of military action without the express authorisation of the United Nations, in contrast, around three-fifths were prepared to consent to war if UN approval could be obtained.[13]

In response to these difficulties, Blair offered an ardent reassertion of his commitment to the new-imperialist trajectory of the United States. In a speech to a Foreign Office conference in early January, the Prime Minister outlined his vision of the current global situation. Warning of the dangers of 'chaos', and proclaiming that the twin issues of WMD and international terrorism posed 'a real, active threat to our security', Blair maintained that it was essential to take a firm stand in order to 'send out a clear signal' to those that would seek to diverge from the norms of the international community. To boost public support for the campaign, the Prime Minister also reasserted the need to calibrate the war on terror as part of a broader reordering of the global political economy, calling for action on WMD to be combined with measures to reinvigorate the Arab–

Israeli peace process and to reintegrate developing nations into the world economy through a process of 'opening up markets'. Lest all this be seen as an attempt to construct a world order based around 'Western values', however, Blair further asserted the need to champion and promote the 'universal values' of freedom, human rights, the rule of law, democracy, and justice. Refuting suggestions that these commitments were antithetical to the overriding strategy of positioning Britain as a transatlantic bridge in order to elevate its influence on the world stage, the Prime Minister also restated his belief that close relations with Europe and America were mutually reinforcing. It was not, he said, a case of becoming tightly adjoined to one pole or the other. That this was looking ever more like a case of wishful thinking, though, was underlined by Blair's parallel insistence that Britain's primary global role was to remain the chief ally of the United States. '[T]he price of influence', he explained, was 'that we do not leave the US to face the tricky issues alone'.[14]

The case for a pre-emptive war with Iraq, however, was at present not being well served by the UN inspections process. Despite furnishing UNMOVIC with intelligence on suspect sites, the actual results currently being achieved remained sparse. The best discoveries—a series of documents relating to Iraq's nuclear programme during the early 1990s (which contained nothing new to the IAEA), a number of empty chemical munitions, and the later uncovering of more than seventy proscribed long-range ballistic missiles (most of which were subsequently destroyed)—hardly constituted the kind of material that US and British officials were warning about, and certainly did not provide them with the 'smoking gun' they so desperately desired. To make matters worse, the Director-General of the IAEA, Muhammed ElBaradei, also informed the Security Council there was 'no evidence' as yet of any Iraqi attempt to reconstitute a nuclear weapons programme.[15]

It does not stop at Iraq

With the inspections process not going according to plan, Washington's patience began to grow perceptibly thinner. Intensifying their efforts to hype the Iraqi threat, senior administration figures stepped up their warnings about Saddam's possession of WMD and his links to al-Qaeda, and insisted that the US would unilaterally disarm Iraq by force if the United Nations continued to procrastinate on the issue. Proclaiming that Iraq was clearly 'a nation with something to hide', Condoleeza Rice declared that the inspections process was 'failing in spectacular fashion', while Bush warned that time would run out in 'weeks rather than months'.[16]

Tony Blair's impatience with the inspections process was also readily detectable. Dismissing Iraq's December declaration as 'an inadequate and probably false document', the Prime Minister pressed on with the political strategy devised during the summer, insisting that although the thrust of the government's policy on Iraq was not directed towards regime change, the focus on WMD would invariably raise such questions given that it was the Iraqi regime itself which was now the chief obstacle to disarmament. The 'main issue', Blair proffered, was 'whether it is necessary to change the regime ... in order to disarm them of WMD'. Adding that this was but part of a wider project of global reordering, the Prime Minister also explained that the overriding aim was about 'sending a signal to the whole of the world ... that people who have these weapons in breach of UN resolutions will be forced to disarm. And it does not stop at Iraq'. That this stance was widely unpopular and ran contrary to the views of the general public, however, was also summarily dismissed. Insisting that the only means of avoiding war was to deploy troops in order to establish the credible threat of force, Blair further maintained that his job was not to represent the general will of the British people, but to determine and implement the policies that were required to defend the national interest. '[P]olls or no polls', he countered, 'my job in a situation like this is sometimes to say the things that people don't want to hear'.[17]

But even so, with the absence of any Iraqi WMD undermining the case for urgent action, and with media coverage of the Iraq issue moving away from the government, the state of domestic opinion remained a matter of some considerable concern for New Labour officials. To this end, in mid-January Blair and Campbell took the decision to produce another information dossier in order to highlight Iraq's ongoing attempts to obstruct and deceive the UN inspectors. This time around, the government's Director of Communications and Strategy himself was given personal control of the process. As with the September dossier, the means by which the new publication eventually came to life also provided a vivid demonstration of the high levels of secrecy and centralisation prevailing inside the walls of central government. Campbell's activities were subject to no monitoring or control by anyone in Whitehall, no government minister (with the exception of Blair) was consulted on either the structure or the contents of the dossier prior to its publication, and although the intelligence material it contained was cleared by MI6, it was not put up for clearance by the JIC. The reason for this, according to Campbell, was that there was simply 'no need'.[18]

The contents of the dossier itself were also deeply flawed. Revealed to the public at the beginning of February and described by Blair in the House of Commons as an offering of 'further intelligence', much of the material it contained was compiled from publicly available sources, and none of the intelligence it contained was clearly designated as such.[19] In effect, this created the impression that the dossier contained a fuller consignment of declassified material, and that it was thus a far more revelatory document, than was actually the case. The dossier's most serious shortcoming of all, however, was that more than half of it had been directly copied, replete with grammatical and typographical errors, from an article in the *Middle East Review of International Affairs* that had been posted on the internet, and which was itself derived from a twelve-year-old PhD thesis on Iraq's WMD capabilities.[20] Worse still, while this material was presented without attribution, and indeed was used without the permission or even the knowledge of its author, Ibrahim al-Marashi, sections of the article were also doctored in order to strengthen the government's case against Iraq. A reference to the 'monitoring' of foreign embassies by the Iraqi intelligence agencies was changed to 'spying', a passage on Iraq's support for 'opposition groups in hostile regimes' was transformed into its active support for 'terrorist organisations', estimates of the size of Iraq's conventional forces were exaggerated, and many of the assertions made about Iraq's concealment activities were not only unverified, but had also been rejected by Hans Blix himself. Further still, subsequent complaints by al-Marashi that the government's actions were not merely 'distorting the intent' of his work but also risked having a 'disastrous effect' on his family in Iraq were dismissed by Campbell, who denied that there had been 'any attempt to mislead', and who insisted that the article had simply been amended 'to reflect the actual situation in Iraq'.[21]

In yet another parallel with the events surrounding the publication of the September dossier, the government's latest attempt to mobilise domestic opinion also proved to be a dramatic failure. Shortly after its release, the revelation that much of the dossier had been plagiarised provoked a wave of derision, with Robin Cook describing it as a 'spectacular own goal', with the Home Secretary, David Blunkett, insisting that it should never have been published, and with Jack Straw also weighing in to deride it as 'a complete Horlicks'.[22] Both the Foreign Affairs Committee and the ISC had harsh words to say about the dossier. The former concluded that it had 'undermined the credibility' of the government's case for war, while the latter sternly chided the government for its failure to abide by the proper procedures for publishing intelligence material.[23] While Campbell eventually apologised to both Richard Dearlove and John Scarlett for the affair, al-Marashi himself received no apology from anyone in the government at all until the summer, when one was belatedly extracted more than four months after the dossier was released. From the government's point of view, however, the most significant point was that the 'dodgy dossier', as it came to be known, had not only failed to engineer a more favourable media atmosphere, but had now seemed to generate an even deeper degree of public suspicion. While around three-quarters of Britons now believed Iraq to be in possession of concealed weapons of mass destruction, around two-thirds thought that the government's case had been weakened by the whole affair, and more than two-thirds continued to believe that Britain should not go to war without the backing of the United Nations. That said, one ray of light for Downing Street was that around two-thirds of the British electorate also stated that they would agree to support military action if only one or two vetoes were wielded against a second, more explicit UN resolution.[24] For Blair, who continued to deny that the status of the dossier had been in any way 'misrepresented', this would prove to be an extremely useful seam of political gold.[25]

Aware that time was now running out, the British government intensified its efforts to justify the use of force and to persuade domestic opinion that this was rapidly becoming necessary in order to deal with the Iraqi threat. Central to this was a renewed attempt to secure a second UN resolution that would explicitly authorise a military attack and thus provide the government with the legal and political cover it desired. With the military plans of the Pentagon still not fully operational, the Prime Minister was able to successfully press for a slight extension to the inspections timetable at another White House summit with Bush at the end of January. This would provide more time for Iraq's elusive WMD to turn up, and more time for the Security Council to reach a solid agreement on the issue. Equally aware that a second resolution might not be forthcoming, the Prime Minister also sought to maintain a politically safe distance from any public commitment to such a necessity. Restating the government's position that a second resolution was preferable but not necessary, Blair now added a further, and highly novel, qualification in terms of international law, insisting that a new resolution would not be required if a Security Council veto was wielded 'unreasonably'. Precisely who would possess the requisite authority to determine whether such an event had occurred, however, would prove to be something of a moot point.[26]

Evasion and deceit

The effort to obtain a second UN resolution focused on a group of unde-cided states on the Security Council—namely Pakistan, Cameroon, Angola, Guinea, Chile, and Mexico. Collectively, they became known as the 'swinging six'. Bearing high levels of domestic hostility towards the United States, the six swingers rapidly found themselves subjected to a concerted campaign of persuasion from the American and British govern-ments, the key to which, alongside the more traditional diplomacy of aid and trade incentives, was an intensive spying operation designed to gain leverage over the proceedings by uncovering the strategic intentions of the waverers. While this was principally driven by the CIA, British involvement in the operation was also courted. At the end of January, the US Defense Chief of Staff, Frank Koza, requested support from Britain's top-secret communications monitoring centre, GCHQ, for what he described as an impending 'surge' against members of the Security Council. The intended aim, he revealed, was to try to glean 'anything useful' about the way in which members of the council planned to vote, about the 'related policies [or] negotiating positions they may be considering', as well as any 'alliances [or] dependencies' that may exist. In short, the CIA was seeking 'the whole gamut of information that could give US policymakers an "edge" in obtaining results favorable to US goals or to head off surprises'.[27]

In conjunction with this, on 5 February the US administration staged its most forceful attempt so far to persuade the world of the danger posed by Saddam Hussein. In a much-anticipated presentation to the UN General Assembly, the US Secretary of State, Colin Powell, purported to offer 'an accumulation of facts and disturbing patterns of behavior' which, he argued, constituted firm evidence that Iraq was in material breach of its UN obligations. Combining rhetorical assertions with an array of photo-graphs, artistic renderings, and fragments of intercepted conversations between Iraqi officers, Powell alleged that there could be 'no doubt' that Saddam Hussein possessed WMD and development programmes, that he had made concerted efforts to obtain nuclear weapons, and that he had active and ongoing links to al-Qaeda. Also drawing attention to the February dossier, which he described as a 'fine paper' containing 'exquis-ite detail' about Iraq's deception, Powell further warned that the failure to discover any WMD was itself a sign of Iraqi guilt, since this was evidently due to the systematic concealment activities of a regime with something to hide.[28]

Similar rhetoric, too, was offered by Jack Straw. Telling the General Assembly that Iraq's claims to have no weapons of mass destruction were blatantly 'a lie', the Foreign Secretary also informed the House of Commons that the draft version of the UNMOVIC dossier currently being compiled on Iraq's WMD was 'a chilling catalogue of evasion and deceit' which lent further credence to the view that containment had failed and that stronger action needed to be taken to ensure disarmament.[29] This, however, was very much to the chagrin of Hans Blix, who protested that the draft report itself contradicted these assertions, and that its central theme was that Iraq did not, in fact, seem to possess any new WMD. As he exclaimed:

> The fact is the UK and the US wanted to demonstrate that Iraq had weapons of mass destruction but that was not what my report said....The fact remains that Mr. Straw quoted from our report selectively, he quoted what suited his conclusions, namely that Iraq was hiding something.[30]

But distinctly undeterred, Straw continued to detail the potential horrors of the Iraqi threat. Now drawing comparisons with the appeasement of Hitler in the 1930s, the Foreign Secretary predicted that the world was entering 'the final, decisive phase in this long crisis', and warned that it was the 'deadly combination of capability and intent' that made Saddam Hussein 'uniquely dangerous'. As he put it:

> Given Saddam Hussein's longstanding support for terrorist causes, does anyone seriously expect us to rule out the terrifying possibility that his poisons and diseases will find their way into the hands of al-Qaeda and its sympathisers?[31]

Yet despite the ferocity of the propaganda barrage, the doubters within the Security Council remained singularly unconvinced by the British and US assertions. Powell's presentation to the General Assembly was described by Blix as being 'ambiguous and unconvincing', the US Senate Committee on Intelligence later concluded that much of the information behind it 'was overstated, misleading, or incorrect', and the mood of the UN Chamber itself was captured in its unprecedented and spontaneous round of applause for the fervently delivered anti-war analysis of the French Foreign Minister, Dominique de Villepin, nine days later.[32] To compound this, the ongoing reports to the Security Council from Hans

Blix continued to provide neither a denouement in favour of the United States nor a vindication of Iraq's claims to innocence. Instead, UNMOVIC charted a slow but steady increase in Iraqi compliance with the inspectors, coupled with a progressive failure to uncover any systematic evidence of WMD or proscribed materials. While large gaps between Iraq's December declaration and its documented evidence remained a cause for concern, Blix again pointed out that it was 'not justified to jump to the conclusion that something exists just because it is unaccounted for'. On 7 March, the US and British claims were further dented with the publication of the final UNMOVIC report, which also revealed that there was no direct evidence to indicate that Iraq had any active WMD or related programmes. At the same time, a further report from the IAEA also reasserted that it had yet to uncover any evidence of an Iraqi nuclear programme.[33]

By now the failure to find any WMD was becoming a cause of deep anxiety for Hans Blix. Later accusing the US and British governments of treating intelligence in 'a lighthearted way', the head of UNMOVIC effused, 'I thought—my God, if this is the best intelligence they have and we find nothing, what about the rest?'[34] On 20 February Blix also told Blair of his concerns in person, complaining that the inspectors 'were not impressed' by the information with which they had been provided. In reply, Blair stated that he, Bush, and the intelligence services were all 'convinced' by the assessments. On the same day, however, a private briefing given to Robin Cook by John Scarlett left the former Foreign Secretary with the distinct impression 'that Saddam Hussein probably does not have weapons of mass destruction'. At around the same time, a similar judgement was also presented to Clare Short, who was informed by the Defence Intelligence Staff that anything Iraq might have in the way of an offensive chemical or biological capability 'almost certainly wasn't weaponised'.[35]

More seriously still, the already anaemic nature of the intelligence behind the government's case against Iraq had been further weakened by a new JIC assessment, presented on 9 February, which informed the Prime Minister that there was no intelligence to suggest that Iraq had provided chemical and biological weapons to al-Qaeda, or indeed that it intended to use them in a terrorist attack. On the contrary, the government was told that the risk of chemical and biological agents being transferred to terrorist groups would in fact now 'be heightened by military action'.[36] In sharp contrast to the prior and strenuous efforts made to squeeze any intelligence material into the public domain that might be useful to their case, government officials now made no attempt whatsoever to promote domestic awareness of this latest assessment. Moreover, despite the clear discrepancy between the reports flowing back from the UN inspectors and the claims being made by the US and British governments, officials also made no attempt to re-evaluate the intelligence on Iraq, and spent just eleven days examining the December report, belying its centrality in determining whether Iraq was in further breach of Resolution 1441.[37] Instead, with the course of events slipping further away from them, US and British officials dug deeper into their trenches. The official line was that the evidence provided by the inspections was simply wrong, that Iraq was continuing to conceal its WMD activities, and that it was therefore in material breach of its obligations on the grounds of omissions and false statements contained in its declaration.

But trenches were also being dug by those on the other side of the argument. A draft resolution tabled on 24 February by Britain, Spain, and the United States proclaiming Iraq to be in material breach provoked a counter-resolution from France, Germany, and Russia, which declared that while the inspections process could not 'continue indefinitely', there was still 'no evidence' to show that Iraq possessed WMD, and there was thus no reason to go to war as things presently stood.[38] This growing bifurcation in the geo-strategic perceptions of the United States and the 'not-yet alliance' was also broadly reflected in the concerns of their respective populations. While the majority of Americans were now in favour of war, the majority of Europeans (both 'old' and 'new' alike in the desultory vernacular of Donald Rumsfeld) were deeply opposed to the prospect, a marked contrast to the public pledges of support to the US currently being extended by many of their leaders.[39]

Worse than you think

As the political gulf between the two continents drew wider, Blair's attempt to uphold the transatlantic-bridge strategy became discernibly strained once more. As it did so, and as the Prime Minister's close alignment with the Bush administration began to arouse further domestic ire, the government found itself facing an acute dilemma. While the need for some form of public demonstration of influence over US foreign policy was becoming ever more apparent in order to justify the closeness of the relationship, the government's capacity to provide it was becoming ever more diminished. A central reason for this was Blair's fear, ensconced through his dealings with Clinton during the Kosovo campaign, that public disclosures of such a nature would merely antagonise the US President (for whom concessions to foreign powers would be seen as a sign of weakness), and would thus prove to be counterproductive. Another—and in this case more pressing—reason, though, was that any political capital that Blair had managed to accumulate with the United States through his unstinting support for the war on terror had now been effectively expended on persuading Bush to go down the UN route and to commit to re-engaging in the Middle East peace process. That these steps had been designed chiefly as a means of easing the Prime Minister's own political discomfiture, itself generated by the very provision of this support, merely compounded the irony of the situation. The result, in any case, was that continuing with the existing policy of providing unqualified public support for Washington merely lent further credence to the notion that Blair was acting as a presidential poodle.

Against such charges, however, the Prime Minister offered a typically vigorous rebuttal. Rejecting an offer from Bush to withdraw from the coalition, Blair insisted that Britain would stay with the Americans 'to the very end', and told reporters that he would have been 'truly committed' to dealing with the problem of Iraq 'irrespective of the position of America'. The situation, he explained, was 'worse than you think ... I believe in it'.[40] Indeed, such was the Prime Minister's commitment to the cause of foreign intervention as a means of global reordering, that on the eve of battle itself an increasingly exasperated Blair said to one observer:

> What amazes me is how many people are happy for Saddam to stay. They ask why we don't get rid of Mugabe, why not the Burmese lot. Yes, let's get rid of them all. I don't because I can't, but when you can, you should.[41]

In a final effort to swing public opinion, the Prime Minister now embarked on a 'masochism strategy'. The prime component of this involved an intense series of media appearances before hostile audiences designed to limit the political damage by cementing his image as a strong, decisive, and principled leader. As Campbell put it, the plan was for Blair to get 'beaten up by the public' in an attempt to take some of the heat out of its opposition.[42] At the core of Blair's defence was the assertion that ignoring the will of the British people was justified since he, as the leader of the country, considered that he was 'doing the right thing'. To bolster this claim, the Prime Minister also began to place a growing emphasis on the moral case for military action, despite having shown scant previous interest either in Iraq's human-rights record or in deposing Saddam Hussein on humanitarian grounds. On 15 February, amid vast international anti-war demonstrations by an estimated thirty million people, and with around two million people descending on London in the biggest demonstration ever seen in Britain, Blair told the Scottish Labour party conference that although the moral consideration 'was not the reason we act ... it is the reason, frankly, why if we do have to act, we should do so with a clear conscience'. Any unpopularity to be incurred in so doing was thus to be borne in a stoical fashion, as 'the price of leadership and the cost of conviction'.[43]

As the situation became ever more strained, the government's efforts at political management began to focus more sharply on the rising disquiet among the Labour backbenchers. On 26 February, a parliamentary vote on the government's Iraq policy produced a massive rebellion, with 121 Labour MPs defying a three-line whip to support a motion stating that the case for war was 'as yet unproven'. Indeed, despite further warnings by the Prime Minister of a 'clear' intelligence picture showing that Saddam continued to regard his WMD programme as 'essential' both for ensuring internal repression and for pursuing 'external aggression', nearly a third of all MPs refused to back the government. Further still, the avoidance of an even greater rebellion was due only to the government's assurances that MPs would now be permitted a substantive vote on any decision to go to war, a move that was in stark contrast to the government's previous assertions, but one that was now deemed to be increasingly necessary in order to quell the discontent frothing within the Labour party. Also swaying wavering MPs was the implicit assumption that the government would, in the event, only commit to war with a second UN resolution, a desire for restraint on which Blair sought to capitalise fully by telling the House of Commons that Saddam Hussein could remain in place provided that he meet with the disarmament demands of Resolution 1441. While this jarred with the Prime Minister's outstanding and secret commitment to support the US policy of regime change, Blair, purporting to 'detest' the Iraqi regime, nonetheless insisted that Saddam could yet 'save it' by complying with the requirements of the United Nations.[44]

The view of the British public, however, also remained sceptical. A clear majority remained firmly opposed to the idea of military action without a second UN resolution, while the Prime Minister's own personal approval rating had now crashed to its lowest level since the petrol crisis some two and a half years earlier.[45] Yet for Blair, there was now no doubt about the inexorable logic of events. Saddam was not going to co-operate, the invasion was going ahead as scheduled, and no amount of undiscovered WMD were going to be allowed to interrupt the proceedings. The support of the general public, for all its desirability as a strategic asset, was by no means considered to be necessary. In any case, the Prime Minister's entrenched belief was that domestic opinion would eventually come round in support of armed action once military operations got under way. The main reason that it had not yet succumbed to the government's propaganda campaign was therefore, in Blair's view, not the merits of its stance on Iraq, but 'a failure to communicate'. While opinion polls could provide 'interesting reflections of where public opinion is', he noted, the role of a Prime Minister was to press ahead with the difficult decisions and tough choices that were essential to defend the national interest, without regard to such ephemera. As he put it:

> there is a certain category of issue upon which your job is to tell people what you genuinely think, and there is nothing else you can do in the end but carry on doing that.... I think we would draw a lot of the sting out of this if people could actually see all those sides of the argument.[46]

By this time, the atmosphere in the Security Council was also becoming increasingly fraught. The outlook of the swinging six was solidifying against the prospect of having to endorse military action, while the not-yet alliance of France, Germany, and Russia was continuing to insist that a resolution for war could not be carried while the opportunity for peace remained to be seized. With a second resolution now dependent on at least nine members of the council voting in favour of it, and on none of the permanent members opting to wield their veto, the prospects of securing a safe passage were looking decidedly slim. In an attempt to breach the impasse, Jack Straw tabled a resolution on 7 March setting a final ten-day deadline for Iraq to comply with Resolution 1441. This, it was hoped, would enable a compromise to be reached by prolonging the life span of diplomacy without turning it into an indefinite process of inaction. Aware, however, that the situation was becoming increasingly grave, the Foreign Secretary also dispatched a memo to the Prime Minister warning that the British government would, in his view, be unable to take part in military action if a vote on a second resolution was lost. Since going to war in such circumstances would ignite an implacable fury on the Labour backbenches, it might, he counselled, be better not to hold a vote at all.[47]

The revival argument

The government's increasingly desperate attempts to make headway in the battle to win over both domestic and international opinion were equally matched by its efforts to establish a firm legal basis for military action. Following a request from Powell and Manning (there is no record of any formal request for a legal opinion by the Prime Minister),[48] on 7 March the Attorney-General Lord Goldsmith informed the government of his current legal thinking on the matter. This was contained in a thirteen-page memo, the contents of which remained a tightly guarded secret prior to being leaked and then fully published by the government a week before the 2005 general election. Lord Goldsmith's advice, however, was far from certain. Stating that the Bush doctrine of pre-emption was not 'recognised in international law', and that attacking Iraq on humanitarian grounds was not 'an appropriate basis for action in present circumstances', the Attorney-General subsequently determined that the use of force could only be justified if this was authorised by the UN Security Council, and that the legality of military action would thus turn on the intricacies of Resolution 1441.[49] As such, Goldsmith's attention duly focused on the so-called revival argument that had formed the basis for the government's military action against Iraq during Operation Desert Fox and other air strikes to enforce the no-fly zones. On this he noted that the view of the British government had been that an Iraqi violation of Resolution 687 could, if it were 'sufficiently serious', restore the authority to use force contained in Resolution 678 which had sanctioned the first Gulf War. The Attorney-General also noted, however, that this line of argument was 'controversial', and that the government had also 'consistently taken the view' that since the cease-fire conditions of Resolution 687 had been set by the Security Council, it would therefore be up to the council itself 'to assess whether any such breach of those obligations has occurred'. 'On the UK view of the revival argument', he maintained, 'only the Council can decide if a violation is sufficiently serious to revive the authorisation to use force'.

To complicate matters still further, the government's chief legal advisor also pointed out that the terms of Resolution 1441 did not imply an immediate revival of the authorisation contained in Resolution 678, since Iraq had been given a 'final opportunity' to comply with its obligation to disarm, and that while he did not believe that a second resolution to explicitly authorise the use of force would be required (given that this was implicit in the clause referring to 'serious consequences'), the actual text of Resolution 1441 was nevertheless 'ambiguous and unclear' as to precisely what would happen in the event of Iraqi non-compliance. Indeed, the argument that the Security Council would, in such circumstances, be required to make a further decision as opposed to holding a simple discussion would, he added, be 'especially powerful' if some degree of assessment as to the degree of Iraq's compliance was necessary.

In his view, then, the Attorney-General put it to Blair that the uncertainty of Resolution 1441 meant that '[a]rguments can be made on both sides' as to whether a further assessment would be required to determine if Iraq was in material breach, but that if an assessment was needed, then 'it would be for the Council to make it'. 'In these circumstances', he explained, 'the safest legal course would be to secure the adoption of a further resolution to authorise the use of force'. Moreover, though prepared to accept, on the basis of discussions with senior British and US officials (discussions with officials from nations opposed to military action having been notably absent), that 'a reasonable case' could be made for claiming that Resolution 1441 was 'capable in principle of reviving the authorisation in 678 without a further resolution', Goldsmith also cautioned that he could not be 'confident' that an independent court would agree with this viewpoint. Insisting, then, that the views of UNMOVIC and the IAEA would be 'highly significant in this respect', the Attorney-General thus warned the Prime Minister that this argument would only be 'sustainable' if there were 'strong factual grounds' for concluding that Iraq had failed to take the final opportunity to disarm, and that the government would therefore 'need to be able to demonstrate hard evidence of non-compliance and non-cooperation'. '[R]egime change', he warned, 'cannot be the objective of military action', and this 'should be borne in mind' when 'making public statements about any campaign'.

In his final note of caution, the Attorney-General also warned Blair that there was no legal basis for utilising the concept of an 'unreasonable veto', and that it would be 'difficult' to categorise any veto wielded by France in such a manner. As such, in the event that the government should fail to secure a second resolution, Goldsmith thus maintained that 'we would need to consider urgently at that stage the strength of our legal case in the light of circumstances at that time'. Concluding with the dangers of acting without a second resolution, the Attorney-General duly warned that there were 'a number of ways' in which legal action could be brought 'against the UK, members of the Government or UK military personnel', and noted that '[w]e cannot be certain that they would not succeed'. In short, Goldsmith's advice to the Prime Minister was that

> you will need to consider extremely carefully whether the evidence of non-cooperation and non-compliance by Iraq is sufficiently compelling to justify the conclusion that Iraq has failed to take its final opportunity.

While this reasoning may have carried sufficient weight for the senior echelons of the New Labour government (although the Cabinet itself was not shown or even told of the advice), the Attorney-General's rather ambiguous survey of the legal geographics was greeted with concern from senior military commanders. Most notably, the Chief of Defence Staff, Admiral Sir Michael Boyce—who was only informed of Goldsmith's advice after pressing Number 10 about the need for 'top cover'—subsequently demanded more concrete assurances that war would be legal, that British troops could not be charged with war crimes as a result, and that if they were, the Attorney-General and the Prime Minister would be 'brought into the frame as well'.[50] The Chief of General Staff, General Sir Mike Jackson, was similarly uneasy about the way events were starting to unfold. As he acerbically remarked, 'I spent a good deal of time recently in the Balkans making sure Milosevic was put behind bars. I have no intention of ending up in the next cell to him in the Hague'.[51]

In a perverse stroke of fortune for the government, three days after receiving Goldsmith's advice the prospects for securing legal cover via a second UN resolution became slimmer still when the French President, Jacques Chirac, announced in a television interview that France would vote against the current proposals before the Security Council, 'regardless of the circumstances'. The reason for this, he explained, was that 'this evening there are no grounds for waging war in order to achieve the goal we have set ourselves—to disarm Iraq'. While accepting that 'war would become unavoidable' if the inspections process proved unable to secure this end, Chirac insisted that this point had not yet been reached, and that the United Nations should therefore be given more time to reach a peaceful solution.[52]

Although the French position clearly referred to the UN situation as it presently stood on the evening of 10 March, a point emphasised by Chirac no less than four times during the course of his interview, the British government seized on the statement as a gilt-edged means of escaping from their political cul-de-sac in the Security Council. By erroneously depicting the French position as a dogmatic refusal to support a second resolution in each and every circumstance, and as a deliberately pitched attempt to wreck their own valiant efforts at resolving the matter amicably, officials would now have the perfect scapegoat for any diplomatic failure at the UN. Deriding Chirac's actions as 'foolish' and 'irresponsible', Blair thus accused the French government of 'undermining' the United Nations, while Gordon Brown, who had now been brought in from his previously disinterested and marginalized vantage point in order to provide heavyweight support for the Prime Minister, told Cabinet colleagues that the government's agreed strategy was to 'pin the blame on France' should Britain fail to obtain a UN sanction for war. In a gleeful repartee to the French Ambassador, the Political Director of the Foreign Office, Peter Ricketts, remarked that Chirac's statement had been a complete 'gift'.[53]

Hard evidence

With the contingency plans for failure now in place, the British government embarked on a last-ditch effort to secure a second resolution. Amid frenzied scenes at the United Nations, officials mooted an idea, initially raised by Hans Blix, of utilising a series of 'benchmarks' against which Iraqi co-operation could be empirically demonstrated and verified. Tied to a fixed thirty-day deadline, it was hoped that the new proposals would satisfy both the United States and the 'not-yets' on the Security Council by enabling Iraq's co-operation to be clearly and explicitly assessed, and by providing a final cut-off point for the inspections process. The key stumbling block for the proposals, though, now hinged not on the recalcitrance of the French, but on the fixed war plans of the American government. With Pentagon officials anxious to avoid having to engage in battle during the scorching heat of the Iraqi summer, with military operations now primed to commence, and with the Bush administration increasingly eager to press ahead with the invasion, the political trajectory for events was effectively set. All hopes for a second resolution were now dashed.[54]

Amid the uncertain legalities of Resolution 1441, the obstinacy of senior military chiefs, and the growing political pressures surrounding the government, the Attorney-General opportunely swooped to the rescue. Having decided to revise his earlier legal advice, Lord Goldsmith had since turned for assistance to Christopher Greenwood, a professor of international law at the London School of Economics well known for supporting the principle of armed intervention on humanitarian grounds.

In Greenwood's view, military action against Iraq would be legal without a second UN resolution on the basis that Resolution 1441 had reactivated the authority to use force contained in Resolution 678, since Iraq had not complied with its long-standing obligation to disarm, and since it did not require the Security Council to 'decide', but merely to 'consider' what, if any, further action should be taken in the event of a material breach. Despite apparently expressing his concerns to various colleagues, on 13 March Goldsmith duly transmitted this more assertive, and wholly more favourable, legal line to the government at an informal and un-minuted meeting with Lord Falconer (then a Home Office minister) and Baroness Morgan, Number 10's Director of Political and Government Relations. But even so, the Attorney-General's residual unease remained apparent. Despite providing Blair with a more sturdy legal structure on which to base a pre-emptive war, Goldsmith again instructed the Prime Minister that the legal authority for such action remained contingent upon the existence of WMD, and that 'strong factual grounds' and demonstrable 'hard evidence' would thus be required in order to conclude that Iraq was in breach of Resolution 1441.[55]

Despite the acute failure to uncover any weapons of mass destruction in Iraq, despite the reports of increasing Iraqi co-operation with UNMOVIC, and despite the government's failure to reassess its intelligence material in the light of these developments, the Prime Minister duly informed Goldsmith that it was his 'unequivocal view' that Iraq was indeed 'in further material breach' of its UN obligations. On this basis, the Attorney-General formally presented his new and improved legal advice to the Cabinet on 17 March, just three days before the onset of hostilities. Reading aloud a written answer that he had given to a parliamentary question earlier in the day (during the course of which he too had claimed that Iraq's failure to comply with Resolution 1441 was now 'plain'),[56] the Attorney-General now delivered the conclusion that Resolution 1441 did, after all, provide the legal justification for military action against Iraq by virtue of the fact that 'the authority to use force under 678 has revived and so continues today'.[57]

The contrast between this and the view presented by Goldsmith just ten days earlier was also evident in the scope of the revised legal argument. In true New Labour fashion, the thirteen-page cocktail of details, caveats, and uncertainties had now been whittled down to a decisive and definitive statement consisting of just 337 words on little more than one side of A4 paper. Nevertheless, the brevity of this legal reasoning provoked little disquiet from the Cabinet, whose members were still unaware of the Attorney-General's prior advice. In a pristine reflection of the degree to which Bagehot's constitutional keystone had now come to function as a device for rubber-stamping Prime Ministerial orders, Cabinet unease about the prospect of war had now largely been transformed into an unyielding body of support for the Iraq policy. As Clare Short would later complain, for all the enormity of the situation before them, 'no-one would allow any discussion'.[58]

Moreover, while the Attorney-General's legal opinion offered political salvation for the Prime Minister, the line of argument it invoked proved to be more than a little contentious. In the view of most experts, the proclaimed authorisation for the use of force lying dormant within Resolution 678 had in fact been limited to ensuring the expulsion of Iraqi troops from Kuwait during the Gulf War, had thus been terminated by the ceasefire of 1991, and could not therefore be revived, resuscitated, or reinvented in any way.[59] Indeed, Kofi Annan himself was of the opinion that military action without the explicit authorisation of the United Nations would be in contravention of the UN Charter, and insisted that only the Security Council as a whole had the right to determine what the 'serious consequences' referred to in Resolution 1441 would or would not be.[60] This assessment was also broadly consistent with the view held by legal advisors at the Foreign Office. The day after Goldsmith's announcement, its Deputy Legal Adviser, Elizabeth Wilmshurst, resigned in protest about the questionable legitimacy of the impending war. In a further reflection of the way in which the government was seeking to restrain debate on the legal issue, however, Wilmshurst herself refused to discuss the circumstances of her departure for fear of official reprisals. As she explained: 'I don't feel free to talk publicly about this sort of thing'.[61]

With the legal justification now in place, Blair set off for a hastily convened war summit with Bush, along with fellow allies in the 'coalition of the willing', José Maria Aznar (the Spanish President) and Jose Barosso (the Portuguese Prime Minister). While the wholly surreal location of the summit—on the Azores islands in the middle of the Atlantic Ocean—neatly symbolised the political isolation of its participants, it also served far more practical purposes. An American proposal to hold the summit in London had been politely but rapidly dismissed by Downing Street for fear that this would attract huge public protests and enrage the much-coveted opinion of rebel backbenchers in the run-up to the parliamentary vote on the war, while conversely, the notion of holding the summit in

Washington was similarly rejected by Number 10 for fear of the negative publicity that would inevitably be created by an image of Blair scuttling off to the White House.[62]

The summit itself was also carved from the stone of political expediency. In an effort to becalm restive Labour MPs, Bush's team of advisors consented to parts of the President's speech being altered by Alastair Campbell, who sought to tone down the rhetoric by turning references regarding the onset of military hostilities from 'when' into 'if' in order to foster the impression that Saddam Hussein still possessed a viable, if practicably impossible, exit route from the crisis. Positive noises, too, were made about the need to involve the United Nations in the process of postwar reconstruction, and about the need to push forward on the 'road-map for peace' in the Middle East. Behind this façade, however, the summit partners were firmly agreed that the diplomatic route had now failed, and that the attempt to secure a second resolution should be formally abandoned. As such it was subsequently determined that the common line to take would be to insist that Resolution 1441 provided sufficient authority for war, and that a second resolution was therefore not required. While this was by no means clearly apparent to most observers, the dangers of this approach were now deemed to be fewer than those involved in pressing ahead with an attempt to secure a second resolution, since any failure would seriously undermine the legal basis for war, and would thus intensify both the legal and political difficulties in mounting the invasion. At a news conference that evening, Bush declared that Saddam now had forty-eight hours to leave Iraq, or the US would commence military action at a time of its own choosing. The following day, the proposed resolution based on the benchmark criteria was formally withdrawn and UNMOVIC began to pull its inspectors out of the country.[63]

The more effective approach

Before the forty-eight-hour deadline had expired, the impending war had claimed its first ministerial casualty with the long-expected resignation from the government of Robin Cook, the Leader of the House of Commons. To ameliorate the political difficulties of the departure, an accord was struck with Downing Street in which Cook agreed to make his resignation speech the day before, rather than immediately prior to the impending Commons vote, and in which the government agreed in return not to set its spin machine to work against the former Foreign Secretary.

But even so, Cook's parting words made uncomfortable listening for the New Labour hierarchy. In a forensic dismembering of the government's case for war, Cook pointed out that none of the intelligence to which he had been privy during his time at the Foreign Office had ever claimed that Iraq possessed WMD, and noted that there was thus 'nothing to conclude that whatever Iraq might still have could be seen to pose an immediate threat to the region, least of all to Britain'.[64] While Cook's departure was accompanied by a flurry of less-threatening resignations, from John Denham (a Home Office minister), Lord Hunt (a junior health minister), and six parliamentary aides, one widely expected departure did not materialise. Instead, having received assurances from Blair that she would still be able to make a useful contribution to the postwar reconstruction effort, Clare Short now opted to remain in the Cabinet. By enabling the Prime Minister to avoid the loss of two Cabinet ministers on the eve of war, this would prove to be a shrewd piece of political management.[65]

Having effectively dealt with the remaining opposition within the Cabinet, Blair now turned his attention to the parliamentary vote itself. While this was an historic occasion, the first time ever that MPs had been granted a meaningful say on whether Britain should go to war, the actual mechanics of the operation proved to be far more rudimentary. The management of the vote was based around a concerted operation of persuasion, with Blair, his advisors, and senior ministers utilising intense personal meetings with wavering backbenchers, and deploying a series of pre-arranged humanitarian, legal, and security arguments specifically tailored to suit each specific 'type' of MP. In an effort to sway the doubters, both Cherie Blair and Bill Clinton were also seconded to the cause as the attempt to secure the support of the Labour backbenchers reached fever pitch. Wisps of rumour, spun into something altogether more solid after the war, added further pressure by suggesting that the Prime Minister might resign if a sufficient majority was not forthcoming.[66] In addition to this, with the repeated use of a three-line whip, the government sought not only to prevent MPs from voting according to the actual wishes of their constituents, but to prevent them from voting according to their consciences on what was now the most grave and exercising of moral issues. As one member of the government observed, 'the arm-twisting was phenomenal'.[67]

Yet interestingly enough, for all the heat of the political cauldron, at no time during the proceedings did any government official make any mention of the core assertions contained in the September dossier that

105

Saddam had WMD ready for firing within 45 minutes, or that he had sought uranium from Africa for the purposes of constructing a nuclear-weapons programme. While these had provided the government with its most striking and fear-inducing claims against the Iraqi regime just six months previously, ministers were now apparently unperturbed about the dangers. Moreover, the fact that no one sought to repeat the charges at the most critical juncture of the entire affair was made still more interesting by the fact that, in a noticeable contrast to Blair's newly discovered moral fervour for war, the motion for taking military action itself centred solely on Iraq's alleged possession of WMD, and made no reference at all to humanitarian or human-rights issues.[68]

Opening the parliamentary debate, Blair attempted to persuade reticent backbenchers, veering across the entire range of arguments in favour of military action. Though having been reluctantly dragged to the division lobby by the political riptide of events, the Prime Minister began by asserting that it was 'right' for Parliament to have a vote on the issue, and by assuring the House that he did 'not disrespect the views of those in opposition to mine'. Having dispensed with the pleasantries, Blair then proceeded to trash the French for having scuppered the government's noble attempt to secure a second UN resolution. Following the agreed strategy, and despite the earlier warnings of the Attorney-General, the line presented was that the benchmarks idea had been 'gathering support' and that this progress had been ruined by Chirac's unreasonable decision to 'veto a second resolution whatever the circumstances'. The French government, he maintained, was 'utterly opposed to anything which lays down an ultimatum authorising action in the event of non-compliance by Saddam.' Of course, this was also totally disingenuous, given that the majority of Security Council members had always been firmly against military action without a second resolution, given that the anti-war position of the swinging six had been hardening prior to Chirac's announcement, and given that France, Germany, and Russia had all publicly accepted the need for military action in the event that the inspections process failed to deliver a peaceful disarmament. Nevertheless, the Prime Minister continued to insist that it was 'palpably absurd' to suggest that Iraq would have unilaterally destroyed its WMD, and hawkishly effused that 'our patience should have been exhausted weeks and months and years ago'. No 'fair observer', he insisted, would 'really dispute that Iraq is in breach and that 1441 implies action in such circumstances'.

Having re-sounded the alarm, Blair then sought to present the proposed action against Iraq as an integral part of the global war on terror. Though conceding that the association between tyrannical regimes with WMD and international terrorist groups was 'loose', the Prime Minister nonetheless asserted that the link was 'hardening', and that the 'real and present danger' facing the world was 'the possibility' (however vague and unquantifiable it might be) that the two might come together. Warning intently of the threat of 'chaos', Blair insisted that the credibility of the West was now at stake, and sombrely impressed upon the House that 'it was dangerous if such regimes disbelieve us'. Iraq, he asserted, was 'the test of whether we treat the threat seriously'. Having thus framed the question of Iraq as the defining measurement of the West's commitment to deal with the issue of international terrorism, Blair again proceeded to position the war on terror itself within 'a larger global agenda', ranging from 'poverty and sustainable development' to 'democracy and human rights'. In sum, he explained, the path that was now chosen by the House would effectively 'determine the pattern of international politics for the next generation'.[69]

In the event, the combined weight of rhetoric concerning Iraq's supposed WMD menace, the misrepresentation of the French, the apparent threat to Blair's premiership, and the comforting legal advice of the Attorney-General (made all the more important by the fact that Parliament itself possesses no legal counsel and no right to commission its own independent legal opinion) eventually swung the balance in the government's favour. Although the Prime Minister's strategy of highlighting the benefits of a strong and centralised form of governance had singularly failed to convince the mass of the British public, two-thirds of which remained unconvinced as to the need for war, the parliamentary power of the executive had helped to ensure that the vote was won, with a seemingly comfortable majority of 179 defeating an amendment stating that the case for war had yet to be made. This triumph, however, masked darker political undercurrents. In what had been the largest parliamentary revolt since the mid-nineteenth century, 139 Labour MPs, around a third of the entire Labour contingent, had voted in support of the amendment. Despite appearances, then, with the government's parliamentary victory having thus only been delivered by the votes of the Conservatives, the foundations of political support for the invasion were anything but solid.

Furthermore, while these events have been widely interpreted as signifying a great constitutional shift, as having enhanced British democracy, and as representing the empowerment of Parliament to the extent that it would now be virtually impossible for a future government to go to war without its express approval, the reality is that it remains to be seen whether the Iraq vote will be regarded as having set any sort of precedent. Indeed, it also remains unclear as to what precisely constitutes a 'war', or whether a future government would feel honour bound to go before Parliament to vote on any lesser action, such as a campaign of air strikes in the same vein as Desert Fox.[70] Yet while much will therefore depend on the particular confluence of circumstances to hand, including the type of military action impending, the character of the Prime Minister, and the state of public and parliamentary opinion at the time, the New Labour executive has explicitly refused to commit itself to allowing a parliamentary right to vote on war. Instead, the power to allow such a vote continues to reside with the Prime Minister, whose ability to exercise the royal prerogative circumvents the need for parliamentary approval to send British troops into action. The prevailing view of central government, then, is that retaining the power and autonomy of the executive in such matters remains the most efficient way of dealing with them. '[T]he pragmatic approach, allowing the circumstances of Parliamentary scrutiny to reflect the circumstances of the armed conflict', it explains, 'continues to be the more effective approach'.[71]

Concluding remarks

The executive management of the run-up to the war with Iraq from September 2002 typified the centralised, hierarchical, and elitist nature of the New Labour government. Central to this was a concerted deployment of state resources in an effort to control the flow of politically sensitive information and to shape the course of political debate in line with the government's objectives. Following the failure of the September dossier to mobilise public opinion behind the need for stronger measures against Iraq, the government's emphasis switched to the UN weapons inspections, which were revived in November under the terms of Resolution 1441. The subsequent failure of the inspections to uncover any weapons of mass destruction, however, was accompanied by an intensification of the propaganda campaign, at the centre of which was the production of a dossier designed to highlight Iraq's programme of concealment and deception. Yet again this served to highlight the largely informal and *ad hoc* character of elite executive activity, as well as the lack of any

feature of the conflict. Accusing the BBC of being biased towards Iraq, Campbell directed particular vehemence at Andrew Gilligan (whom he accused of having 'low' standards and a 'sneering contempt' for information put out by the coalition), at John Humphries (who was attacked for his general 'contempt' for elected politicians), and at Rageh Omar (for being 'determined to present military success as a disaster'). In one portentous outburst, Campbell made it known that 'the Prime Minister has also expressed real concern about some of the reports he has seen and heard', and in a thinly veiled remark, he predicted that 'if the BBC reporting continues as it is, this will become a public controversy, which I am sure neither of us particularly want'.[8]

Right across the world

Though stepping back from such directly pointed attacks on the media, the Prime Minister remained intensely assertive about the conduct and the merits of the military campaign. Stung by criticism of the logistical arrangements, and in stark contrast to the anarchic scenes that would soon mark the birth of the post-Saddam era, Blair fervently insisted that the invasion had been subject to 'the most careful planning and consideration', and that 'the essential strategic picture' was 'unfolding exactly according to plan'. Defending the principle of the war itself, Blair further insisted that the government had been careful 'to operate within the context of international law and the demands of the United Nations', and warning of a split between Europe and America, described the idea of a multi-polar world as 'a profoundly dangerous concept' that would make it 'far harder to make the international order stable and secure'. That the war with Iraq would also further the new-imperialist strategy being driven by the United States was thus similarly presented in beneficial terms. As the Prime Minister put it, the invasion was 'the right thing to do', since the removal of Saddam's regime would 'send a huge signal not just to the people of Iraq but a signal right across the world'.[9]

In order to avoid sending out the wrong signal, however, the Prime Minister was also careful to play down the prospects of rapidly discovering large stocks of WMD on the technical basis that Iraq was 'very very big'. 'The idea that we can suddenly discover this stuff', he explained, 'is a lot more difficult in a country the size of Iraq'. While also admitting that some of Iraq's weapons systems had been 'dismantled', and that this would act as 'an inhibition' to its use of WMD, the Prime Minister was also keen to reassure people that such material would eventually turn up, since there was 'absolutely no doubt at all that these weapons of mass destruction exist'.[10] To compound matters further, Blair's hoary legal problems also re-emerged during the course of the war. On 26 March, just a week into the conflict, the Attorney-General delivered an assessment to the Prime Minister warning that all US and British postwar activity in Iraq beyond the essential maintenance of security would be illegal without the express authorisation of the United Nations. While Resolution 1441 had provided the legal justification for war, its legal mandate, he reported, did not stretch to postwar reconstruction. As such, Goldsmith extrapolated that a new UN resolution would thus be required 'to authorise imposing reform and restructuring of Iraq and its government', and that a failure to obtain this would undermine the legitimacy of the invasion. As he put it:

> the longer the occupation of Iraq continues, and the more the tasks undertaken by an interim administration depart from the main objective, the more difficult it will be to justify the lawfulness of the occupation.[11]

Unsurprisingly, Blair and Goldsmith agreed to keep this judgement confidential in order to avoid arousing further political discord, keeping both Parliament and the general public in the dark about the conclusions reached. Yet again, this centralised control of information also reflected the tightly constricted style of the New Labour government, with Blair now choosing to conduct the war effort itself through informal links with senior officials (primarily Hoon, Straw, Scarlett, and Sir Michael Boyce) rather than through a conventional, formally structured, and properly minuted War Cabinet.[12] Nevertheless, from mid-April, the Prime Minister's popularity was given a much-needed boost by the collapse of the Iraqi regime, with a much-vaunted 'Baghdad bounce' prompting a rise in public support for the war to a peak of almost two-thirds of the British electorate in favour. From this point on, however, the ratings began to slide back. By August, around half of British voters were of the view that the government had exaggerated the case for war, and by September fewer than two-fifths agreed that the invasion had been the right thing to do.[13] Central to this deflation of public support was the deteriorating security and humanitarian situation in 'postwar' Iraq. The initial stabilisation plan—a three-stage process of handing control to the US Office of Reconstruction and Humanitarian Assistance in conjunction with the Pentagon, leading to the creation of an interim Iraqi administration and thence to democratic elections at an as-yet-unspecified date—soon began to unravel amid the widespread looting and disorder that rapidly followed the disintegration of the Iraqi regime.

The initial postwar involvement of the United Nations was also enormously limited. Although sanctions and the oil-for-food programme were both abolished, and although legal recognition of the US-led occupation was retrospectively established under Resolution 1483, the UN itself did not play any significant role either in helping to maintain peace or in the process of postwar reconstruction. Instead, the United States began to carve up the task itself by awarding the majority of rebuilding contracts to American companies with no competitive tendering. As large contracts were quickly bestowed upon firms with close ties to the Bush administration—the most notable of which was Halliburton, the world's largest oilfield services company, once run by Dick Cheney (and in which the US Vice-President continued to hold millions of dollars' worth of shares)—the suspicion grew that US elites had embarked on the path of war at least in part as a means of feathering their own personal nests.[14] Moreover, although an interim Iraqi government (the Iraqi Governing Council) began a limited sharing of power with the United States from mid-July, hopes that the situation would soon stabilise were further undermined when twenty UN staff, including Kofi Annan's Special Envoy, were killed by an insurgent attack on its Baghdad headquarters, prompting the United Nations to withdraw from Iraq entirely. To add to the general sense of conflagration, hopes accompanying the much-awaited 'road-map for peace' in the Middle East, finally published at the end of April, also soon began to fade amid a renewed wave of violence.[15]

The postwar reconstruction process also led to the belated resignation of Clare Short. Bemoaning a lack of any influence over the course of events, and protesting about the lack of UN participation, in her resignation speech Short mounted a direct assault on Blair's handling of the Iraq crisis. She placed much of the blame for the poor situation currently prevailing on 'the style and organisation of our government', which, she claimed, had moved from the spin-driven control-freakery of the first term to a second term characterised by 'the centralisation of power in the hands of the Prime Minister and an increasingly small number of advisors who make decisions in private without proper discussion'. Accusing Blair of governing by 'diktats' in place of collective decision-making through the Cabinet, the now ex-Secretary for International Development added that much of this was due to the Prime Minister's personal obsession with ensuring 'his place in history'.[16]

For reasons Blair would much rather forget, this place was soon to be very secure indeed. As questions began to mount about the ongoing failure to discover any weapons of mass destruction in Iraq, the Prime Minister was again forced into mounting a politically evasive rearguard action. Repeatedly implying that he had inside information of WMD poised to materialise at any moment, Blair continued to maintain that more time was required in order to uncover the stockpiles, a discernible contrast to his prewar insistence that no more time could be given to the UNMOVIC inspections. By May, with more than half the sites identified by US intelligence as worth examining having been searched, and with no WMD having yet been found, the clamour for answers was becoming ever more demanding. With the pressure on the British government mounting, and with the questions starting to stack up, the need for a postwar offensive on the home front was becoming increasingly pressing. Within a matter of days, it would be a matter of urgency.[17]

A little patience

As the aftermath of the war pitched and rolled among the growing failure to uncover any weapons of mass destruction, events in Britain were taking a very unexpected turn. On 22 May the BBC journalist Andrew Gilligan met with one of the government's foremost weapons experts, Dr David Kelly, at a North London hotel, for a general discussion about matters relating to Iraq. At this meeting, Kelly informed Gilligan about the disquiet surrounding the production of the September dossier, outlining some of the tensions and issues relating to the use of intelligence material. A week later, in a live and unscripted broadcast at seven minutes past six in the morning, Gilligan broke the news on Radio 4's *Today* programme that one of the 'senior officials' involved in drawing up the dossier had alleged it to have been 'sexed up' by the government. In the week prior to its publication, Gilligan maintained, the dossier had been 'rather a bland production', at which point Downing Street had ordered it 'to be made more exciting', and had 'ordered more facts to be discovered' so as to strengthen the case against Saddam Hussein. The 'classic' example of this, he told listeners, was the inclusion of the 45-minute claim, which, he alleged, the government 'probably knew' to be wrong 'even before it decided to put it in'.[18]

Three days later, Gilligan pointed the finger for this transgression firmly at Alastair Campbell, alleging in an article for the *Mail on Sunday* that the government's Director of Communications and Strategy had been primarily responsible for the transformation.[19] Over the next few days, similar reports about the use of intelligence in the September dossier (further sourced from Dr Kelly) were also being run on BBC 2's *Newsnight* programme. The reaction of government ministers, though, was to dismiss calls for a public inquiry into the prewar use of intelligence on the grounds that they 'did not think it was necessary'.[20] With Parliament itself possessing no power to initiate such proceedings, the task of holding an inquiry instead fell to the Foreign Affairs Select Committee (FAC). Five days after the initial '6:07' broadcast, this committee announced its decision to hold an inquiry into whether the government had 'presented accurate and complete information to Parliament in the period leading up to military action in Iraq, particularly in respect of weapons of mass destruction'.[21]

The government's immediate response to the BBC reports combined blanket denials with a concerted attempt to distort the nature of the claims being made. Asserting that everything in the September dossier had been cleared by the JIC and that its contents had been based on 'their judgement—not my judgement', Blair retorted that the idea that the government 'made our intelligence agencies invent some piece of evidence' was 'completely absurd', and strenuously rejected any notion that anyone had attempted to 'insert' concocted information into the September dossier in order to strengthen the case for war.[22] Although this was technically true, it was also a misrepresentation of the central allegations being made, which were not that the government had actually 'invented' intelligence to put in the dossier, but simply that there had been concerns from within the intelligence community about the way in which some of the information, especially that pertaining to the 45-minute claim, had been used during the course of its construction. Indeed, as government officials were only too well aware, the real strengthening of the dossier came not so much through the insertion of information, but through its removal via the stripping out of caveats and uncertainties from the assessments of the JIC. As Gilligan protested: 'The government merely denied a story that had never been. They denied a number of claims that had never been alleged'.[23]

What is more, the 6:07 broadcast apart, none of Gilligan's reports for the BBC made any mention of the 'probably knew' claim, and at no time did any BBC broadcast seek to apportion any blame over the dossier to any particular individual. And this despite the fact that Dr Kelly himself had told *Newsnight*'s Science Editor, Susan Watts, that the Number 10 press office had played a key role in strengthening the dossier, and that Alastair Campbell was 'synonymous with the press office because he's responsible for it'.[24] Nevertheless, contrary to the feigned apoplexy and indignation regarding the severity of the allegations that was to come, and contrary to Blair's insistence that the *Mail on Sunday* article had produced a 'raging storm' and had put 'booster rockets' on the story,[25] the BBC claims aroused little initial interest. Not only this, but the Downing Street machine itself made no formal complaint about the matter, with the only objection emanating from one of its minor press officers, Anne Shevas, who insisted that the allegations were 'serious and untrue', and who claimed that the BBC had given insufficient coverage to the government's denials.[26]

Alastair Campbell's own protestations were also restricted. There were no communications at all to the *Mail on Sunday*, and just two private letters to the BBC, written a week and a fortnight respectively after the initial broadcasts. Moreover, these complained not of the actual substance of the story, but of technical inaccuracies pertaining to Gilligan's description of the JIC as being a Number 10 committee, and to his claim that Campbell had apologised to Richard Dearlove for the February dossier by letter, when he had in fact done so by phone. At no time was Gilligan's 6:07 broadcast singled out for any special attention, at no time did Campbell call for any sort of apology from anyone concerning the substantive allegations, and at no time was there any attempt from any government official to pursue the matter either through the Broadcasting Standards Commission or through the complaints procedures of the BBC itself.[27] Yet with senior New Labour officials aware of the potential dangers of the story, efforts were nevertheless made to secure an official refutation of the allegations in order to choke off any possible threat. In a plan hatched by Campbell, the government's Director of Communications approached John Scarlett, asking him if he would write a formal letter to dismiss the claims and to put the record straight. This idea fell flat, however, when Scarlett, still smarting over the February dossier affair, replied that it would not be 'appropriate' and that 'it would certainly not have been normal for any chairman of the JIC to make that sort of statement in public'.[28]

Instead, with the government unable to convincingly refute the BBC allegations, and with the political pressures concerning the absence of WMD continuing to close in, the Prime Minister was now forced to seize upon every possible indicator of a weapons arsenal, regardless of its

118

veracity, in the hope of quelling discontent about the invasion. In one of the most notable examples of this, Blair reported on 2 June that 'our experts' had found 'two mobile biological weapons facilities', which he claimed 'were almost certainly part ... of a whole set of those facilities'. The far more mundane reality, though, was that the trailers were not actually examined for another three days, and in the event turned out to have been nothing more deadly than a portable system for the production of helium for weather balloons. As the Prime Minister's desperation grew, the failure to uncover any WMD was also explained away on the grounds that Saddam Hussein had clearly gone to 'extraordinary lengths to dismantle, conceal, and disperse the weapons and any evidence of their existence'. Of course this did little to support the view that the impending danger from Iraq had been of such an order as to require the termination of the inspections process and the launching of an invasion against the will of both the international community and domestic opinion. It was not a little ironic, then, that the Prime Minister now called on the British people 'to just have a little patience' with the inspections process.[29]

A very, very bad direction

In a further effort to neutralise the political disquiet, the government also now opted to establish its own inquiry into the prewar intelligence. In order to regain some measure of control over the political debate, it was determined that this undertaking should be conducted by the Intelligence and Security Committee rather than the Foreign Affairs Committee. A major advantage of this was that the secretive nature of the ISC would permit the investigation to be conducted away from the scrutinising gaze of the press and the general public, and would ensure that the proceedings would be undertaken in a rather less confrontational and politically abrasive environment than would be provided by the open forum of the FAC. Furthermore, by charging the ISC with an examination of whether the intelligence on Iraq 'was adequate and properly assessed and whether it was accurately reflected in Government publications', the inquiry would also home in on the credibility of the September dossier, and hence the dispute with the BBC, at the exclusion of the political decision-making processes during the run-up to the war.[30]

To enhance its influence over events still further, the government also sought to constrain the operation of the 'independent' FAC inquiry. Requests to interview a range of senior officials, including John Scarlett,

Richard Dearlove, David Omand (the Cabinet Office Intelligence Co-ordinator), Martin Howard (the Deputy Chief of Defence Intelligence), as well as Blair himself, were all refused by the government. A request to examine Alastair Campbell was also rejected, with the most ostensibly radical and modernising Prime Minister of recent times now resorting to the use of precedent to justify such actions. It had, as he told the House of Commons, 'never been the case that officials have given evidence to Select Committees'.[31] With requests to see draft copies of the September dossier along with other intelligence material relevant to the case being similarly refused (with Blair again explaining that '[i]ntelligence papers have never been provided to committees in this way'), and with the FAC possessing no legislative authority to compel senior members of the executive to appear or to order the release of sensitive documents, the FAC was instead forced to rely on a privately given oral presentation by the Foreign Secretary, outlining from 'some extracts' what he deemed to be the 'relevant' sections of JIC intelligence assessments.[32]

The official reason for such a high level of secrecy was that this was a necessity borne of national security considerations. Notwithstanding the fact that during the course of the Hutton Inquiry, far more sensitive material than the FAC could ever have dreamt of seeing was posted on the internet for the viewing pleasure of the entire world (with apparently no detrimental effects on the national security position), David Omand later explained that 'the close examination of the process of putting together the dossier would reveal more about the nature of the intelligence underlying the assessments than we thought would be safe'. A somewhat more systemic and technocratic reason for the secrecy surrounding the construction of the September dossier, however, was divulged by John Scarlett, who maintained that 'the JIC would not be happy for the drafts to be released to the FAC' since 'the process of formulation of advice by officials ... should remain confidential for the good conduct of Government business'. Or, as Jack Straw put it, the FAC, as a parliamentary committee composed of elected representatives, was not an 'appropriate' body to look at such issues.[33]

Yet despite this official obfuscation, the FAC inquiry still proved to be greatly damaging for the government. Adding to the steady stream of negative media reports both of the war itself and of the events preceding it, the investigation generated further unease over the government's handling of intelligence in the run-up to the conflict. In a particularly damning testimony, Robin Cook told the committee that there had been little to indicate 'a new, alarming, urgent and compelling threat' from Iraq, that there had been 'no compelling and urgent reason to believe that containment was not working', and that the government had failed to present 'the whole picture' concerning the intelligence in order to meet the political objective of securing British support for a US-led invasion. The 'fundamental problem', as he saw it, was that

> instead of using intelligence as evidence on which to base the conclusion of a policy, we used intelligence as the basis on which we could justify a policy on which we had already settled.[34]

An even more vociferous criticism of the government was meted out by Clare Short. Accusing the Prime Minister of indulging in a series of 'half-truths' and 'exaggerations' in order to get Britain to war, Short purported to have been informed by 'senior people' that Blair had committed himself to war during the spring of 2002, and that consequently the intelligence had been 'exaggerated politically' in order to create the impression that the threat was 'more imminent' than it actually was. In her view, since Blair had considered it to be an honourable course of action to support the United States, the Prime Minister had thus performed an 'honourable deception' in order to get Britain into war behind the Americans. '[O]ur country', she protested, 'was deceived about what the plan really was'.[35]

Throughout the latter half of June, the government was in a palpable state of alarm about the political damage being wrought by the inquiry. According to Godric Smith, one of the Prime Minister's official spokesmen, the issue was now 'dominating the news agenda almost to the exclusion of everything else'. According to Sir Kevin Tebbit, the Permanent Under-Secretary at the Ministry of Defence, his political master, Geoff Hoon, was now 'very concerned' about the finalisation of the FAC's report, while Alastair Campbell too was now of the opinion that 'the FAC was moving in a very, very bad direction for the Government'. There was, he noted, 'a fire storm developing which was causing considerable difficulty with MPs, with the press and by now with the media right around the world'. Observing a strong desire in official circles to 'change this dynamic that was currently prevalent in the media', Campbell further noted that Blair himself was becoming increasingly desperate to 'get back onto a domestic political agenda'.[36]

In a renewed effort to bring the situation under control, the government now sought to broker an informal deal with the BBC, offering to acknowledge that the Corporation had been within its rights to have broadcast the allegations if it publicly accepted that the story itself was wrong. The prospects of any deal being reached, though, were soon dashed when Greg Dyke and Gavyn Davies (the Chairman of the BBC) both refused to accept the government's offer on the grounds that it would compromise the BBC's impartiality.[37] With this avenue closed, the government decided instead to adopt a more direct approach. The first part of this strategy was to present Gilligan's 6:07 broadcast as being the definitive version of the wider story relating to the government's use of intelligence in the run-up to the war. Second, the government sought to define this as constituting a charge that Number 10 in general, and Alastair Campbell in particular, had deliberately lied in order to get Britain into the war. Third, the government then strove to secure a public refutation of this charge in order to discredit the entire BBC story. In so doing, officials hoped to ease the political disquiet over Iraq by deflecting attention away from the failure to find WMD, and by establishing that the intelligence had not been pumped up and distorted with a view to misleading Parliament and the general public. The government would thus be able to counter the failure to uncover any WMD by demonstrating that it had acted in 'good faith' on the basis of the information that was being presented to it by the intelligence agencies.

Four weeks after the Gilligan story was initially broadcast, and with the government having yet to make any formal complaint about its content, officials began to claim that the allegations made in the 6:07 report were of such magnitude and severity that it had left them with no option but to seek a public retraction. The first phase of the attack was launched at the FAC on 24 June with a preparatory strike from Jack Straw. Insisting that the government had never sought to present the threat from Iraq as being 'immediate', but that it was merely 'current', Straw maintained that the 45-minute claim had not been 'remotely' central to the government's case. The reason that this had not been repeated since the publication of the September dossier, he claimed, was due not to its inaccuracy, but to the fact that it was not needed given the 'overwhelming' amount of other evidence that was being presented.[38]

The following day, the offensive was stepped up by Alastair Campbell, who, in a complete turnabout by the government, was now allowed to appear before the FAC inquiry. The government's Director of Communications and Strategy began by conceding that the February dossier had been an error, by insisting that 'the totality' of the government's output on Iraq's WMD should not be defined by 'one mistake', and by then proceeding to denigrate the entire output of the BBC for precisely the same thing. While accepting that he had made drafting suggestions for the September dossier ('in common with other officials'), Campbell denied that he had tried to 'sex it up', insisted that there had been 'no question of interference' with the JIC, and, presenting a parodied version of the BBC's story based purely on the 6:07 broadcast, stated that the central allegation was that 'the Prime Minister, the Cabinet, the intelligence agencies, people like myself, connived to persuade Parliament to send British forces into action on a lie'. Calling on the BBC to thus apologise, the Director of Communications added that he had been 'trying to get an acknowledgement from the BBC that the story is wrong for weeks'.[39] That day, Campbell wrote in his diary that he 'felt a lot better' and that he 'had opened a flank' on the organisation.[40]

Of public interest

In a series of letters sent to Richard Sambrook (the BBC's Head of News) over the next few days, Alastair Campbell pressed further for an apology. Releasing the most virulent of these letters to the press in order to gain further publicity for his campaign, Campbell insisted that the 6:07 report was '100 per cent wrong', that it had been based on 'wholly false and inaccurate information', and, with apparently no sense of irony given the provenance of the 45-minute claim, accused the BBC of 'poor professional judgement and competence' in relying on a single source without making any further checks about its reliability.[41] In response, Sambrook accused Campbell of having 'seriously misrepresented the BBC's journalism', and maintained that the Corporation had never accused anyone in the government of lying, but was simply reporting the allegations made by its source on 'an issue of public interest'.[42] Faced with the BBC's refusal to concede that it was wrong, on 27 June Campbell, ostensibly gripped by a 'mounting sense of anger and frustration', raised the temperature still further in a live interview with Channel 4 News. Lambasting the 6:07 allegations as 'a fundamental attack upon the integrity of the Government, the Prime Minister, [and] the intelligence agencies', he again insisted that 'there were no errors of fact' in the September dossier, and once more demanded that the BBC apologise for its conduct.[43]

While Campbell's assault on the BBC proved to be successful in diverting press attention away from the failure to find WMD in Iraq, the alleged charges of the 6:07 broadcast had still to be discredited. At the end of June, an unexpected opportunity for the government to change the situation emerged when Dr David Kelly informed his line manager at the Ministry of Defence (MoD) that he might have been the source for the BBC's story. Maintaining, contrary to his conversation with Susan Watts, that he had no knowledge of the 45-minute claim before the dossier was published, and denying claims that he had accused Campbell of transforming it, Kelly's admission thus presented the government with an effective means of destroying the 6:07 allegations.[44] If the scientist was indeed Gilligan's source, and if this information could be made publicly available, then the government would be able to irreversibly discredit the BBC's story by demonstrating that Kelly's views had been distorted and misrepresented. As Campbell prosaically observed, it would 'f**k Gilligan' if Kelly proved to be his source.[45] Geoff Hoon, on the other hand, made the point somewhat more diplomatically. The view in official circles, he observed, was that Gilligan was 'being less than frank' with BBC chiefs about the nature of his source, and that there would therefore need to be a 'correction of the public record'. The working assumption, as he saw it, 'was that at some stage his [i.e. Kelly's] name would come out'.[46] As Hoon subsequently explained:

> We spent a lot of time discussing ... how we could find a way of encouraging the BBC to accept that it was in both our interests to identify Andrew Gilligan's source.[47]

Indeed, this view now had wide currency among government officials. According to Richard Hatfield (the MoD's Personnel Director), it was now 'very clearly expected that Kelly ... at some stage ... would need to be publicly associated with his account', and as Sir Kevin Tebbit later revealed, the general premise was that there was 'a very strong case for correcting, clarifying, amplifying the public record', and that, in short, 'it was inevitable that his name would become public at some stage'.[48] The same point was also put by David Omand, who maintained that the inaccuracies in the BBC's story would need to be 'publicly acknowledged'. Hence,

> there would indeed be an obligation on him to help clear up the matter ... given the very intense public interest and the fact that very great damage had been done to the credibility of the Government and credibility of Government institutions as a result of this whole furore.[49]

Thus aware that Kelly might be the BBC's source, and believing that it would be politically useful if this was more widely known, key figures in the government now sought to pass this information on to the Foreign Affairs Committee. In total contrast to its prior obstructionism, the official reason for this new-found willingness to assist the FAC inquiry was that the government would have been accused of instigating a cover-up had it not informed the committee that someone purporting to be the source for Gilligan's story had come forward. Jonathon Powell, for example, contended that officials were concerned about 'being accused of withholding information from the FAC', Hoon attested to have been 'very concerned' that they would need to make any relevant information about Kelly known to the committee 'quite quickly', while Tebbit maintained that 'the Government were increasingly in danger of being vulnerable to the charge that it was suppressing, withholding, covering up very relevant information'.[50]

A more prescient reason for wanting to make Kelly known to the FAC, however, was that the committee would subsequently want to interview him, and that, in all likelihood, this would lead them to conclude that the BBC's story was wrong, thus exonerating government officials of having acted in a duplicitous fashion during the run-up to the war in Iraq. As Campbell explained, both he and Hoon now 'wanted to get it out that the source had broken cover' to claim that Gilligan had 'misrepresented him', that 'the source was not in the intelligence community', and that he was 'not involved [in] drawing up [the] dossier'. The aim, as he put it, was to get Kelly before the FAC in order to secure 'a clear win not a messy draw' in the battle with the BBC.[51]

While Blair, too, was now becoming increasingly keen to bring the matter to a decisive conclusion, the Prime Minister's initial instincts were to proceed with caution in order to avoid worsening the political situation. As Campbell records, while he and Hoon both 'wanted to get the source up', Blair 'was nervous about it' and felt that 'the bureaucracy' (namely, Tebbit and Omand) should remain in charge of the process. As the Prime Minister himself explained, although there was 'a fair possibility' that the information 'would leak in any event', a central concern was that passing Kelly's name to the FAC 'could lead them to re-opening the inquiry' on a broader level, thus raising further controversy about the government's use of intelligence material.[52] Nevertheless, according to Tebbit, Blair 'was following this very very closely indeed'. '[T]he implication', he observed 'was that he wanted to do something about it.'[53] This impression was also noted by David Omand, who concurred that since the dispute with the BBC had 'dominated political debate in the country for a considerable time', and since it was showing 'no signs of diminishing', the issue was becoming 'a matter of intense interest and concern to the Prime Minister'.[54]

Orderly and measured

On 7 July, still unaware of Dr Kelly's admission, the FAC published its much-anticipated report. Strongly criticising the government's conduct during the run-up to the war with Iraq, it concluded that the September dossier had been 'more assertive' than traditional intelligence-based documents and that it had contained a series of 'undue emphases', including an executive summary that was stronger than the text.[55] In particular, the committee stated that the 45-minutes claim had been given an excessive degree of prominence in the dossier, and that the uranium-from-Africa claim 'should have been qualified to reflect the uncertainty' of the intelligence. The committee further noted that it was 'very odd indeed' that the government had yet to produce its own non-forged documentation in relation to this matter. Moreover, although finding that 'allegations of politically inspired meddling' could not 'credibly be established' in relation to the construction of the dossier, the FAC nonetheless complained that it had been 'entitled to a greater degree of co-operation from the Government on access to witnesses and to intelligence material' during the course of its inquiry, and pointed out that this lack of access not only amounted to 'a failure of accountability to Parliament', but also meant that the committee itself had been unable to ascertain for certain whether the intelligence 'was in any respect faulty or misinterpreted'. Further still, members of the committee were also sharply divided on Campbell's personal involvement with the dossier, explaining that they were 'neither equipped nor willing to arbitrate' in his dispute with Gilligan, and clearing him of exerting an undue influence only on the casting vote of the Labour chairman, Donald Anderson.[56]

On Campbell's involvement in the February dossier, however, the FAC was far less reticent. Describing this entire affair as 'a disaster', and concluding that it had been 'fundamentally wrong' for such a document to be presented to Parliament and widely circulated 'without ministerial oversight', the committee found that Campbell had failed to clear the document with the JIC, had failed to indicate clearly that the dossier had been his responsibility, and had failed to pay 'sufficient attention to detail' during its construction. The lack of accountability evident in the production of the dossier was also highlighted, with the FAC pointing out that the key 'contributory factors' in this process had been the free rein granted to Campbell's production team, as well as 'the lack of procedural accountability' within Whitehall itself. The process of compiling the dossier, it maintained, 'should have been more openly disclosed to Parliament'.[57]

The report of the FAC was nevertheless presented as a victory by both the government and the BBC. Alastair Campbell insisted that the allegations against him had been shown to be 'untrue', and Jack Straw asserted that the FAC had 'heard all the evidence' and that the government had now been cleared of misusing intelligence in the run-up to the war, while the BBC maintained that the report had shown its story to have been in the public interest and refused to yield to renewed governmental demands for it to apologise.[58] With the dispute remaining very much unresolved, the government's desire to undermine the 6:07 broadcast by ensuring public awareness of Dr Kelly's identity became ever-more pressing. In this context, senior officials became increasingly keen to discover whether or not Dr Kelly himself would support the government's line on Iraq's WMD in the event that he should appear before a committee of inquiry. As John Scarlett explained, since the government clearly had 'an interest' in knowing what Kelly's views would be 'in advance', 'it would thus be useful to know what he would or would not say' in the event of such an examination. In order to assess this, it was therefore determined that Kelly should undergo a further round of questioning at the MoD, designed to elicit his views on the matter more thoroughly. While Blair continued to insist on the need to follow the 'proper procedures' in all of this, in keeping with the government's informal style of business there were no discussions as to precisely what these procedures should be. For Scarlett, the interpretation was that Kelly would now need 'a proper security-style interview', while as Dominic Wilson (Sir Kevin Tebbit's private secretary) put it, a 'key issue' was to ascertain

> Kelly's readiness to be associated with a public statement that names him and carries a clear and sustainable refutation of the core allegations on the '45 min' intelligence.[59]

At the ensuing examination, Kelly assured his inquisitors at the Ministry of Defence that his views on Iraq's WMD were very similar to the government's, and was in turn notified that his name might become public knowledge 'in due course'.[60] With officials now virtually convinced that Kelly was indeed the source of the BBC's story, the wheels of ensuring that his identity, and hence his views, became publicly known were now carefully set in motion. As Tebbit pointed out, it would not be sufficient simply for the government to declare that someone had come forward with a

127

version of events which contradicted the claims of the BBC, since 'the authenticity would have depended on the individual being named'. Thus:

> The central point was that if we were certain that Dr Kelly provided the explanation for a story which had a fundamental influence on public confidence and trust in the Government's policies, then there was a strong case, one might almost say a duty, to bring that information forward.[61]

Indeed, such was the government's desire for it to be known that Kelly's views diverged from the BBC's story that, as Tebbit also noted, 'there was a feeling that even if he was not the source ... this nevertheless was information of sufficient importance to be brought into the public domain'.[62] However, with Kelly himself unlikely to come forward voluntarily, with the Prime Minister anxious about the potential consequences of him appearing before the FAC, and with further informal contacts with the BBC proving fruitless at either brokering a deal or at persuading the corporation to reveal the name of its source, New Labour officials (with Peter Mandelson now threatening that the BBC 'would have the full force of the government's PR machine thrown at it') moved to their next preferred option.[63] In contrast to the official line that Kelly needed to be given to the FAC in order to avoid accusations of a cover-up, the government's intention was now to put him up for examination before the Intelligence and Security Committee.[64]

The official reason for this *volte-face* was that placing Kelly before the ISC rather than the FAC would enable his identity to be kept secret, given that the government was as yet not completely certain that he was Gilligan's source. Since the widely held view, however, was that Kelly would, and indeed should, be named in any case, a more substantial advantage was that the secret nature of the ISC would enable Kelly to give his evidence in private, thus allowing the government to get the more favourable of his views into the public domain in a controlled and organised manner.[65] In this way, the government would be able to discredit the BBC's story, and thence the wider claims about misleading the public over the war, with less trouble and controversy than if Kelly appeared before the open and more combative Foreign Affairs Committee. As Omand put it, proceeding through the ISC 'would be likely to lead to a conclusion which could then be made public, and that could be done in an orderly and measured way'.[66]

The strategy adopted, then, was to issue a public letter to the ISC stating that an individual claiming to be the source for the BBC's story had come forward, and to suggest that the committee might therefore like to interview this person. As Omand again explained, while this would be 'an unusual step', it would nevertheless enable the process to be 'done openly and in words over which we had control'.[67] Or, as Campbell put it, there was a clear need 'to have some element of control over the process.... You cannot just let this sort of dribble out in a way that you are not clear how it is then going to unfold.[68] In the event, however, Blair's attempt to 'sort out the source issue' via the Intelligence and Security Committee was rapidly dashed by the chair of the committee itself, Ann Taylor, who made it known that she would not want to receive the letter if it would be made public, since this would publicise the activities of the ISC, would create the impression that the government was dictating who the committee could examine, and would be a wholly 'unwelcome break with precedent'.[69] With this avenue now blocked, the government instead turned to the more direct tactic of releasing Kelly's name itself. As Godric Smith explained, the 'collective view' was now that 'we had reached the point where we were going to have to put this into the public domain'.[70] Or, as Campbell observed, Taylor's rejection 'meant do it as a press release'.[71]

The way of the world

Over the next two days, Blair chaired no less than four informal and un-minuted meetings of senior officials at which the issue of Dr Kelly was dis-cussed. At the last of these meetings, on 8 July, Campbell, Scarlett, and Jonathon Powell were dispatched to draft a press statement detailing the situation concerning the suspected source.[72] Yet again, and despite the government's concern to avoid any involvement from the FAC, the official line that was later promulgated in defence of this strategy was that the government needed to communicate the fact that Kelly had come forward lest it be seen to be dissembling or hiding information. Tom Kelly, one of the Prime Minister's two official spokesmen, for instance, explained that 'everybody concerned' was now 'anxious to avoid any suggestion of a cover-up', while, as Blair put it,

> I don't believe we had any option ... but to disclose his name, because I think that had we failed to do so then that would have been seen as attempting to conceal something from the committee [i.e. the FAC] that was looking into this at the time.[73]

This, of course, is an erroneous claim, given that the FAC had by now issued its report and was not, in fact, looking into the matter at the time the decision to release Kelly's name was made. Indeed, a less munificent reason than that of wanting to help the FAC was later revealed by Sir Kevin Tebbit, who maintained that 'the reason' for the public statement was the government's desire to get the Kelly information out in order to set the record straight, a move that officials believed would discredit the BBC allegations. 'Correcting the public record', he explained, 'could only be achieved by that single anonymous source being named as the individual who can provide the explanation'. Thus:

> it was felt, not just in the Ministry of Defence but very strongly in No.10 and in the Cabinet Office that it was necessary for a statement to be made, that the information could not be held on to…. [T]here was a very strong feeling that we needed to come forward with the information.[74]

In conjunction with the press release, officials also put together a selection of question-and-answer (Q&A) material, outlining a prearranged set of responses to anticipated questions from journalists in order to enable the MoD press office to deal with any queries put to it. While the initial Q&A material drawn up following Kelly's confession had been relatively innocuous and had contained no information that could have possibly led anyone to discover his identity, over 8 and 9 July (following remarks from Powell that it would be possible 'to think of better questions'), this was exposed to a rigorous redrafting process involving officials from Number 10 and the MoD, including Campbell, Scarlett, Tebbit, and Martin Howard.[75] Upon completion, the updated version of the Q&A material now contained a range of new information about Dr Kelly. This included the disclosures that he had been in the MoD for three to four years, that he had been a member of UNSCOM prior to this, that he had recently visited Iraq for a week, and that he had contributed to a section of the September dossier chronicling the UN weapons inspections in Iraq. Keen to downplay Kelly's status in respect of intelligence material as a means of further undermining the BBC's story, the new Q&A items also described him as a 'middle-ranking official'. More crucially than this, however, the Q&A material had also now shifted from its original position, in which it was observed that there was 'nothing to gain by revealing the name of the individual', to one in which the MoD press office was now instructed to confirm Kelly's name if it was correctly put to it by journalists.[76]

This revamping of the Q&A material was later justified by the government on the grounds that it would have been improper not to have confirmed Kelly's name in such circumstances. Richard Hatfield, for example, told the Hutton Inquiry that 'the MoD cannot deny things that are true', Martin Howard concurred that it would have been 'intellectually dishonest and evasive', while Tebbit insisted that the MoD could not rightly deny that Dr Kelly was believed to be the source if journalists presented them with the correct name, since 'it was an issue of vast public importance'. Furthermore, the possibility of adopting a dead-bat approach and of simply refusing to comment on any names put to the MoD was incredulously dismissed by Geoff Hoon on the grounds that it would have been 'tantamount to admitting the name in question was the right name'.[77] More pertinently, perhaps, as Alastair Campbell put it, while it would have been possible to batten down the hatches and to simply refuse to answer any questions on the matter, Kelly's name would still have come out 'because these things do'. It was, he lamented, 'just the way of the world'.[78]

On the evening of 8 July, the MoD issued its press statement containing the information that an individual who claimed to be the source for the BBC's story had come forward. With this also having now been revised into a 'higher risk' form to contain more details about Dr Kelly,[79] the release, in line with the Q&A material, revealed that the individual concerned was an expert on WMD, had worked in the MoD, and was not 'one of the senior officials in charge of drawing up the dossier'. Adding that Kelly was 'not a member of the intelligence services', that he had not discussed the production of the September dossier with Andrew Gilligan, and that he agreed with the government's views on Iraq's WMD, the statement also disclosed that his identity would be given to the ISC in the event that the committee should wish to interview him. An hour later, however, the BBC issued their own counter-statement claiming that Gilligan's informant did not in fact work for the MoD, thus implying that the government had not managed to correctly identify the source.[80]

The government's response to the BBC statement was to arrange a series of lobby briefings conducted by Tom Kelly and Godric Smith, ostensibly to correct the discrepancies which the government was now claiming had called the credibility of the MoD into question. In so doing, the Prime Minister's official spokesmen duly divulged still more information pertaining to the identity of Dr Kelly. The briefings disclosed that the scientist had worked in various government departments, and that while he was currently working for the MoD, his salary was actually being paid by another department. In what could be construed as a broad hint to journalists, Number 10's official spokesmen also pointed out that the name of this department could not be revealed, since 'providing such information would make it easy to identify the person' given that 'there were only a few people that were paid a salary by this particular Department but who worked for other Departments'. Although Kelly and Smith also denied that the briefings were held to 'give information or drop clues' about the identity of Dr Kelly, as Geoff Hoon himself admitted the disclosure of this information would indicate that the government believed the source to belong to a small group of people, and that this 'inevitably meant' that press interest in this matter 'would be heightened'.[81]

With the field helpfully narrowed for any intrepid journalist seeking to uncover Dr Kelly's name, the Defence Secretary also wrote to Gavyn Davies, Chairman of the BBC, informing him directly of Dr Kelly's identity, and asking him flatly to confirm or deny if Kelly was the BBC's source. Evidently, it was hoped that this would spring a trap on the Corporation, since confirmation that Kelly was indeed the source would instantly reveal that he was not a senior intelligence official, and would thereby help to discredit the Gilligan story.[82] Though admitting that one of the aims in writing to the BBC had been 'to publicise the fact that an official had come forward', and that one advantage of disclosing Kelly's name to the ISC would be that this 'might encourage the BBC to reveal their source', Hoon later denied that the government had tried to 'force' the BBC to disclose the name of their informant, but insisted that the officials had merely sought to give them 'an opportunity, if they judged it appropriate, to reveal their source'.[83]

A similar anxiety was also shared by other government officials. Alastair Campbell, for example, was now of the view that the government should simply name Dr Kelly and be damned. As he noted: 'We kept pressing on as best we could at the briefings but the biggest thing needed was the source out'.[84] Tom Kelly and Jonathon Powell were of like opinion, with the former insisting that the government needed to get the source information out in order 'to establish the facts', and remarking to colleagues that the situation was 'now a game of chicken with the Beeb'. '[T]he only way they will shift', he warned, 'is if they see the screw tightening.'[85]

Tricky areas

While New Labour officials have fervently denied that any of this amounted to a deliberate and concerted strategy to reveal Dr Kelly's name, the general view within government circles at this juncture was not only that the disclosure of this information would prove to be extremely useful in undermining the 6:07 broadcast, and hence in exonerating the government of the charge of having misused intelligence, but that the measures presently being undertaken would themselves assist in this process. Martin Howard, for instance, was later forced to concede that the combined details of the press statement, the Q&A material, and the lobby briefings 'may well have helped' a competent journalist to identify Kelly, and while Geoff Hoon maintained that there was 'not the slightest shred of evidence' of a strategy to out his identity (adding that the Q&A clause to confirm his name was 'not quite the same as releasing it'), the Defence Secretary was also later forced to acknowledge that, with hindsight, 'the answers to some of those questions might have assisted journalists in that process', and that it was in fact 'surprising' that Kelly was not discovered sooner.[86] Purporting to be equally 'astonished' that Kelly had not been identified more rapidly, Richard Hatfield mused that once the press release had been dispatched,

> I did not expect … even without the detail … it would take very long, given all the other clues … for somebody to say, either from a good guess or from deduction, they thought it was Dr Kelly.[87]

Armed with the information provided by the government, from the early evening of 9 July journalists began to accurately guess Kelly's name. Of the first three to do so, James Blitz of the *Financial Times* and Richard Norton-Taylor of the *Guardian* both tracked Kelly down by using the various details that had been divulged by the government. The third, Michael Evans of the *Times*, simply went through a list of civil servant names until the MoD's press office confirmed he had the right one. At the same time, the Foreign Affairs Committee submitted a request to interview the scientist for themselves, meaning that Kelly would now have to appear before two separate inquiries. While Geoff Hoon maintained that the government now had 'no alternative' but to assent to this request given the intense political interest in the issue, the view in official circles, for all the apparent concern about needing to avoid accusations of a cover-up, was that Kelly's appearance at the Foreign Affairs Committee should nevertheless be tightly constrained. Remarks from Tony Blair outlining the fact that the scientist would 'need to be properly prepared' were reflected in the subsequent advice given to Dr Kelly by the MoD, which detailed several 'tricky areas' that he should steer clear of. Naturally, one of these was his personal assessment of the September dossier. In relation to this, the MoD impressed upon Kelly that he should stick to what he had told

Gilligan, and that he should not be drawn on his own personal opinions about the war. To emphasise this further, the Defence Secretary himself informed the FAC that Kelly could only be interviewed 'on the clear understanding' that he would be questioned

> only on those matters which are directly relevant to the evidence that you were given by Andrew Gilligan, and not on the wider issue of Iraqi WMD and the preparation of the dossier.[88]

On 15 July, Dr Kelly appeared before the assembled ranks of the FAC, where, in notable contrast to the government's sustained efforts at restricting the FAC's access to information, officials were now entirely content for him to provide all the information the committee desired on the question of the Campbell–Gilligan dispute. Kelly looked extremely uncomfortable throughout the whole of his ordeal, and his testimony was a mixed blessing for the government. While the scientist stated that he did not believe the September dossier to have been transformed by Alastair Campbell, that he had no doubts over its veracity, and that he had been unaware of the 45-minute claim prior to its publication, Kelly also refused to accept that he was the main source for the Gilligan story, claiming that he did not see how this could have been based on his conversation with the BBC reporter.[89] Nevertheless, government officials were now keen to declare that the BBC's allegations had been fully discredited. As David Omand put it:

> the false allegation that the dossier had been sexed up, with the 45 minutes put in at Alastair Campbell's request, or whatever ... has now been pretty convincingly found to be false.[90]

As is now well known, two days after giving his evidence to the FAC, Dr Kelly himself committed suicide in a field near his Oxfordshire home. In what has since become a grim and familiar juxtaposition, at this precise moment Tony Blair was now enjoying the first phase of a global tour as the guest speaker at a joint session of the US Congress. While the Prime Minister ignored growing criticism that his focus on foreign affairs was leading to a neglect of domestic concerns, his remarks to the esteemed gathering also flew in the face of public opinion. Interspersed with no less than nineteen standing ovations, Blair's speech expressed his confidence that history would forgive Britain and the US, if they turned out to have been wrong on the question of Iraq's WMD, on the grounds that they had destroyed an evil regime, and reaffirmed his commitment to maintain the special relationship with the US, asserting that it was America's 'destiny' to ensure the spread of freedom, and that it was Britain's role to support it in this world-historic endeavour. 'Our job', he told his hosts, 'is to be there with you'.[91]

The celebratory tone of the Prime Minister's tour was immediately transformed by the news of Dr Kelly's death. Plunging the cortège into crisis-management mode, the shock announcement was followed by an instinctive reaction from Blair, who sought to distance himself from the events surrounding the release of Kelly's name by telling journalists on board a flight to Hong Kong that any suggestion of him having authorised the disclosure was 'completely untrue'. In an endeavour to retain some control over the course of events and to shut the story down as fast as possible, Blair and his advisors, chiefly Peter Mandelson and Lord Falconer (now the Secretary of State for Constitutional Affairs), also moved quickly to announce a public inquiry into Kelly's death. As Falconer himself later explained, had the government decided not to hold an inquiry then this would have led to a politically untidy prolongation of the controversy, whereby

> bits and pieces would have come out in an incomplete way ... which would have led to a whole series of apprehensions and misapprehensions ... [about] the circumstances of what happened'.[92]

With the decision to establish an inquiry having thus been made, it was also determined that the investigation itself would be chaired by Lord Hutton, a judge with impeccable establishment credentials, and whose background as a Chief Justice in Northern Ireland rendered it unlikely that he would be openly critical of the government or the intelligence services. As a further precaution, the remit of the inquiry was also tightly drawn in order to keep it away from the broader political questions concerning the use of intelligence by the government. Directing Hutton 'urgently to conduct an investigation into the circumstances surrounding the death of Dr Kelly', Blair averred that any deviation from these terms of reference would not, in his view, be 'sensible'.[93]

Yet despite these constraints, the establishment of the Hutton Inquiry was greeted with a fanfare of expectation. While public opinion remained distinctly sceptical (more than two-thirds believed the government to have acted dishonestly, wanted the remit of the inquiry to be widened, and did not believe that it would get at the truth),[94] the prevailing view throughout the media was that Lord Hutton would prove to be an independent-minded and vociferous explorer of the truth, and that the facts behind the use of intelligence preceding the Iraq war would now be revealed.

A combative approach

Throughout the course of the summer, the government's difficulties seemed to multiply. A steady stream of revelations about New Labour's internal machinery flowed from the Hutton Inquiry, the security situation in Iraq continued to worsen, and the search for WMD remained fruitless. Moreover, while the Prime Minister was forced to continue his back-peddling on the issue, now telling the House of Commons Liaison Committee that he had 'absolutely no doubt at all' that the Iraq Survey Group (ISG) would uncover 'evidence of weapons of mass destruction programmes',[95] the FAC reported that the war might have exacerbated the short-term risk of terrorist attacks, and that its advantages in the war on terror were therefore questionable.[96]

On 9 September, the government was granted a brief respite from its troubles as the ISC published the report of its inquiry. This concluded that the September dossier had not been 'sexed up', that the JIC had 'not been subjected to political pressures', and that its independence and impartiality had 'not been compromised in any way.' But even so, despite having enjoyed access to far more material than the FAC inquiry had done, the ISC was also critical both of the way in which the 45-minute claim had been used, and of the government's failure to disclose the concerns within the intelligence community over the use of classified material. In particular, the committee claimed to have been 'disturbed' by Geoff Hoon's failure to inform it about the level of unease within the DIS concerning the production of the September dossier, an omission that was considered to have been 'potentially misleading'. In his defence, the Defence Secretary proclaimed that there had been no need for the ISC to have been told of these concerns since the matter had been resolved from within the intelligence service itself.[97]

But even this brief parting of the political storm clouds was soon reversed. Ten days after the publication of the ISC report, the Labour party suffered its first by-election defeat for fifteen years, losing the former safe seat of Brent East and a majority of more than 13,000 to the Liberal Democrats. Moreover, Alastair Campbell's long-expected resignation from the government at the end of the month, conveniently timed to deflect attention away from Blair's evidence to the Hutton Inquiry, was followed in early October by the interim report of the ISG, which revealed that it had yet to find any weapons of mass destruction in Iraq after three months of intensive searching. Further still, from November the parliamentary opposition also began to sharpen considerably following the Conservatives' regicidal deposition of their leader Iain Duncan Smith, and his replacement by Michael Howard, while an ill-timed state visit from George W. Bush compounded matters yet further, drawing a predictable wave of public protest and sparking terrorist attacks on British targets in Istanbul. Opinion polls, too, made continually depressing reading for the government. More than half the British public now wanted the Prime Minister to resign due to the illegitimate reasons given for the war, while a quarter of Labour backbenchers were now in favour of Blair stepping down either before or just after the next general election.[98] Blair was increasingly exasperated by the refusal of domestic opinion to support the Iraq policy even on humanitarian grounds, and his frustration now spilled over. As he remarked to one observer, 'we are interventionists ... I don't see why people on the left are not putting us under more pressure to intervene in Zimbabwe or Burma'.[99]

Against this background, Blair's own doubts about his future as Prime Minister also appeared to be growing. At a meeting with Gordon Brown and John Prescott in November, Blair apparently informed the Chancellor that things were now 'very difficult on trust', and that while he would eventually be 'vindicated' over Iraq, he would nevertheless be unable to turn the situation around 'for a very long time'. On this basis, Blair seems to have told the Chancellor that he intended to quit before the next election, but that he required his help 'to get through the next year' before doing so.[100]

For all these private misgivings, however, the Prime Minister's public persona remained nothing if not resolute. Following the advice of Alastair Campbell that the best means of handling the failure to find WMD was to focus on the process of discovery and to adopt 'a combative approach' on the broader issues surrounding the war,[101] Blair told the Labour party conference at the end of October that the invasion had been 'the right thing to do', and continued to implore his critics to await the final report of the Iraq Survey Group before passing judgement on the matter. Yet further, Blair also insisted that the war in Iraq had been justified as much by the need to ensure the credibility of the West and to set an example to others as by the need to remove the threat from Saddam Hussein. The invasion, he explained, 'was justified in either case', since there would never be any serious action on the question of WMD unless it was made 'absolutely clear' that the 'international community' was going to enforce its demands. Also reasserting the need for Britain to continue playing a prominent role in world affairs, Blair once more sought to draw upon the virtues of strong and decisive leadership in an attempt to bolster his position. Proclaiming that 'the British people will forgive a government mistakes … but what they won't forgive is cowardice in the face of a challenge', Blair explained that

> All you can do in a modern world … is to decide what is the right way and try to walk in it.… It's the only leadership I can offer. And it's the only type of leadership worth having.[102]

To further underline his adherence to the elitist principles of the British political system, Blair also refused to countenance any possibility that he might have been wrong to take Britain to war with Iraq against the wishes of the general public. While this decision, and the events that had flowed therefrom, had engendered a widespread loss of trust in the government, had led to a rising sense of public anger, and had put his own premiership in crisis, the Prime Minister insisted that critics of the war had simply failed to grasp his reasons and motives for taking military action. The problem, as he saw it, was not that the policy itself was wrong, but that people had misunderstood it. Pitching this argument at the launch of the 'Big Conversation', an apparent exercise in public consultation designed to show that the government was reconnecting with the voters, Blair's comments were distinctly revealing. As he opined: 'What I think erodes trust is not taking difficult decisions, but when people do not understand what motivates people taking difficult decisions'.[103]

Concluding remarks

The initial aftermath of the Iraq war saw the New Labour government utilise every means at its disposal to effectively channel and shape the course of political debate, to reduce the threat of any meaningful scrutiny of its actions, and to eschew any sense of democratic accountability. Faced with growing concerns about the politicisation of intelligence material during the build-up to the conflict, and with domestic opinion moving further against the government, senior officials unleashed a full-frontal assault on the BBC in an attempt to divert attention away from the absence of WMD in Iraq and to discredit any notion that the government had ever been anything less than entirely truthful with the British people. At the core of this strategy was a sustained media campaign designed to frame the postwar debate around the wholly unique and manifestly unrepresentative allegations contained in Andrew Gilligan's 6:07 broadcast. This was coupled with a keen desire to ensure the disclosure of the identity, and hence also the views, of Dr David Kelly, whom the government believed to have been misrepresented by Gilligan. Through the combined efforts of an MoD press statement, carefully scripted Q&A material, and a series of lobby briefings, Dr Kelly's identity was directed into the public domain, leading to his subsequent examination by the inquiries being conducted by the ISC and the FAC. In revealing his identity, the government sought to undermine the Gilligan story by demonstrating that Kelly's views had been distorted, and to thereby show that the government had not misled the country over the threat posed by Iraq's weapons of mass destruction.

At the same time, the government also sought to constrain the inquiry being conducted by the FAC in order to avoid any close scrutiny of the September dossier. By refusing to allow it access to intelligence material, to official documents, and to some of the key actors involved in the process of constructing the dossier, the government was able to severely reduce the ability of the FAC to effectively scrutinise the conduct of the executive, and thus to hold its members to account for their actions. In contrast, the government's own inquiry, being conducted in parallel by the highly secretive ISC, was permitted to examine a range of classified material. So too was the Hutton Inquiry, which was set up to examine the circumstances surrounding Dr Kelly's suicide. This provided a clear demonstration of the executive's ability to mould the course of political debate by placing the inquiry within the confines of a tight remit that would not touch upon the political context behind the decision to go to war. That all this was further accompanied by an emphasis on the benefits of strong and decisive leadership was, of course, perfectly in keeping with the elitist principles on which British democracy is based.

7

Business as Usual

From the publication of the Hutton Report through to the general election of May 2005, the government was engaged in a sustained attempt to divert the political agenda away from the intractable difficulties of the Iraq war and back onto domestic issues. This, however, proved to be largely unsuccessful. The Hutton Report was widely regarded as a whitewash, the report of the subsequent Butler Inquiry, despite being critical of the government, was also considered to have been a let-off, and concerns about the nature of the Attorney-General's legal advice continued to surface throughout this period. Though forced to acknowledge that no weapons of mass destruction would now be found in Iraq, and despite the high levels of hostility and the lack of trust now surrounding Tony Blair, the government also continued to defy the expressed views of the British people by continuing to defend the decision to go to war, and by continuing to insist on the benefits of strong and decisive leadership. Yet for all this, with the Conservatives still unable to make any substantial political headway, New Labour were eventually returned to power for a third consecutive term, albeit with a vastly reduced majority. Questions over the war in Iraq, however, refused to abate. Just nine weeks after the election, the issue was again thrust into the forefront of the political agenda as a series of terrorist attacks brought chaos and devastation to the streets of London.

Glaring headlines

By 2004 the government's difficulties were starting to mount. The security situation in Iraq showed little sign of improving despite the capture of Saddam Hussein, the Labour party had slipped behind the Conservatives in the polls, and success remained elusive in the hunt for WMD. Tony Blair's desperation to find something tangible with which to legitimise the war was also increasingly evident. In a Christmas interview for the British

Forces Broadcasting Service, the Prime Minister declared that the Iraq Survey Group had found 'massive evidence of a huge system of clandestine laboratories, workings by scientists, [and] plans to develop long range ballistic missiles', only to have the claim embarrassingly rebuffed by the US-appointed Administrator of Iraq, Paul Bremer. Unaware that the remarks had been made by the British Prime Minister, Bremer stated that this was not in fact the view of the ISG, and that the comments were 'a bit of a red herring'.[1] In matters far worse than this, the prevailing view among political commentators was also that the Hutton Inquiry was drawing towards a damning and potentially fatal conclusion for the Prime Minister. Indeed, on paper, the week beginning 26 January looked like being the toughest yet of Blair's premiership. Starting on the Tuesday with a potentially huge backbench rebellion in the vote to introduce university top-up fees, on Wednesday the government faced the publication of the Hutton Report. It was by no means certain that Blair would still be in office by the weekend.

In the opening act of the drama, an advance copy of the Hutton Report was handed over to the government, giving Blair twenty-four hours to examine its contents prior to publication. To ensure a free and fair debate on the matter, the leaders of the main opposition parties were given copies of the report on the Wednesday morning, permitting them six hours of reading time to prepare. The British public, courtesy of a leak to the *Sun* newspaper, unexpectedly discovered that they too had a similar period in which to digest the findings. The previous evening, with Gordon Brown having mustered his political infantry in belated support for the Prime Minister, the government had just cleared the first hurdle of the week by scraping through the top-up-fees vote with a majority of three. It was about to clear the second by a much greater margin.

The publication of the Hutton Report on 28 January gave the government an impeccably clean bill of health. Completely exonerating it of any improper conduct, less-than-pure motives, or poor judgement, the report delivered a singularly clear verdict on the row between New Labour and the BBC, coming down decisively in favour of the former. In a statement to the House of Commons, Blair praised the report as being an 'extraordinarily thorough, detailed and clear document' which left 'no room for doubt or interpretation', and maintained that it had now cleared the government of any allegations of deception, duplicity, and deceit with regards to the falsifying of intelligence in the run-up to the war. This was followed by an acrimonious blast from Alastair Campbell, who proclaimed that the report showed 'very clearly' that the Prime Minister, the government, and he himself had 'told the truth', and that the BBC evidently had not. Decrying the behaviour of Gavyn Davies, Richard Sambrook, and John Humphrys as 'unforgivable', Campbell indicated that it would now require 'several resignations at several levels' in order to sufficiently rectify the situation. As he ebulliently declared, the Hutton Report had been 'better than my best-case scenario'.[2]

Stunned by the ferocity of Hutton's criticisms, the governing regime at the BBC swiftly imploded. Resignations from Gavyn Davies, Greg Dyke, and Andrew Gilligan were accompanied by an 'unreserved' apology from the BBC's new acting Chairman, Lord Ryder. In one fell swoop, the Hutton ruling also cut away the ground from under the opposition leaders, leaving Michael Howard, who had set much store by the Prime Minister's lack of honesty over Iraq, visibly emasculated by the experience. In the court of public opinion, though, Lord Hutton's verdict carried considerably less weight. A YouGov poll found that more than half the British public felt that the report had been a complete whitewash and that Number 10 had, in fact, sexed up the September dossier. More than two-fifths also said they would continue to trust the BBC more than the government, and nearly two-thirds declared that they no longer had any trust at all in the Prime Minister.[3]

The key reason for this backlash against the Hutton Report stemmed from the obvious discrepancies between its findings and the evidence actually presented during the course of the inquiry itself. Completely accepting the government's framing of the issue as centring on the 45-minute claim contained in Andrew Gilligan's 6:07 broadcast, the report subsequently ignored whole swathes of critical material. The openly expressed desire on the part of government officials to get Kelly's identity into the public domain was disregarded as being 'not decisive on the main issue', while Blair's denials of culpability on board the plane to Hong Kong were similarly dismissed as casting 'no light on the issues'. This was despite the fact that the Hutton Report itself had judged that the MoD press statement that had been 'authorised by the Prime Minister' had 'led onto the MoD confirming Dr Kelly's name'. Furthermore, Hutton also overlooked much of the e-mail traffic pertaining to the construction of the September dossier, said little about the concerns raised by members of the intelligence services during this process, was equally sparse on the events surrounding the publication of the February dossier, and refused to examine the reliability of the intelligence behind the government's case against Iraq, contrary to Blair's claims to have been exonerated on this point.[4] Indeed, as it later transpired, the Hutton Inquiry itself had not even been informed about the fact that the intelligence behind the 45-minute claim had been 'on trial', and that it had been officially withdrawn by MI6 during the summer for being 'unreliable', with neither John Scarlett nor Richard Dearlove choosing to mention these facts in their evidence.[5] Justifying the omission, Number 10 later claimed that such a disclosure would have been 'improper', given that the intelligence was 'still being investigated as a sensitive operational matter', and maintained that questions of wider intelligence were, in any case, not relevant to the death of Dr Kelly. This particular instance, it was claimed, was merely one component in the overall 'picture' of Iraq's WMD.[6]

While Gavyn Davies later accused Lord Hutton of being 'inept',[7] the reality was, however, that he had performed his role only too well. Recognising that the inquiry would have a profound impact on the future of the government, Hutton chose to stick to the letter of his already narrow remit, later informing the House of Commons Public Administration Committee that questions concerning the use of intelligence and the relations between the government and the intelligence services 'did not fall within my terms of inquiry'. Moreover, Hutton also pointed out that even should he have been minded to examine such issues, the remit for the inquiry itself would not have allowed sufficient time, noting that he had been 'asked to conduct the inquiry urgently' and that an analysis of 'all the very widespread matters of intelligence ... would have been very lengthy indeed'. What is more, Hutton also pointed out that it would not in any case have been 'appropriate' for a single judge to have conducted such an investigation, since this could only be properly undertaken by a panel and not by one judge sitting alone.[8]

But even so, none of this was considered to be a bad thing. While being forced to acknowledge that the reliability of the intelligence material published by the government had been essential to the 'context' of Dr Kelly's death, Hutton nevertheless observed that a narrowly drawn focus had 'certain advantages', explaining that for the purposes of practicality, 'you have to draw a line' somewhere.[9] Indeed, contrary to the expectations of the press, such a deferential attitude towards the government was even discernible during the course of the inquiry itself. Despite proclaiming that his role was to act 'without having regard to political consequences', Hutton had refused to allow Blair to be cross-examined, regardless of his centrality in the entire affair, on the grounds that this would have been seen as 'playing to the gallery'. It would not, as he put it, have been 'appropriate' for the Prime Minister to be treated in such a manner, since there would have been 'glaring headlines' the next day.[10]

Controlling events

While the Hutton Report offered a technical vindication of the government, it did not provide any long-lasting political catharsis. Indeed, on the same day as it was published, David Kay (the ex-head of the ISG) stated that he did not expect any weapons of mass destruction to be found in Iraq, and called on the US government to establish an independent inquiry to examine the failure of intelligence. This suggestion was rapidly taken up by the Bush administration, itself now under growing criticism for its inability to discover proscribed weapons materials in Iraq, and with the President also having been forced to beat a series of embarrassing retreats on the justification for war. By now this had transmogrified from Saddam's possession of *actual* WMD to his possession of WMD *programmes*, from thence to his WMD-*related* programmes, and finally to his WMD-related programme *activities*.[11]

With the government having just survived the treacherous waters of the Hutton Inquiry, however, calls for a similar inquiry in Britain fell on deaf ears. The official line, as presented by Lord Falconer, was that 'little would be achieved by constantly looking and re-looking at what the intelligence shows at a particular time'.[12] Facing an intense public backlash, though, within forty-eight hours of the US announcement, the government had determined that a new inquiry was now unavoidable if the issue of Iraq was ever to be dislodged from the political agenda. Nevertheless, despite being forced to perform a spectacular U-turn, officials remained grimly determined to prevent the new inquiry from examining the political decision to go to war, constraining it within another strategically drawn remit—namely, to examine the 'accuracy' of the prewar intelligence on Iraq's WMD, and to examine any 'discrepancies' between this and the subsequent findings of the Iraq Survey Group.[13]

While Blair now insisted that the 'time was right' for 'a proper inquiry into the intelligence', he also maintained that it should not be permitted to examine the wider issues concerning the decision to go to war itself, since the various rights and wrongs of this was 'something that we [i.e. Parliament] have got to decide'.[14] This view was also supported by Jack Straw, who, despite the fact that the Hutton Report had abjectly failed to address the issue of WMD, asserted that there was no point in 'revisiting the issues so comprehensively covered by Lord Hutton', and who, despite the fact that MPs had not actually been aware of the full facts at the time of the vote on war, maintained that the decision to go to war was one 'for which we, as elected representatives, took responsibility and will continue to take responsibility'.[15] Somewhat more prosaically, the idea that a judge could be appointed to examine the political decision-making process was derided by one member of the government as 'complete bollocks'.[16]

To tighten the corset still further, the Prime Minister's inner circle also determined that the hearings and evidence presented to the new inquiry would take place in secret, and that any 'sensitive' parts of its report would be withheld from publication on the grounds of 'national security'. Delivery of its findings, too, would be due before the end of July, a timetable described by the inquiry team itself as being 'very tight', but one that would leave sufficient time for any controversy to subside before the next general election.[17] To top this off, the government also appointed Lord Robin Butler to head the investigation. Butler was a former Cabinet Secretary whose establishment credentials had been memorably evidenced during the Scott Inquiry on arms to Iraq, to which he had professed that Whitehall's ingrained culture of secrecy was 'in the interests of good government'.[18]

The establishment of the Butler review, however, did little to dissipate the brooding political atmosphere that continued to envelop the government. The Liberal Democrats refused to participate in the inquiry on the grounds that its terms of reference were 'unacceptable'; the Conservatives withdrew their support several weeks later, following an announcement by Lord Butler that the inquiry would focus on processes and systems rather than on the actions of specific individuals;[19] and public hostility towards the government over the whole question of Iraq remained undimmed. Support for the war continued to decline, the majority of domestic opinion continued to favour the idea that there should be a full and independent inquiry into the government's conduct surrounding the war, and the view that Tony Blair should resign remained widespread.[20]

Renewed public criticisms from Clare Short and Robin Cook also added to the government's difficulties. While the former was now alleging that Britain and the United States had routinely bugged Kofi Annan during the attempt to secure a second UN resolution, the latter was now directly accusing Blair of having 'misled' the British people over the threat posed by Iraq's WMD. 'The reality', he mused, was 'that intelligence from

Iraq was rifled in order to find the scraps to support a political decision'.[21] To make matters even worse, it further emerged during the parliamentary debate on the Hutton Report that Blair had apparently been unaware that the 45-minute intelligence had referred to battlefield weapons rather than to full-scale WMD.[22] Nevertheless, with the parliamentary opposition now in disarray, and with MPs only permitted to express their view on the report through a vote on the adjournment rather than through a substantive motion, the executive management of the fallout effectively neutered any prospects of a more damaging outcome for the government.

Concerns also continued to surround the legal advice given to the government by the Attorney-General in the run-up to the invasion. Amidst allegations that he had been pressured to change his opinion in order to justify the war, government officials reacted with extreme sensitivity to any suggestion that Lord Goldsmith's full advice should be publicly disclosed. In a high-profile display of state secrecy, in mid-February the government's reluctance to reveal the Attorney-General's advice led to the collapse of the trial of Katherine Gunn, the former GCHQ operative charged with leaking details of the UN spying operation, once it became clear that the advice was to form a key part of the defence, and that its public disclosure might therefore be required. That the decision to abandon the trial before it had even started was made by the Attorney-General himself merely added to the conspiratorial atmosphere permeating throughout the whole affair.[23]

In addition to this, the security situation in Iraq also continued to deteriorate. Escalating attacks on coalition forces by insurgents, a sharp rise in hostage-taking, and a prisoner-abuse scandal involving US forces at the notorious Abu Ghraib prison all contributed to a palpable sense that the situation was now spiralling out of control. In May, a leaked memo from the Foreign Office revealed the government's own concerns about the course of events, complaining that the 'heavy-handed' tactics being employed by the United States had 'lost us much public support inside Iraq' and had 'sapped the moral authority of the coalition'.[24] With the controversy surrounding the war refusing to relent, the spring of 2004 proved to be Blair's political nadir. Now assessing that he would 'never turn it around' on Iraq, Blair's view was that he should step aside as Prime Minister during the autumn and allow a successor to take the reins for a sufficient period before the next general election. In a reflection of his wavering authority, Blair also found himself being forced to execute another spectacular reversal of policy, this time pledging to hold a referendum on the newly designed European constitution for fear that continuing to reject the idea would benefit the Conservatives during the forthcoming European and local elections, which were now widely seen as a crucial barometer of New Labour's electoral future.

Indeed, while the considered verdict of the electorate was not unexpected, it was nevertheless a harsh one. Despite the absence of the Prime Minister's image from campaign material, the view could not be dispelled that Blair was now an electoral liability, and having scraped together a mere 26% of the vote in the local elections, and just 23% in the European poll, the Labour party slumped to its worst result in a national election for over eighty-five years. This disastrous showing, however, was ameliorated by the equally catastrophic performance of the Conservatives. Squeezed by the UK Independence party, the Tories now crumbled to their worst share of a national vote since the Great Reform Act of 1832, receiving just 38% in the local elections and a desultory 27% in the European campaign. Stirred by the lack of edge to the Tory threat and realising that a repeat performance in a general election would still leave Labour with a three-figure majority, given the distortions of first-past-the-post, Blair took few lessons from the polls. Instead, now buoyed by the failure of the Conservatives to make any electoral headway, Blair's mind was no longer directed towards quitting as Prime Minister, but rather towards remedying the prevailing sense of malaise with a dose of even stronger government. 'The public', he explained, 'needs to know that we are controlling events, not events controlling us'.[25]

The front line

Transposed onto the issue of Iraq, this meant implementing the next phase of the postwar 'strategy'. On 28 June, in a move brought forward by two days in an effort to head off an expected outburst of fresh attacks from insurgent forces, Iraqi sovereignty was formally handed over to an interim authority, thus enabling the British and US governments to frame the maelstrom of violence as a battle between the emergent forces of democracy and those of chaos and disorder. As Blair put it, Iraq was now 'the front line in the battle against terrorism and the new security threats we face'. Nevertheless, while the handover of formal sovereignty might have helped to relieve some of the political pressures on the coalition, the move was less than unequivocal. The new Iraqi Prime Minister, the US-backed Iyad Allawi, immediately requested that more than 150,000 coalition troops should remain in support of the interim authority, which itself possessed no ability to repeal the economic contracts and neo-liberal measures, including the unlimited repatriation of reconstruction profits by US companies, that had been hitherto imposed by the United States.[26]

But while the slow winds of change were breathing new life into Iraq, the political climate in Britain remained decidedly frosty. Preparing the ground for a formal admission from the government that no weapons of mass destruction would now be found, on 4 July Sir Jeremy Greenstock, the former British representative to the United Nations, acknowledged that there was 'no doubt' that stockpiles of WMD 'are not there', though he insisted in the government's defence that the intelligence 'was quite compelling at the time'. Although the government had clearly got it wrong in a practical sense, it had, he attested, been 'right on the intention'.[27] Two days later, Blair himself finally yielded to the inevitable truth during his biannual appearance before the Liaison Committee. As usual, however, the Prime Minister's words were less than straightforward. While accepting that WMD might not now be found, Blair continued to propagate the line that had been developed to persuade the British people of the need for war, refusing point-blank to accept any possibility that the weapons may never have existed in the first place. In total contrast to the JIC reports that were being supplied during 2002, the Prime Minister insisted that he had been 'very, very confident' of finding WMD in Iraq 'because all the intelligence and evidence we had was that these WMD existed'. Explanations for their absence, therefore, centred around more exotic lines of reasoning. As he put it:

> We do not know what has happened to them; they could have been removed, they could have been hidden, they could have been destroyed.... I genuinely believe that those stockpiles of weapons were there.[28]

Moreover, despite the absence of any actual WMD, the Prime Minister also continued to assert that the war had been justified on the basis of the potential threat posed by Saddam Hussein, by Iraq's failure to abide by the stated will of the international community, and by the need to continue fighting the war on terror. Maintaining that the ISG had uncovered 'very clear evidence of strategic intent and capability and a desire to carry on developing these weapons', the Prime Minister further averred that the war had been fought on 'the basis of enforcing United Nations resolutions in respect of WMD' (conveniently overlooking the fact that the majority of the Security Council had been opposed to the war), and continued to warn of the confluent perils of this 'new form of global terrorism' and 'unstable rogue states with WMD'. Furthermore, Blair also continued to emphasise the humanitarian dimension of the war on terror, referring yet again to the importance of embedding this within 'the rest of the world's agenda' (namely, 'the whole issue to do with Israel and Palestine and poverty and development, and so on') and arguing that the war in Iraq had been beneficial for the world. Not least was this due to the important progress made in relation to Libya, Iran, and North Korea, the first of which was now committed to abandoning its WMD programme in return for re-entry into the international community.[29]

The broader question of the transatlantic-bridge strategy, and more particularly Britain's ability to influence the United States in its handling of the Iraq issue, also proved to be a source of some tension for the Prime Minister. Although Blair insisted that the government had exerted 'a very great deal of influence in respect of all of this', the central problem remained that any capacity to affect decisions in Washington had been effectively discharged by the Prime Minister in exchange for actions designed to ease his own political pressures—namely, the need to restart the Arab–Israeli peace process and to deal with the Iraq issue through the United Nations—leaving scant reserves available to exert influence on other matters, such as the direction of postwar reconstruction. Thus unable to offer a single example of where British influence had yielded fruit, Blair retorted to the liaison committee that it was 'pathetic' to try and dissect the transatlantic relationship in terms of who-got-what, and continued to insist that, in any case, the need for a strong relationship with the United States transcended the views of the British people (more than two-thirds of whom now favoured a more distant relationship with their American cousins).[30] The notion that this could be construed as being somewhat undemocratic was also brushed aside in a distinctly Kafkaesque manner, with Blair justifying the need for a close relationship on the grounds that this was essential for enhancing democracy. As he remarked:

> Let the people say whatever they like about it, in the end I believe it is an important relationship that delivers for us because we share their values and because we share their view that the best security we ultimately have is the spread of freedom, democracy and justice throughout the world, and that is what we are trying to do.[31]

Although public opinion remained openly hostile, New Labour's political difficulties were eased slightly during the early part of July. The first ray of light was the publication of the report from the US Senate Committee on Intelligence (SCI), which had been charged with examining the accuracy of America's prewar intelligence on Iraq. Though not without its dissenting views,[32] this report cleared the Bush administration of having exerted undue political pressure in an attempt to distort intelligence material during the run-up to the war, and instead placed the blame squarely on the shoulders of the US intelligence services. Having engaged in a collective bout of 'group-think', the American agencies, it claimed, had systematically prejudged, exaggerated, and misrepresented the threat from Iraq's WMD.[33] Nevertheless, despite these conclusions, the Senate's report provided further ammunition for critics in Britain. Among these, the ex-head of the JIC itself, Dame Pauline Neville-Jones, was particularly assertive. Warning that the JIC had become too close to the policy-making process, and that it was thereby susceptible to improper political influences, Neville-Jones also claimed that ministerial resignations should now be forthcoming regardless of whether officials had themselves been directly involved in the manipulation of intelligence. Given the overall responsibility vested in the hands of the executive, she complained, 'I don't think the political layer in any country can escape the consequences of a systemic failure'.[34]

In good faith

The second, and somewhat more substantial, ray of light for the government was the publication of the Butler Report in mid-July. On one level this offered a highly critical account of the intelligence on Iraq's WMD, of the processes used for its assessment and presentation, and of the policy-making style of the New Labour government more generally. Criticising the JIC for having based its assessments on 'intelligence of dubious reliability, reinforced by suspicion of Iraq, rather than up-to-date evidence',[35] the report revealed that 'serious doubts' had emerged about the reliability of some of the intelligence, and that the particular stream behind the 45-minute claim had recently been withdrawn for this precise reason. Also criticising the fact that DIS experts were not allowed to see the new 45-minute information upon its late arrival, Lord Butler concluded that the September dossier had taken the available intelligence to 'the outer limits', and that as a result 'more weight was placed on the intelligence than it could bear'.[36] Beyond this, the report also levelled a series of attacks at the governing style of Blair's inner court, noting that the centralised and elitist structure of the New Labour government had acted 'to concentrate detailed knowledge and effective decision-making in fewer minds at the top', and that the 'informality and circumscribed character of the Government's procedures' had risked 'reducing the scope for informed collective political judgement'.[37]

Such criticisms aside, the report proved to be more beneficial than not for the government. Mirroring the conclusions of the Senate report, Lord Butler also claimed to have found 'no evidence of deliberate distortion or of culpable negligence' over the government's handling of intelligence on Iraq's WMD, and no evidence that JIC assessments had been deliberately 'pulled in any particular direction to meet the policy concerns of officials'.[38] Indeed, one of the central hallmarks of the report was its studied refusal to apportion any blame or responsibility to any specific individuals. Though the report uncovered an array of misgivings and concerns, and though it drew attention to the tightly controlled and highly centralised character of the policy-making process, the critical emphasis instead focused on the communal nature of any mistakes, noting, for example, that the error of letting the JIC get too close to government officials during the production of the September dossier 'was a collective one'. Despite adding that there was now 'a strong case' for the JIC Chairman to be 'someone with experience of dealing with Ministers in a very senior role, and who is demonstrably beyond influence' (the implication, of course, being that John Scarlett was not), the report also refused to directly criticise Scarlett for his role in the affair, and indeed expressed the hope that his planned promotion to be head of MI6 would not be jeopardised as a result of its findings.[39]

Blair's response to the report was defiantly bullish. Having set the remit of the Butler review to examine the issue of WMD in an international sense as well as in relation to Iraq, the Prime Minister was able to draw on the report to justify the government's stance on the war on terror, highlighting a series of success stories concerning the threat of WMD proliferation (including Libya and the AQ Kahn network), before praising its 'invaluable analysis' on this matter, and on the 'potential acquisition of WMD by terrorists'. On the question of Iraq itself, while acknowledging 'that at the time of invasion, Saddam did not have stockpiles of chemical or biological weapons ready to deploy', and while purporting to accept 'full responsibility for the way in which the issue was presented and therefore for any errors made', the Prime Minister again sought to misrepresent the charges levelled against the government, insisting that Lord Butler's report (which he described as 'comprehensive', 'voluminous', and filled with 'balance and common sense') had now unequivocally proved that 'No-one lied. No-one made up the intelligence. No-one inserted things into the dossier against the advice of the intelligence services', and that everyone involved had 'genuinely tried to do their best in good faith'. Notwithstanding the fact that the real charge against the government was that intelligence had been left out or removed rather than having been 'made up' or inappropriately 'inserted', the Prime Minister also failed to provide any explanation as to why the caveats accompanying the intelligence had been taken out, and in stark contrast to the kind of full responsibility taken by Gilligan, Dyke, and Davies, he remained impervious to any suggestion that he should consider relinquishing his position.[40]

At the same time, Blair's prolonged shift away from the original justification for war on the basis of WMD and towards its legitimation on humanitarian grounds continued to proceed apace. Though ardently insisting that the intelligence assessments 'really left little doubt about Saddam and weapons of mass destruction' (although it was now also revealed that Blair did not apparently know that the 45-minute intelligence had been withdrawn), the Prime Minister added that while the nature of the Iraqi regime was not the reason for the war, it was nevertheless 'decisive for me in the judgement as to the balance of risk for action or inaction'. As to the criticism that key policy decisions were being made by a small clique of ministers and special advisors without proper Cabinet consultation, Blair announced an end to 'sofa-style' government, stating that future crises would be dealt with by a formal *ad hoc* Cabinet committee, that the new head of the JIC would be someone 'beyond influence' from ministers, and that JIC assessments would be kept separate from the government's case in any future dossier.[41]

For all this, however, John Scarlett was still permitted to take up his new post at the end of July as planned, and some nine months later the Intelligence and Security Committee itself was moved to complain that proposals to implement the recommendations of the Butler Report had 'only just been agreed' by the government. Expressing its 'disappointment' with the collective discussion of intelligence, the ISC also noted in its annual report of April 2005 that the Ministerial Committee on the Intelligence Services (the only cabinet committee with an overview of this area) had not met for over four months (the previous meeting to that having been the first for over seven years), that 'collective discussion by ministers of intelligence priorities and developments' was only evident at times of crisis or on 'single-issue meetings', and that a late distribution of the JIC Chairman's annual review had diminished its 'timeliness and usefulness'.[42]

As with the Hutton debacle, the broader response to the Butler Report was also infused with anger and incredulity. Polls revealed that more than half of the electorate continued to believe that Blair had lied over the war, and a similar figure now purported to trust the Prime Minister even less in the wake of the Butler Inquiry.[43] Public dismay was also reflected in two weak by-election performances, which saw the Labour party narrowly hold on to Birmingham Hodge Hill with a majority of more than 11,000 falling to just 461, and which saw its majority of more than 13,000 wiped out in Leicester South as the anti-war Liberal Democrats went on to claim the seat. Putting the government's usual spin on events, the Health Secretary, John Reid, optimistically described the results as a 'score draw'.[44]

Hostility to the report was particularly marked from those who had suffered directly at the hands of Lord Hutton. Andrew Gilligan maintained that Lord Butler's findings had verified the substance of his 6:07 broadcast, Greg Dyke proclaimed that the report had justified the BBC's decision to run the story (which he insisted that he would continue to 'defend forever'), while Gavyn Davies later accused Lord Butler of having 'bottled out of assigning responsibility' despite having published 'more than enough evidence to show that there had been political interference in the intelligence dossier'.[45] A similar point was also made by Robin Cook, who expressed renewed dismay at the fact that no one in the government was to be held accountable for any of the controversies surrounding the Iraq conflict, despite the clear evidence from both the Hutton Inquiry and the Butler Report showing that Parliament had been 'misled into voting for war on the basis of unreliable sources and over-heated analysis'. When asked if Blair, Hoon, and Straw should have resigned over the Iraq affair, Cook acerbically remarked, 'I have a lot of respect for Jack Straw'.[46]

To add further weight to the criticism now being piled on top of the government, Hans Blix lent his own inimitable contribution to the debate. Claiming that Blair had not acted in 'good faith' and that the removal of the intelligence caveats during the construction of the September dossier had produced 'a spin' which had 'distorted the contents', Blix maintained that the government had 'put exclamation marks where there had been question marks'. The result, he explained, was 'that the public were led to believe something that was not accurate'. Moreover, that the Butler Report had subsequently chosen to let the government off the hook, Blix wryly observed, was all part of the 'British tradition'.[47] And so too, it seemed, was the government's more substantive, though somewhat less publicised, response to the Hutton and Butler Reports. In notable contrast to their half-hearted reform of the intelligence sphere, New Labour officials now moved swiftly to strengthen their hand in respect of any further investigations. Among the proposals contained in the new Inquiries Bill were plans to allow ministers to suspend or terminate an inquiry, or to withdraw its funding if it was felt to have exceeded its remit.[48]

Yet for all this, the parliamentary opposition lay in ruins. While Blair's credibility continued to sink, so too did that of Michael Howard, whose latest attempt at skewering the Prime Minister by announcing that, had he known the true state of the intelligence, he would not have supported the parliamentary vote on the war (despite being in support of the war itself) was widely derided as being lamentably opportunistic.[49] Indeed, despite drawing positive support from little more than a third of British voters, New Labour continued to maintain a five-point lead over the Conservatives in the polls, a gap more than sufficient to return them to power with a healthy majority.[50]

Further still, Blair was increasingly emboldened by the inability of his opponents to make any substantial capital out of the government's woes, and his protracted turnabout on his earlier decision to quit as Prime Minister was also now complete. On 18 July the heir-apparent, Gordon Brown, was duly informed of Blair's view that he needed 'more time' before quitting, and that leaving at the present juncture 'would make it look like I've been defeated over Iraq'. At the end of the month the decision was announced publicly, with Blair stating that he would serve a full term if New Labour were re-elected, but that he would not fight a fourth election campaign as Prime Minister. Effectively marking the end of the long-standing 'Granita deal', the move further soured the already tempestuous relationship at the heart of the New Labour project, and infused it with an ever more profound degree of enmity. To the Chancellor, whose frustrated ambitions continued to smoulder, it was nothing short of a personal betrayal. 'There is nothing that you could ever say to me now', he told Blair, 'that I could ever believe'.[51]

The crucible

In the wake of the Butler Report, the government launched into a strident attempt to rehabilitate the credibility of the Prime Minister, to re-legitimise the war on terror, and to refocus public attention away from Iraq and back onto domestic issues. In the first of these manoeuvres, calls for a full and independent inquiry into the political decision-making behind Britain's involvement in the Iraq war were predictably dismissed. Instead, the Prime Minister now insisted that both he and the government had been cleared of any wrongdoing by four independent inquiries, despite the fact that neither the FAC, the ISC, the Hutton Inquiry, or the Butler Inquiry had been allowed to examine the political issues behind the decision to go to war. Beyond this, ministers also reprised the threat of international terrorism, advising people to stock up on supplies of food and water in case of an al-Qaeda strike, and, in a renewed attack on the 'liberal consensus' of the 1960s, sounded the charge for a renewed wave of measures centred on law and order coupled with a programme of welfare reform bound up in the notion of establishing an 'opportunity society'. In a sop to the left wing of the Labour party, still vexed by the war and by the government's increasingly illiberal approach towards civil liberties, this further strengthening of the state and the extension of the government's neo-liberal economic plans was accompanied by a renewed drive to outlaw fox-hunting, with the government invoking the Parliament Act to force the act banning it through the House of Lords before the next general election.

The government's commitment to maintaining a form of strong executive governance was further evidenced in its response to a recent report by the Public Administration Committee (PAC) calling for a reduction in ministers' prerogative powers. Though insisting that the government welcomed 'scrutiny of any of its actions', the predictable response was that the wide range of prerogative powers, such as the Prime Minister's capacity to declare war without parliamentary approval, remained essential on the basis that these offered 'much needed flexibility to govern' and enabled ministers 'to react quickly in possibly complex and dangerous circumstances'. Unsurprisingly, then, the government declared itself to be 'not persuaded' by the argument that replacing the prerogative powers with a statutory framework 'would improve the present position'.[52]

But while the question of Iraq may have started to move down the political agenda, the issue was never too far away from the headlines. A leaking of the spring 2002 memos detailing the government's secret discussions with Washington and the Prime Minister's commitment to regime change, a declaration from Kofi Annan that the Iraq war itself was 'illegal' and that the United States and Britain had 'shamelessly disregarded' international law, and a high-profile (though ultimately doomed) attempt by disgruntled MPs to impeach the Prime Minister for misleading Parliament over the war all helped to sustain the controversy throughout the autumn. So, too, did the ongoing firestorm in Iraq itself, which continued to raise questions about the lack of forethought and planning for the postwar situation. In a vigorous rebuttal of such charges, Blair's explanation for the ongoing carnage was that 'we have unfolded that plan, but there are people in Iraq who were determined to stop us'.[53] Having presumably failed to foresee that there would be those keen to disrupt the US and British liberation party, Blair then sought to resolve the problem by resorting to the tried-and-tested method of rebranding it. Describing the intensification of violence as a 'new Iraqi conflict', the Prime Minister now tried to redefine the parameters of the political debate in an attempt to portray as unreasonable all those opposed to Britain's involvement in the war. Presenting it as a battle for human freedom, and insisting that 'disagreements about the first conflict in Iraq' should now be set aside, Blair stated that the only side to be on was 'the side of liberty and democracy', and called on all 'sensible and decent' people to support the government's efforts to restore peace and security in what, he claimed, had now become 'the crucible in which the future of this global terrorism will be determined'.[54]

Further still, the Prime Minister was also coming under growing pressure to apologise for mistakes leading up to the war. An initial refusal, on the grounds that an apology would be 'insincere and dishonest', was followed within a fortnight by an attempt by Blair to create the impression that he had indeed apologised, when he had not actually done so, by stating that it was 'absolutely right that we've apologised to people for the information that was given being wrong'.[55] With the tones of political discord becoming increasingly rancorous, and with the question of the Iraq war continuing to derail the government's attempts to return to a domestic agenda, Blair was finally forced to issue an apology of sorts at the Labour party conference in September. The Prime Minister scrapped the inclusion of the word 'sorry' at the last minute, however, and his speech stated merely that he felt able to apologise for the intelligence being wrong, but that he nevertheless remained convinced that the war itself was justified. As he put it:

> The evidence about Saddam having actual biological and chemical weapons, as opposed to the capability to develop them, has turned out to be wrong. I acknowledge that and accept it. I can apologise for the information that turned out to be wrong, but I can't, sincerely at least, apologise for removing Saddam.[56]

156

Indeed, despite the fact that the Prime Minister had admitted that the problem of diminishing trust in the government was due 'to the decisions I have taken', and despite confiding in his audience that he was apparently 'fallible and capable of being wrong', his refusal to deviate from the elitist norms of British democracy remained clearly evident. Insisting that the duty of leadership was not to merely represent the views of the people in a delegatory fashion, but that it was about pressing ahead with one's own views and judgements regardless of the opposition, Blair explained that 'caring in politics' was 'about doing what you think is right and sticking to it'.[57]

With the Prime Minister's statement of regret failing to lance the boil, however, the unpleasant task now fell to Patricia Hewitt, the Trade and Industry Secretary, who was obliged to offer a more fulsome apology on behalf of the government the following week. At the same time, Hewitt was also charged with the logically challenging task of defending the decision to wage war on the grounds of intelligence, given that the intelligence had now been shown to have been comprehensively wrong. Wisely avoiding an attempt to resolve the conundrum, Hewitt stuck to a simple, if unenlightening, formulation. As she explained:

> All of us, from the Prime Minister down, who were involved in making an incredibly difficult decision, are very sorry and do apologise for the fact that that information was wrong, but I don't think that we were wrong to go in.[58]

Yet despite this *non sequitur*, the question of trust and integrity continued to be a burning issue across the country. Less than a quarter of the British public now trusted ministers to tell the truth, only one in ten felt that MPs acted to further the interests of the community rather than their own or those of their party, and more than two-thirds of British voters now believed the government to be fundamentally dishonest. Contrary to the Prime Minister's own repeated assertions, more than half also believed that the Iraq war had been the wrong thing to do, while Blair's own personal ratings had now slumped to the levels enjoyed by Thatcher during the last days of her own spectacularly implosive tenure at Downing Street.[59]

I will not apologise

In early October the question of trust was compounded still more as the ISG delivered its final report into the search for WMD. Coming in the wake of another embarrassing by-election result in the supposedly safe seat of Hartlepool, which was retained with another vastly reduced majority, the wholly unsurprising conclusion that it reached was that there were no WMD in Iraq (and indeed that there had been no WMD production in Iraq since 1991), but that Saddam Hussein had intended to reconstitute his weapons activities at some unknown future point once the sanctions regime had been lifted.[60] In an equally predictable fashion, the report also led to renewed criticism of the invasion. Hans Blix stated that the ISG had now conclusively shown that the policy of containment had been working and that Saddam had been 'a diminishing danger to his neighbours and the world', and the Liberal Democrats maintained that the report had now demonstrated 'beyond doubt' that Britain had gone to war 'on a false premise'. Gavyn Davies railed that British democracy was now moribund, that Number 10 had ended up 'controlling' both the 'supposedly independent' Hutton and Butler Inquiries, and that the press was now the only substantive means of checking executive power given the relative weakness of Parliament. 'The attacks by Campbell on the BBC last year', he raged, 'mostly reflected the pent-up frustration that the fourth estate was the one remaining estate of the realm that would not dance to his tune'.[61]

Nevertheless, Blair seized on the ISG report as offering a renewed justification for the invasion. Speaking during a whistle-stop tour of African nations designed to showcase his talents as an international humanitarian (despite a discernibly weak response to arguably the world's greatest humanitarian crisis presently unfolding in Sudan), the Prime Minister stated that

> I have had to accept that the evidence now is that there were no stockpiles of actual weapons ready to be deployed. I hope others have the honesty to accept that the report also shows that sanctions were not working.[62]

Questions over the Prime Minister's 'apology', though, continued to dog the government. On 12 October an official spokesman from Number 10 told a press briefing that while Blair regretted 'mistakes in intelligence', this did not in any way 'undermine the key point about the reason for going to war', while two days later Lord Falconer insisted that there was no need for the Prime Minister to apologise, since he had already 'made it absolutely clear that he is sorry about ... the information issue'. 'We know the intelligence on which it was based is flawed', he said, 'and we are sorry about that'.[63] On the same day, Blair himself finally issued an actual, albeit qualified apology to the House of Commons, stating, 'I take full responsibility, and indeed apologise, for any information given in good faith that has subsequently turned out to be wrong'. Nevertheless, despite the fact that the apparent *raison d'être*, as well as the stated legal basis for the conflict, was Iraq's supposed possession of WMD, despite the fact that all such assertions had since vanished into thin air, and despite the continuing violence in Iraq, Blair steadfastly refused to accept 'that there was any deception of anyone', and bluntly refused to apologise for taking the country to war. As he told the House:

> I will not apologise for removing Saddam Hussein. I will not apologise for the conflict. I believe it was right then, is right now and is essential for the wider security of the region and the world.[64]

If Blair hoped that the final extraction of some form of an apology would provide a degree of respite over Iraq, then he was immediately and sorely disappointed. Within forty-eight hours of the Prime Minister's display of apparent contrition, controversy over the war had again boiled to the forefront of the political agenda following an announcement that British troops had been asked to stand in for American forces in Baghdad while the US strengthened its offensive against the rebel stronghold of Fallujah. Amid concerns that the move was designed, at least in part, to assist George W. Bush's presidential re-election campaign by sending out a message that the US were not acting unilaterally, the Defence Secretary, Geoff Hoon, added further fuel to the fire by claiming, along with Blair, that no decision had yet been made, while simultaneously declaring that it was Britain's 'duty' as a good ally to provide troop support to the United States.[65]

The following month, Blair was granted the honour of being the first world leader to meet with the newly re-elected President Bush. Restating his belief that maintaining a strong US alliance and continuing to fight the war on terror were essential for Britain's national interests, the Prime Minister also reaffirmed his view that the international promotion of democracy and freedom offered the best means of ensuring peace and security in unstable frontier zones of the global political economy.[66] While the evident flaw in deploying an argument that democratically elected leaders were more likely to prefer peaceful means of resolving political difficulties appeared to have been lost on the premier, two months later this also formed a central theme in Bush's own inauguration speech. Amid rumours that Iran and Syria were now being lined up as possible targets for US military action, the newly re-elected President enthused that the United States had a messianic calling 'from beyond the stars', and proclaimed that it was standing ready to help spread the 'fire of democracy'.[67]

Good government

By 2005 the ancient feud between Tony Blair and Gordon Brown was reaching new depths. With revelations about their widening rift percolating throughout the media, and with the Prime Minister having recently moved to sideline the Chancellor by reappointing his own close supporter, Alan Milburn, to head up the forthcoming general-election campaign, the political crevasse at the heart of the New Labour government became increasingly unmissable as each vied to outdo the other in the humanitarian stakes following the Boxing Day tsunami disaster in the Indian Ocean. With daggers drawn, the political enmity reached its peak in January as Downing Street rescheduled the Prime Minister's monthly press conference to coincide with a keynote speech being given by the Chancellor on plans to assist developing nations.[68] Astutely sensing the national cat-calls that accompanied the unedifying spectacle, the respective camps now deigned to call a hasty truce in an attempt to calm the media headlines and to re-establish a workable co-existence for the impending re-election drive.[69]

The following month, preparatory moves for the widely expected May poll began in earnest. At the centre of these manouvres was yet another attempt to direct the political agenda onto domestic affairs. Unveiling New Labour's six key election pledges (all of which centred on domestic issues) during a one-day dash around the country, Blair signalled the government's clear intention to focus on its economic record and on its programme of investment in public services. This was posed in marked contrast to the large and destabilising programme of tax cuts, accompanied by a vague and uncertain drive for more efficiency savings, that was being proposed by the Conservatives. To drive the message home, the release of official papers relating to Britain's exit from the Exchange Rate Mechanism in 1992, a release widely believed to have been orchestrated by Alastair Campbell (now working as New Labour's Head of Strategic Elections Communications), served as an effective reminder of the economic degeneration that had accompanied the years of Tory rule.[70]

Yet domestic issues, too, were proving to be a source of some discomfort for the government. In response to a High Court ruling that its current policy of detaining foreign nationals without trial was in clear breach of the

Human Rights Act, the Home Secretary, Charles Clarke, announced that the government was now negotiating to have the existing detainees deported to their home countries despite fears that they would be subjected to torture, or even worse, upon their return. Defending this approach, and now apparently willing to take undemocratic and oppressive regimes at their word, officials insisted that no detainees would be returned to their country of origin without the government having first received 'assurances' that they would not be mistreated in any way. At the same time, the government also faced strong opposition to a new raft of proposed anti-terrorist measures. With Blair raising the spectre of 'terrorism without limit', these included the use of control orders involving electronic tagging and bans on the use of telephones or the internet by those suspected of being engaged in terrorist activities. In addition, in an extension of its earlier anti-terrorist legislation, the government now also permitted the Home Secretary to detain suspects under house arrest without charge or trial, and without even knowing the evidence against them, on the 'balance of probabilities' that they might constitute a risk to national security.[71] Though eventually being forced to concede that the Home Secretary should make a judicial application for the imposition of a control order in an effort to squeeze the anti-terror bill through Parliament before the end of the current session, the government remained insistent that it would reintroduce further security measures, including a controversial scheme for national identity cards, should it remain in power after the general election. Indeed, the following month, the ISC reported that the terrorist threat to Britain was 'real and current', and that the security services were being expanded 'significantly' in order to deal with the threat.[72]

In a further display of its authoritarian, illiberal, and elitist tendencies, the government was also at this time embroiled in renewed controversy over its refusal to publish the full advice given by the Attorney-General on the legality of the Iraq war. Triggered by a wave of requests under the long-awaited Freedom of Information Act, and by their rather predictable rejection by government officials, the dispute hinged upon whether publication was or was not in the 'public interest'. In stark contrast to the proclaimed necessity of having to release Dr Kelly's identity on these precise grounds, the official line from the government was that Goldsmith's advice was subject to the constraints of client confidentiality. Christopher Simon, the Freedom of Information Officer for the chambers of the Attorney-General, maintained, for instance, that publication of the advice would mark an unwarranted break with precedent, while Lord Falconer explained that the secrecy surrounding Goldsmith's opinion was 'right for ensuring good government' since 'every government needs space to take advice'.[73]

Indeed, such was the government's desire to keep Goldsmith's vacillation under wraps that it later transpired that the Butler Inquiry itself had faced difficulties in obtaining the information. As Lord Butler explained, there had been 'a bit of tension with the government about whether they were going to disclose documents to us', and it was only the 'important leverage' gained by the threat of going public about this obfuscation that had, in the end, persuaded officials to change their mind.[74] Further still, the official justification for refusing to publish Goldsmith's advice also conveniently ignored the fact that precedents for the disclosure of such material had been previously set during the Factortame and Westland affairs, and that the government itself had not baulked at setting precedents aside during the publication of the September dossier, in granting the House of Commons a vote on the war, in allowing Alastair Campbell to appear before the FAC, or, indeed, in publishing its own 'selected extracts' of Goldsmith's legal opinion. As the Cabinet Secretary, Sir Andrew Turnbull, himself pointed out, 'There are precedents for publishing summaries of advice. There are probably even precedents for going further than that'.[75]

With calls mounting for the government to reveal the full view of its chief legal adviser, and with Clare Short now openly accusing the Attorney-General of having succumbed to political pressure and of having 'misled the Cabinet' by failing to disclose his uncertainty and reservations about the legal situation,[76] the controversy was further inflamed towards the end of March following the disclosure of the letter of resignation from Elizabeth Wilmshurst, the former Deputy Legal Advisor at the Foreign Office. Following another request under the Freedom of Information Act, this was initially produced by the government with a paragraph missing, with Jack Straw explaining that the redacted section contained references to confidential legal advice (widely believed to be that of the Attorney-General), and that it was 'entirely proper for the Government to withhold information'. The implications for 'good government' of publishing such confidential material, he augured, were 'very grave indeed'. The next day, however, the offending paragraph was subsequently leaked to Channel 4 News, its contents revealing that both the Foreign Office and the Attorney-General had indeed held reservations about the legality of going to war without a second resolution.[77]

162

To no small degree, this prevailing sense of confusion surrounding the Attorney-General's legal advice was engendered by government officials themselves. A Number 10 spokesman, for example, had stated that the Attorney-General had 'set out his reasoning but not the detailed advice', and Blair insisted that Goldsmith had given 'a fair summary' of his opinion and that this had been set out 'in detail', while Sir Andrew Turnbull informed the Public Administration Committee that there was 'not a longer version' of the advice given by Goldsmith, and that the text provided to ministers on 17 March had been the definitive version.[78] Furthermore, while the Attorney-General himself vehemently insisted that the advice given had been his 'genuine and independent view', Lord Goldsmith also appeared to be somewhat confused over the nature of his own opinion. Initially stating in November 2004 that his advice had been 'a summary of my view of the legal position, rather than a detailed consideration', by February 2005 his stated position was now that the advice 'did not purport to be a summary of my confidential legal advice to government'.[79]

All this amounted to a rather uncomfortable dilemma for the government. If the advice given to the Cabinet on 17 March was indeed a shortened summary of the Attorney-General's views, then the government would be charged with having failed to provide ministers with the complete legal assessment on the eve of war. If nothing else, this would mark a clear breach of the Ministerial Code which stipulates that full legal advice must be disclosed to ministers whenever they are presented with a summarised version. On the other hand, however, if the advice really was Goldsmith's complete legal opinion, then this would show that the country had been pitched into battle supported by the briefest of textual analyses.[80]

An incredibly tough decision

Even with the announcement of the election having been delayed by an ill-timed confluence of a royal wedding and the death of a Pope, its revelation came as no surprise to anyone. Indeed, after three months of pre-election campaigning, and with little interest having yet been aroused, the declaration was received with a great deal more relief than excitement. Firing the starting pistol as the Labour party enjoyed its biggest lead in the polls for four months, Blair proclaimed that there was a 'big choice' to be made, and that 'the British people are the boss'.[81] Nevertheless, the early stage of the campaign proper remained a leaden affair. Despite Blair's later insistence that the 'great thing about an election' was the opportunity to go out and 'talk to people for week upon week',[82] New Labour's opening strategy was based around a series of carefully managed and choreographed set pieces designed to minimise the risk of any senior government figure, least of all the Prime Minister, coming into contact with potentially hostile voters. Instead, the aim was to deliver a sanitised version of the party message on public investment and the economy direct to the masses. But on this, Labour tacticians were rapidly outflanked by the Conservatives, who successfully managed to drag the government into a series of bloody dogfights on the traditionally right-wing issues of asylum and law and order. Although this, too, failed to ignite any real interest in the campaign, the gap between the two parties began to narrow.[83]

With the Labour campaign threatening to stall, and with levels of public trust in the Prime Minister remaining perceptibly weak, Blair was once again forced to turn to Gordon Brown for assistance. With polls showing that Labour's lead would more than double if Brown were installed as the party leader,[84] the Chancellor was now pitched back into the front line of the election foray to serve as the Prime Minister's 'human shield', and to help refocus the public debate onto the government's economic record. Paradoxically, this was also aided in mid-April by the unexpected collapse of Rover, which gave the government a clear opportunity to demonstrate its commitment not to play fast and loose with the economy by refusing to bail out the fatally stricken car firm.

Although Iraq remained a key doorstep issue for large numbers of voters, the war itself did not as yet feature highly in the election campaign. While both the pro-war Labour and Conservative parties remained anxious to avoid raising the subject for obvious reasons, the persistently anti-war Liberal Democrats, packaging themselves as 'the real opposition', were now increasingly keen to avoid being characterised as a one-issue party. Where government officials could not avoid the topic, however, events were parleyed through a thick veneer of positive gloss. New Labour's manifesto commentary, for example, offered but a brief celebration of the fact that 'the butchery of Saddam' was over, and that the roots of democracy were starting to take hold within Iraq. Implicitly, the manifesto also sought to justify the war by restating the government's underlying principles on foreign policy, describing the threat of WMD and their use by rogue states or terrorist organisations as 'a pressing issue', asserting that Britain's national security was best ensured by 'the spread of liberty and justice over-seas', and proclaiming that under New Labour, 'a strong Britain will force international terrorism into retreat and help spread democracy and freedom around the world'. To assuage the fears of those on the left, concerned that the Prime Minister might help to light further Bushfires around the world during a third term in office, the manifesto also pledged that the government would 'always uphold the rule of international law', and that it would take a leading role on international development issues, including aid to Africa and global poverty.[85]

The question of Iraq finally emerged as a serious campaign issue with little more than a fortnight to go before polling day. On 20 April, the Prime Minister faced the BBC interviewer Jeremy Paxman in the first of a series of interviews with the main party leaders. In an angry, aggressive, and often confrontational performance, Blair maintained his defiant stance on the war, insisting that the JIC assessments had been 'absolutely plain' about the fact that Iraq had WMD, that they had been 'absolutely right' in what they reported at the time, and that the government had been vindicated over the question of misusing intelligence by 'four separate inquiries'. In what would become the official mantra throughout the remaining days and hours of the campaign, the Prime Minister also sought to establish a justification for the war based on the supposed benefits of strong and decisive leadership. Insisting that he had been forced to take 'an incredibly tough decision' and that there had been 'no fence to sit on', Blair claimed that the invasion had been 'the right thing to do' since to have threatened action and to have then failed to act would have undermined the credibility of the international community, and would have left Saddam Hussein and similar deviants immeasurably emboldened. That this was an entirely disingenuous argument, given that the American-led attack was not in the slightest way conditional upon British involvement, and given that Saddam would have been overthrown regardless of whether a single British soldier had set foot in the Gulf, was by this time well and truly beside the point.[86]

Within a matter of days, the question of the war, and with it the question of Blair's integrity, had galloped up the electoral agenda following a leak of the Attorney-General's March 7 advice to Channel 4 News. Now deigning to publish the full document as an exercise in damage limitation, the government sought to play down the affair, with the Prime Minister describing it as 'a damp squib', and insisting that Goldsmith's advice had shown the war to be lawful. Ministers also insisted that there had been a full and proper Cabinet debate on the matter, despite the fact that the Cabinet itself had not seen the earlier and far more equivocal advice, and despite the fact that there had been no actual discussion of the view presented to the Cabinet by Goldsmith himself. Nevertheless, according to

Gordon Brown, it was a 'myth' to suggest 'that there was no Cabinet involvement in this discussion'. 'Not only did we have the data available to us', he carefully explained, 'but we had the opportunity to quiz the Attorney General on every aspect of it'.[87]

Not surprisingly, Lord Goldsmith, too, stuck to his guns, insisting that the advice showed how he had simply passed through the normal processes of thought and had taken stock 'of all the arguments' involved before arriving at a firm and final conclusion. Moreover, that this definitive viewpoint was markedly different from his earlier account of the situation was also explained away as a necessary product of circumstances. The nuanced and ambiguous views of 7 March, he explained, had in fact been inadmissible as a valid opinion, given that 'the military and civil service needed me to express a clear and simple view whether military action would be lawful or not'.[89] Of course, that Goldsmith himself had close personal links to the Prime Minister, having been made a life peer and appointed to his post by Tony Blair, did nothing to lessen suspicions that he had been pressured to change his mind.

Buoyed by the disclosure, which they claimed showed that Goldsmith had inexplicably changed his advice (given that he had provided no real explanation as to precisely why he changed his long-standing view during ten days in March), the Tories stiffened their personal attacks against the Prime Minister. For all their best efforts, however, Michael Howard's attempt to vilify Blair by directly accusing him of having lied over the war ran into a political quagmire. Ironically, the invasion, too, was now proving to be an unwrenchable albatross for the Conservative leader, whose strong support for the war regardless of the WMD issue trapped him in the logically untenable position of having to defend an illegal policy of regime change. Howard's explanation for this, as incomprehensible as it was hopeless, was that he was in favour of 'regime change plus'.[89] With the Conservatives unable to capitalise on the government's difficulties, the main beneficiaries again proved to be the Liberal Democrats. In response, the government launched into a last-ditch scare tactic, warning any potential deserters from the New Labour fold that casting a protest vote against the Prime Minister would merely dispense 'a Tory vote by the back door'. Given that the first-past-the-post electoral system was so heavily biased against the Liberal Democrats, and that only the Labour and Conservatives parties had any realistic prospect of forming a government, the 'big choice' before the nation, then, was between a third term of Blair's New Labour and a return to Tory rule.[90]

The worst election

As with all the events surrounding the invasion of Iraq, the general election itself exemplified the principles of centralised, hierarchical, and elitist government in Britain. Indeed, for all the tub-thumping bluster about getting the voters out that marked the end of the campaign, the vagaries of the Westminster electoral system ensured that the large majority of these voters had been effectively disenfranchised from the very outset. With the final outcome of the election—a historic third term for New Labour—being virtually assured from the beginning, and with the precise scale and manner of its arrival to be effectively determined by a series of battles in a relatively small number of marginal constituencies, for most voters the key question before them was not so much who to vote for as why to bother voting at all.

In the event, the government's margin of victory on 5 May was far smaller than most people had expected. With its parliamentary majority slashed from 167 to 66, the New Labour machine was also forced to endure a series of individual shocks throughout election night. These included the ousting of Barbara Roche (an ex-Home Office minister), the defeat of Stephen Twigg (the Enfield executioner of Michael Portillo's political career in 1997), the wholesale rejection of an attempt by New Labour command to foist an external female candidate onto the constituents of Blaenau Gwent, and the outlandish victory of George Galloway, the stalwart Labour MP who had been excommunicated from the party for his vehement criticism of the war. Returned to Parliament for Respect on an explicitly anti-war ticket, Galloway spectacularly deposed the Blairite MP Oona King in East London's Bethnal Green and Bow constituency with a swing of more than 26%. Yet among the individual sights of the evening, none would live in the memory longer than that of a ghostly white Prime Minister being forced to endure an embarrassing denunciation at his Sedgefield constituency declaration from Reg Keys, the anti-war campaigner whose son was killed in Iraq, and who managed to poll a highly respectable 10% of the vote in Blair's own political backyard.

As antipathy towards the government reverberated across the national battleground, the main story of the election, however, proved to be that of the election itself. Described by the Electoral Reform Society as 'the worst election in the history of democracy in Britain',[91] this was characterised by a palpable discontinuity between the expressed will of the British people and the actual outcomes delivered by the electoral system. The most obvious of these discrepancies was the clearly disproportionate relationship between the seats gained by the respective parties and their level of popular support. While the Conservatives secured a roughly proportional 30% of the seats with just under a third of the national vote, the Liberal Democrats were rewarded for their 22% of the vote with less than 10% of the seats, while New Labour itself received 55% of the seats from just 35% of the vote. In contrast, a system of proportional representation would have produced a markedly more equitable composition of Parliament, giving 227 seats to New Labour, 208 to the Conservatives, and 142 to the Liberal Democrats, thus resulting in a situation of no overall control. Worse still, with voter apathy continuing to reign supreme and with turnout rising but marginally to just 61%, the Labour party had effectively managed to regain the seat of executive power backed by little more than a fifth (21.6%) of the British electorate. While this was the lowest level of popular support for a democratically elected majority government ever seen in Britain, it was also the first time that a British government had ever been elected by fewer people than those who had not voted at all.[92]

The unjust nature of the electoral system was also evident in other ways. The average number of votes that each MP needed in order to win election, for example, differed wildly due to the peculiarities of first-past-the-post. While Labour MPs required an average of just under 27,000 votes to win a place in Parliament, Conservative MPs required two-thirds more, around 44,500 votes, while astonishingly, Liberal Democrat MPs required more than 96,000 votes—some three-and-a-half times more than their Labour counterparts—to gain entry to the House of Commons. In addition to this, the total number of wasted votes throughout Britain, defined as those cast for losing candidates or as being surplus to requirements for those successfully elected, also reached alarming levels. In all, more than 70% of the votes cast in the 2005 general election had no ultimate impact upon the final result.

To compound this, while New Labour's share of the vote had fallen by 6% since 2001, the quality of the electoral support being bestowed upon the government was also degrading. Active support for New Labour was now draining away at both ends of the electoral spectrum, from professional middle-class and unskilled working-class voters alike. The number of seats with a Labour majority of less than 5% (the so-called 'super-marginals') had more than doubled from 20 to 43 since 2001, and more than half of those voters choosing to support the government claimed to have done so due to a negative impression of other parties, rather than to any positive feelings towards the New Labour project itself. Indeed, more than half of those casting their vote for Labour now also wanted the government to be re-elected with a smaller majority.

Acknowledging this fact, Blair's victory speech bore little relation to the triumphalism of 1997. Trying to draw a line under the war by admitting that Iraq had been 'a deeply divisive issue', but stressing that the British people now wanted 'to move on', Blair nonetheless appeared to have been chastened by the election experience, which was the first time that support for the Labour party had regressed at a general election since 1983. Indeed, by many observers, the Prime Minister's reduced majority was now thought to augur a new style of government, ushering in an era of collegiate and consensual politics in contrast to the authoritarian and presidential style that had hitherto defined the New Labour government. In part, this expectation also reflected the widespread assumption that Blair himself would soon step down, at least as party leader, in order to provide his successor with a sufficient period of time to become established before the next general election.

The political reality after 5 May, however, gave little indication that the government was starting to move in a more inclusive and responsive direction. While professing to have listened and learned during the election campaign, and to have developed 'a very clear idea of what the British people now expect from this government', the Prime Minister also stated his desire to 'focus relentlessly' on 'the priorities the people have set for us'. Notwithstanding the fact that nearly four-fifths of 'the people' did not actually vote for a New Labour government, the result was interpreted by Blair as having provided a mandate for the implementation of a radical programme of reforms ranging from public services to pensions, and from immigration to law and order. Still further, the enduring nature of the Prime Minister's elitist style of political management was also displayed in the first Cabinet reshuffle of the third term. The long-expected departure of Geoff Hoon from the Ministry of Defence was accompanied by the controversial appointment of Andrew Adonis, an unelected Downing Street advisor, to the post of Junior Education Minister, and by the return to office of David Blunkett as the Minister for Work and Pensions, just five months after being forced to resign as Home Secretary for fast-tracking a visa for his child's nanny. In a notable contrast to this lack of internal democracy, the New Labour government also continued to emphasise that its commitment to 'promoting democracy' abroad remained 'at the heart' of its foreign policy.[93] Yet while the events of the election, as with all of the preceding issues concerning Britain's participation in the Iraq war, flew in the face of democratic propriety, such developments were perfectly in keeping with the underlying norms and values of the British political system. Despite raising serious questions about the legitimacy of the New Labour government and of the democratic process in Britain more generally, the various distortions and inequities of the election system effectively secured the continuation of strong majority government, and with it the continuation of elite executive rule.

The rules of the game

As the controversy over the war in Iraq finally seemed poised to subside from the political agenda, events again took a dramatic and unexpected twist. On 7 July, less than twenty-four hours after London was celebrating its victorious bid to host the Olympic Games in 2012, the capital was rocked by the worst terrorist attacks ever seen on the British mainland. In a co-ordinated series of bombings, four 'Islamic' suicide bombers devastated three tube trains and a double-decker bus, killing fifty-two innocent people and injuring more than seven hundred others. Two weeks later, an attempted series of copy-cat strikes brought further chaos to the streets of London, and an already febrile atmosphere became still more highly charged following the subsequent shooting of an innocent Brazilian, Jean Charles de Menezes, in a botched operation by the Metropolitan Police, who ostensibly mistook him for a terrorist bomber.

Almost immediately after the 7 July bombings, the question of a possible connection to Britain's participation in the invasion of Iraq began to be raised. Clare Short, for example, purported to be in 'no doubt' that British foreign policy throughout the Middle East had been a key factor behind the attacks, George Galloway remarked that London had 'paid the price' for its role in the conflict, Robin Cook added that the war could no longer be presented as having 'protected us from terrorism abroad', while Hans Blix concurred that the invasion had provided fertile ground for 'breeding terrorism'.[94] Eleven days after the atrocities, a report by Chatham House (formerly the Royal Institute of International Affairs) also highlighted the Iraq connection, claiming that Britain's alliance with the United States and its role in the invasion had created 'particular difficulties' for the United Kingdom and had given 'a boost' to al-Qaeda.[95]

More worryingly still, it also transpired that government officials themselves had been warning of the heightened risks of a terrorist attack posed by Britain's involvement in the war. Alongside the earlier warnings from the JIC and the FAC, a leaked letter to Andrew Turnbull from Michael Jay, the Permanent Under-Secretary at the Foreign Office, revealed that the government had been further informed of this possibility in May 2004. In the '[e]xperience of both Ministers and officials working in this area', he stated, 'one of the potential underlying causes of extremism', and 'a key driver' in its expansion, was the 'recurring theme' of British foreign policy, 'especially in the context of the Middle East peace process and Iraq'. In an accompanying strategy document, the government was also warned that both Britain and the United States were now increasingly being viewed as 'Crusader states', and that hostility towards the West from the Muslim world was 'worse than ever'.[96] In addition to this, Britain's intelligence agencies, too, continued to warn of such risks. Three weeks after the initial attacks, a report produced by MI5's Joint Terrorism Analysis Centre (described by the government as its 'centre of expertise on assessing the threat from international terrorism')[97] itself acknowledged that Iraq had become 'a dominant issue' for Islamic extremists, and warned that the war was still acting 'as a focus of a range of terrorist related activities in Britain'.[98]

The government's response to the attacks, however, again exemplified its desire to frame and manage the course of political debate around the virtues of a strong and decisive executive. Striking a discernibly Churchillian posture, the Prime Minister condemned the attacks as 'barbaric', and broke off from his negotiations at the G8 summit in Gleneagles to assume direct control of the crisis. Insisting that he would not yield 'one inch' to terrorism, Blair pledged that such attempts to 'impose extremism on the world' and to destroy 'our values and our way of life' would 'never succeed'.[99] Moreover, despite the fact that 'al-Qaeda' attacks had predominantly followed a pattern of targeting Western interests, chiefly those of the United States and its allies, the government pointedly refused to accept the politically dangerous conclusion that the bombings had been related to the Iraq war. Instead, ministers sought to highlight the global and the longer-term nature of the terrorist threat, and firmly rejected any idea of a link to Iraq. Emphasising the fact that terrorists had 'struck across the world', Jack Straw, for example, pointed out that there had been atrocities in countries unrelated to the Iraq war, such as Kenya, Tanzania, Indonesia, and Turkey.[100] Charles Clarke dismissed the idea of a link to the war as suffering from 'a serious intellectual flabbiness', given that terrorists had been carrying out attacks 'before the Iraq war was engaged upon',[101] while

171

Blair himself derided the notion of an Iraq connection as complete and utter 'nonsense'.[102]

In contrast, the official analysis of the situation as presented by the Prime Minister was that 'the underlying causes' of terrorism were not to be found in the actions of the main Western powers, but in the 'perverted and poisonous' doctrine of Islamic extremism. As such, he maintained, they were 'obviously a lot deeper than anything that is happening in this country'.[103] On this basis, the solution to the crisis was deemed to entail a comprehensive dismantling of not just the material but also the ideational resources being utilised by the terrorists. Asserting that the doctrine of extremism would need to be 'pulled up by the roots', Blair announced that the country was now engaged in 'a battle of ideas, hearts and minds', and called on the 'decent mainstream majority' to 'stand up and confront the ideology of this evil'. Concomitantly, the Prime Minister also re-emphasised the need to address a range of international issues, such as Africa, global poverty, and the Middle East peace process, as a means of depriving Islamic militants of any cause that could be used against the West. As he explained, 'if you want to deal with the root causes of this you have got to do ... the other things like ... showing that we care and are compassionate about people less fortunate than ourselves.'[104]

As a further corollary of this analysis, the Prime Minister also asserted that any solution to the crisis could not therefore be found in a change of Western foreign policy, but would instead require a more vigorous reasser-tion of global reordering. Changing 'one single bit of any policy' in response to terrorism, he warned, would be 'a disastrous signal to send out'. In an equally predictable fashion, the centre of this renewed war on terror also fell on the Middle East. Given that 'part of the roots' of the ter-rorist problem were to be found 'in the way that the Middle East has devel-oped oppressive systems of government', Blair declared that any effective response would require 'a greater sense of democracy and human rights' throughout the region, and warned that 'the political systems in those countries have got to change'. In sum, as he put it, the nations of the civilised world would need to go after the terrorist threat with 'far greater vigour' than they had been 'prepared to do so far'.[105]

Aligned with this project to reconfigure the global and ideological land-scape, a further aspect of the government's response focused on the need for tougher and more effective anti-terrorist measures at home. The raft of proposals floated in the wake of the attacks included the further use of control orders, the possibility of introducing longer periods of detention

172

without charge, the deportation and exclusion of foreign nationals suspected of fostering hatred or of advocating and justifying terrorist acts, and
plans to clamp down on those engaged in inciting terrorism, preparing a
terrorist attack, or giving or receiving terrorist training. The government
warned that, if necessary, it would also consider derogating from sections
of the Human Rights Act should the judiciary seek to use its provisions in
order to block the will of the executive in this matter.[106] While many of
these measures attracted a great amount of criticism from human-rights
and civil-liberties groups, and although none of them would have been
sufficient to prevent the London bombings given that there had been no
prior intelligence about the intended strike, and given that the suicide
bombers themselves were 'home grown' rather than outside extremists,
the government nevertheless insisted that the balance between national
security and individual freedoms would now have to be recast in favour
of the former. 'The rules of the game', as Blair starkly maintained, 'are
changing'.[107]

Yet the success of the government's strategy was somewhat mixed. On
the one hand, Blair's firm response to the crisis prompted a rise in his own
approval ratings, New Labour's lead in the polls remained undiminished,
and the general public remained largely supportive of most of the proposed anti-terror measures. Despite this, and for all the government's
rhetoric, however, around two-thirds of voters were also of the view that
the London attacks had been linked to Britain's participation in the Iraq
war, and a similar proportion duly believed that the Prime Minister himself bore some share of the responsibility.[108] Moreover, while the
government's difficulties over Iraq continued to persist, the problem was
now more than a matter of political endurance. Indeed, given that any
effective response to the terrorist threat would require a rethinking of
Britain's foreign-policy strategy, as well as a broad-based and co-ordinated
effort involving the active support of civil society and the general public
itself, the marked refusal to accept any link to Iraq, coupled with the continuing low level of trust in New Labour, represent a serious impediment
to the government's ability to successfully negotiate the crisis. While the
introduction of firmer measures may well be necessary as a temporary
expedient, and while the balance between national security and civil
liberties may legitimately need to be recast, the risk that individual freedoms may now be set aside and never regained remains a matter of
genuine concern to those anxious for the future of Britain's already weakened democratic system, and one that is further exacerbated by the appar-

ently endless nature of the 'war on terror' itself. In this context, then, a central question to be asked is whether New Labour, having treated both Parliament and the electorate with such complete disdain over the Iraq war, can ever be trusted again.

Concluding remarks

The final phase of New Labour's Iraq crisis was characterised by the enduring norms of elitist governance in Britain. Despite exposing the inner machinery of the New Labour government to reveal the informal, centralised, and highly closed nature of its decision-making processes, and despite revealing a wide range of executive misdemeanours ranging from the production of the September dossier to the events surrounding the naming of Dr David Kelly, the outcome of the Hutton Inquiry decisively failed to land a telling blow on the government. Bound by the confines of a tight remit designed to avoid any examination of the broader issues surrounding the war with Iraq, Lord Hutton's conclusions were widely derided as a classic case of whitewash. While the government's response to the ongoing controversy—the establishment of the Butler review—led to a far more critical assessment and raised concerns about the centralised and elitist nature of the government's policy-making processes, this inquiry too was constrained by its terms of reference, and was similarly unable to encroach upon the political context behind the decision to go to war. Although the New Labour heirarchy purports to have now been cleared by four separate inquiries, the reality is that it sought at every stage to block and constrain any meaningful scrutiny of its actions. By restricting access to a range of critical information on the decision-making process behind the invasion of Iraq (including its aims and motivations and the evolution of government policy), on the intelligence material that had apparently informed this decision, and on the legal advice on which the war had ultimately been prosecuted, the government severely undermined the ability of Parliament and the wider public to make a fully informed assessment of its conduct.

Faced with rising public antipathy over Iraq, the government responded by renewing its efforts into steering the course of political debate back onto domestic issues, by rebranding the conflict as a battle for freedom and democracy, and by stubbornly refusing to accept that the invasion had been wrong in any way. On the contrary, it was now seen to demonstrate the virtues of strong and decisive leadership. Despite the fact that every

174

reason given for the conflict had turned out to be wholly false, the Prime Minister not only refused to apologise for the war but continued to insist that it had been the right thing to do, that it was his duty to take tough decisions to safeguard the national interest, and that failure to have taken military action would have left an emboldened Saddam in power to the detriment of global stability. Moreover, even the ultimate mechanism of democratic accountability—namely the general election—proved to be a perfect embodiment of the unresponsive nature of British democracy. Demonstrating a clear lack of concern with ensuring the effective representation of the general will, this rewarded New Labour with a third consecutive majority in Parliament despite having drawn the support of scarcely more than a fifth of the entire electorate.

The persistently propagated line emphasising the benefits of a strong executive has also dominated the government's response to the emergent terrorist crisis following the London bombings of 7 July. Steadfastly refusing to recognise any connection to the war in Iraq, the government's strategy has instead focused on the malevolent role of radical Islamic ideology, on the need to intensify the process of global reordering, and on the need for harsh anti-terrorist measures and a redrawing of civil rights as a defence against any further attacks. Yet while this has proved to be a relatively popular response to the crisis, the majority of the British people remain convinced of a link between the London bombings and Britain's participation in the Iraq war. For all the best efforts of the government, then, it would seem that the question of Iraq, and with it questions about the nature of New Labour itself, will not easily be dispelled.

8

Conclusion: The Reform Agenda

Democratic values

If the ancient Chinese are to be believed, 'interesting times' are far more of a curse than a blessing. For many who have followed the events of the past few years, such sentiments will undoubtedly ring true. Yet the fact that an old Chinese saying can find new life at the dawn of the twenty-first century is but one of the contradictions of our time. We live, indeed, in an age which is thick with irony. That a 'war on terror' can only be fought by obliterating thousands of innocent people, that global order can only be maintained by splitting the community of nations, that international law can only be upheld through the perpetuation of an illegal conflict, and that a self-proclaimed government of the centre-left can so closely align itself with one of the most vehemently right-wing regimes on earth—these are all fitting epithets for this most 'interesting' of periods in our history. But amid all this there is also continuity. Britain's participation in the Iraq war was in many ways facilitated by the underlying norms and values that are perpetuated by, and deeply entrenched within, its political structures. Conditioned by the principles of centralisation, hierarchy, and elitism, these ideational and institutional contours act to sustain a model of government based on the virtues of a strong and decisive executive, a limited notion of representation, and a relative paucity of effective checks and balances. Imposing a form of selective bias upon the strategic actions of the political class, this has served to ensure a high degree of conformity with these dominant modes of operation and has thereby helped to ensure the reproduction of these systemic constraints. We have crossed the threshold of the millennium only to find that the British political tradition is very much alive.

The impact of this behavioural discipline upon the Labour party has been dramatic. Provoking an intensive programme of internal restructuring designed to strengthen the role of the party leadership and to re-establish its credibility as a governing force, the elitist configuration of Britain's political architecture has subsequently conferred a largely untrammelled degree of freedom upon senior members of the party in office. The result has been the amplification of its underlying principles and their elevation to new commanding heights. This has been reflected in the adoption of a political strategy designed to sustain New Labour in government, to enhance Britain's position within the global political economy, and to augment the autonomy of the core executive itself. More specifically, these overarching goals have been pursued via an entrenchment of free-market economics set within a support mechanism of depoliticisation, by an informal and highly centralised form of policy-making, by the enforcement of tight party discipline, and through an ongoing programme of media management designed to control the flow of politically sensitive information and to shape the course of public debate. In external terms, this strategy has also involved the pursuit of an interventionist foreign policy designed as a means of projecting British power and influence on the world stage, and set within the adoption of a transatlantic-bridge approach; the government has sought to shape the contours of the international system via the promotion of free markets, the provision of military and diplomatic support for key allies, and by promoting the spread of 'freedom' and 'democracy' as an ostensible means of ensuring world peace and prosperity.

An important part of this strategy has involved ongoing efforts to address conditions within unstable 'frontier zones' that are seen to pose a threat to the US-led 'Western alliance' of core capitalist states. More importantly still, the government's attempt at creating an international environment conducive to Britain's geo-strategic interests has also involved a series of military ventures, the most recent of which has been the pursuit of regime change in Iraq, seen as a key, if potential, node of instability within the global political economy. The elimination of Saddam Hussein was thus viewed as a useful way of establishing the credible willingness of the alliance to use force in defence of its interests, and of thereby sending out a strong signal to would-be transgressors that any actions to the contrary would not be tolerated. In the event, this led Tony Blair and members of the New Labour elite to align themselves with the new-imperialist trajectory of the Bush administration, on the grounds that this provided the best route towards furthering their interventionist ambitions. That this view of the 'national interest' was one that was not shared by the majority of the British people, however, merely demonstrated the elitist and unresponsive character of the New Labour project.

All this, of course, is not to imply that the influence of Britain's political structures should be interpreted in a deterministic fashion. While imposing a selective bias upon the central actors involved, the underlying norms and values of the system did not predestine any specific course of action, and despite exerting an influence upon political behaviour, they did not preclude or foreclose a role for agential dynamics, such as the beliefs and values of individuals themselves. Neither did they prevent influence by other contingent factors, such as the weak nature of the parliamentary opposition, or the internalities of the Labour party itself, particularly the absence of any strong ministerial objections to the Iraq policy, and the lack of any broader party constraints on the activities of the leadership. The importance of Britain's political structures in the Iraq affair, then, is to be found in the way in which they formed the strategic terrain in which these views and contingencies combined, and in the way in which they influenced the development and the implementation of core executive policies. Indeed, while it seems unlikely that a Conservative government would have taken an alternative course of action (although the possibility cannot be ruled out), it is almost certain that this would not have been pursued with quite the same level of disdain for constitutional propriety as that which has been displayed by New Labour, with its deeply ingrained penchant for highly centralised, informal, and secretive decision-making. Given the developmental path experienced by the Conservative party itself, with its absence (until recently) of any prolonged electoral estrangement, and its lack of willingness to submit to the same degree of internal transformation as that adopted by the Labour party, the likelihood is that while the outcome may well have been the same in terms of support for the United States and the pursuit of regime change, the 'processology' of events would have been much different. It is the combination of a facilitative constitutional architecture and an extremely centralised ruling party that has set the necessary, if not the sufficient, condition for the events of recent years.

New Labour and the war with Iraq

Britain's participation in the war with Iraq provides a perfect demonstration of the centralised, hierarchical, and elitist nature of both the New Labour government and the British democratic system. Having provided the strategic terrain in which New Labour's political strategy was formed, and having thereby conditioned the emergence of the Iraq policy itself as a component of this wider design, the constitutional architecture of the British state also provided senior members of the executive with a relatively high degree of freedom with which to pursue their aims in an informal, tightly controlled, secretive, and ultimately unaccountable manner.

While the desire to secure regime change in Iraq was initially precluded by a series of political and legal obstacles, the rise of the neo-conservative Bush regime from the end of 2000, combined with the events of 9/11, created a window of opportunity for senior New Labour officials, and the Prime Minister in particular, to pursue this policy objective with more vigour. In a series of secret negotiations with Washington during the spring and summer of 2002, senior officials agreed to support a US-led policy of regime change and began to devise a strategy to create the required conditions for doing so. Constructed by a small and informal cabal based around Number 10, this centred on the issue of Iraq's alleged possession of WMD, on a renewal of the UN weapons inspections process, and on a propaganda campaign designed to convince domestic and international opinion of the need for tougher measures. While public consent was not an essential requirement for the implementation of the Iraq policy, the widespread opposition to the idea of taking military action was nevertheless a political concern, given the need to maintain an impression of democratic governance and to dispel any notion that the public mood could be completely disregarded. Still, however important public and parliamentary opinion may have been in determining the means of implementing the policy, at no point during the entire episode was there any sense that those involved in driving it forward believed that this would be of sufficient importance to determine the overall end. At no point was the Cabinet made aware of these underlying policy developments, and still less were its members invited to partake in any form of collective decision-making. Nor were ministers shown the actual intelligence that was apparently informing the government's approach, which remained far weaker than the more assertive claims that were now being publicly made by the Prime Minister.

The chief element in the government's propaganda campaign was the now-infamous September dossier, detailing the threat posed by Iraq's WMD. The construction of the dossier also revealed the unduly close and malleable nature of the relationship between the political and the intelligence spheres of the British state, as well as the absence of any rigorous safeguards against a politicisation of intelligence material. The dossier affair also highlighted the ability of the executive to effectively influence the flow of politically sensitive information, and to thereby shape the course of political debate. This was clearly demonstrated by the process of strengthening intelligence material, including the removal of JIC caveats, the overlooking of concerns from within the intelligence community, and the extensively spun presentation of intelligence, which went up to the very limits of, if not in fact beyond, any meaningful connection with the truth. Yet with no alternative sources of information available, and with no means of objectively assessing the government's claims, the Cabinet, Parliament, and the wider public were all forced to take the line being presented by Number 10 at face value. Furthermore, with no information about the motives and actions of the executive concerning the development of the Iraq policy itself, the ability of MPs and the wider public to make a fully informed assessment of the government's conduct was severely curtailed.

The government's attempt to ensure the required political and legal conditions for enforcing regime change was intensified following both the failure of the September dossier to sway public opinion and the inability of the UN inspectors to uncover any weapons of mass destruction in Iraq. This involved the production of another dossier, now detailing Iraq's concealment and deception, which was again produced in an informal, secretive, and centralised manner. This was accompanied by a concerted emphasis on the apparent virtues of strong executive leadership, and by a scapegoating of the French government for the failure to secure a second UN resolution that would explicitly authorise the use of force. All this was also backed by the legal advice of the Attorney-General, which was hardened on the eve of battle to unambiguously justify an invasion on the basis of existing UN resolutions, and by a process of intensive party pressure designed to ensure success in the parliamentary vote on committing troops to war. Equally, however, both ministers and MPs remained unaware of the underlying intelligence behind the government's public rhetoric, of the Attorney-General's earlier legal opinion—also replete with caveats and uncertainties—and of the actual French position in the United Nations. The House of Commons, too, was only granted a vote on the matter in the hope that this would quell discontent over the issue, while MPs were subjected to the disciplining effects of an intensive three-line whip. The result was that the views of the general public were not translated into political action by its elected representatives, who instead voted in favour of going to war.

180

The course of postwar events was also marked by the government's persistent efforts to channel and mould the course of political debate and to further constrain any attempts to scrutinise its actions during the run-up to the conflict. These efforts were designed to deflect attention away from the inability to uncover any weapons of mass destruction, and to discredit the growing suspicion that the government had misused intelligence material to strengthen the case for war by rounding on the BBC. By framing the 6:07 report by Andrew Gilligan as the definitive version of the allegations against the government, and by working to ensure that the identity and the views of Dr David Kelly entered the public sphere through a combination of an MoD press statement, carefully designed Q&A material, and a series of lobby briefings, members of New Labour's inner circle now hoped to exonerate themselves of any wrongdoing and to relieve the political pressure that was now starting to mount.

At the same time, officials also sought to impede scrutiny of their activities by denying the inquiry of the Foreign Affairs Committee access to critical information on the process behind the decision to go to war, while establishing a parallel inquiry through the secretive Intelligence and Security Committee. The government's attempt to avoid any detailed examination of its actions was also evidenced in the constrained remits of the subsequent Hutton and Butler Inquiries, which served to direct their judgements away from any politically dangerous areas, and which enabled the government thereafter to cite the fact that it had been cleared by four 'independent' investigations. As part of the strenuous efforts now being made by the government to redirect the flow of political debate back onto domestic issues, this was accompanied by an attempt to rebrand the Iraqi conflict as a fight for freedom and democracy, and by an ongoing insistence on the advantages of strong and decisive leadership. Despite the fact that New Labour secured a third consecutive majority in the general election of May 2005, albeit with the support of little more than a fifth of the British electorate, these themes have also defined their response to the emergent terrorist crisis. While most people in Britain believed the London bombings of 7 July to have been linked to the country's participation in the Iraq war, the government has pointedly rejected any such claim. Focusing instead on the role of extreme Islamic ideology, the officially sanctioned solution to the crisis has posed yet another threat to British democracy by calling for a dose of still more resolute and hard-line executive action.

Whither British democracy?

The central argument of this book, then, is that the centralised, hierarchical, and elitist underpinnings of the British political system provided the strategic terrain in which the Iraq policy was both developed and implemented by senior figures within the New Labour executive. This analysis provides a contrasting interpretation of Britain's involvement in the Iraq war in two key ways. The first of these concerns the underlying reasons behind the conflict itself. Based largely on the interaction of agential and contingent factors, many accounts of the war have sought to portray the New Labour executive, and Tony Blair in particular, either as having acted as poodle-like sycophants to the United States, or as having been driven by genuinely and sincerely held concerns about the need to address the issues of WMD, rogue states, and global terrorism. Instead, the analysis presented here contends that the desire to pursue regime change in Iraq was present within the New Labour government prior to the emergence of the Bush regime, and that the motivations informing this were bound up with a desire to enhance and project British power and influence as a means of moulding the global political economy.

In terms of British democracy, this analysis is also somewhat different. While to many observers the events surrounding Britain's participation in the Iraq war are seen to provide a veritable catalogue of flaws and discrepancies that highlight the failings of the British democratic system, the argument presented here is that such events are a demonstration not so much of the weakness of British democracy as of the enduring success and resilience of its underlying structural and ideational foundations. In other words, the key feature of the Iraq episode is not so much that it reveals the failure of British democracy, as that it signifies the triumph of its essentially undemocratic underlying norms and values. While to some extent these represent two sides of the same coin, the difference is more than a case of mere semantics and raises fundamental questions about the nature of any democratisation strategy. Following the standard line of argument, the reinvigoration of British democracy is seen to require a programme of reform designed to address and eradicate its institutional defects, and typically based around the adoption of a codified constitution, a Bill of Rights, the provision of greater powers for Parliament, and the establishment of a more meaningful system of checks and balances on the use of executive power. These include more substantive freedom of information, a more rigorous and formalised relationship between the political and the intelligence spheres of the British state, a strengthening of the select com-mittee system, the abolition or at least the dilution of the prerogative powers, and a civil-service act designed to formalise relations between ministers, civil servants, and special advisors. A process of electoral reform also features highly on the list of recommendations in order to replace the anachronistic and disturbing system of first-past-the-post for Westminster elections with some form of proportional representation.

However, while such reforms would undoubtedly enhance Britain's democratic credentials, a central problem of such an analysis is that it remains highly unlikely that such a programme would of itself prove to be sufficient to alter the underlying selective bias of the British political system towards the principles of centralised, hierarchical, and elitist governance. There is, in short, no guarantee whatsoever that the introduc-tion of these various changes would address the ideational forces that lie deeply embedded within its institutions and processes. Merely establishing a codified constitution, for example, would not of itself produce a more responsive and participatory form of government (as is well demonstrated by the politics of the United States), and nor would the introduction of proportional representation have produced an alternative course of events over Iraq, given that both the Labour and the Conservative parties were strongly in favour of going to war. Nor too would the introduction of increased parliamentary powers or a strengthening of the select committee system have been likely to alter the eventual outcome given the political corset of internal party discipline, and hence the need for a strong and centralised structure of command.

Given these limitations, two possible outcomes thus present themselves. The first of these is a perceptibly bleak vision of Britain's democratic future in which any attempts at political reform are resisted and curtailed, resulting in superficial modifications at the expense of meaningful change, and thereby enabling the continuation of executive dominance. Yet while this may well be the path that is most likely to be taken given the deeply embedded constraints imposed by Britain's institutional structures and processes, given the absence of any widespread discrediting of the political system (despite all the controversy generated by the Iraq affair), and given the lack of widespread, sustained, and organised pressure for wholesale change (pressure most certainly absent from within the political establish-ment itself), the potential for a successful transformation of Britain's constitutional arrangements cannot be completely foreclosed. As such, a second and more positive vision of Britain's democratic future based on the emergence of a more participatory, representative, and responsive form of governance remains at stake.

Whatever form this might take, however, its realisation will require a broadening of the reform agenda itself to include a wider confrontation at the level of the ideational as well as the institutional. Put simply, a process of reform which does not seek to address the underlying norms and values of Britain's political system, and which thereby ignores, and hence retains, its 'Burkean gap' between the electors and the elected, cannot hope to supplant the enduring model of strong executive decision-making with one based on a more inclusive and progressive modality. To reformulate the problem, then, the challenge for reformers, given the firmly ingrained selective bias of the political system and the unlikelihood of any radical change in the near future, is one of how to dissolve this deep-rooted structural context from within the confines of the structural context itself.

This difficulty may appear to be insurmountable, and the key to overcoming it will only be found in a campaign of sustained pressure on all points of Britain's core political life. This would require a programme of reforms such as those outlined earlier, coupled with more thorough-going measures designed to tackle the stultifying edifice of the party system, to dislodge the dominant notion of representation and to replace it with one based on a more delegatory conception. Such measures might include the use of secret voting for MPs, more frequent general elections (involving staggered elections for a second chamber), the resolution of specific issues by national referenda (incorporating advances in communications technology for speed and accessibility), and the introduction of mechanisms by which the general public could themselves act to remove representatives from office between elections on the grounds of poor performance. In other words, a key part of the democratisation agenda will require a concerted effort to promote the view that representatives are not elected to act as they see fit and are not in place to blindly accept diktats from a party machine, but, rather, are returned to office in order to represent and implement the views and wishes of the people themselves. In this way, although the size of the task should not be underestimated, it is nonetheless possible that such a broad-based process of reform could gradually loosen and dislodge any systemic resistance from the executive, progressively force a more consensual style of politics, reconfigure the selective bias of the system itself, and thus build up a slow but sustained momentum towards creating a form of political behaviour that is more responsive to the popular will than that which currently prevails. While to some all of

184

this may well appear to be fanciful, the question of which form British democracy will take over the course of the next century is one that will have serious ramifications both within and beyond the domestic political realm. As the events surrounding Britain's participation in the Iraq war have made abundantly clear, the consequences of any failure to reform are potentially grave. They should be apparent to us all.

Notes

Chapter 1. Introduction: A Sign of the Times

1 See www.costofwar.com
2 See R. Stein, '100,000 civilian deaths estimated in Iraq', *Washington Post*, 29/10/04; D. Cortright, 'Iraq: the human toll', *Nation*, 24/7/05; also see www.Iraqbodycount.net
3 See for example Cook (2004); Galloway (2004); Rangwala and Plesch (2004); Short (2004); Sands (2005).
4 See Ramesh (2003); Stothard (2003); Bluth (2004); Coates and Krieger (2004); Kampfner (2004); Naughtie (2004); Riddell (2004); Stephens (2004); Tyrie (2004); Woodward (2004); Doig (2005); Glees (2005); Hoggett (2005); Seldon (2005).
5 For the analogy of a 'barium meal' see Weir and Beetham (2003).

Chapter 2. The Democratic Consequences of New Labour

1 Examples from within the voluminous literature include James (1992); Judge (1993); Blackburn (1995); Barberis (1996); Pilkington (1999); Hennessy (2000, 2005); Webb (2000); Rogers and Walters (2004).
2 For holistic analyses, see, for example, Birch (1979); Beer (1982); Dearlove and Saunders (2000); Kavanagh (2000); Wright (2000); Budge *et al.* (2001); Kingdom (2001); Weir and Beetham (2002).
3 On institutional analyses, see Hall and Taylor (1996); on the notion of strategic selectivity, see Hay (1996) and Kerr (2001).
4 On the notion of Britain's political tradition, see Marsh and Tant (1989); Tant (1993).
5 On the historical origins of the British political system, see Tant (1993), Chapters 2–3.
6 For some of the chief proponents of this view see MacKenzie (1955); Birch (1979); Beer (1982); Rose (1985).
7 Figures calculated from Leonard and Mortimore (2004), Table 2.1, and Appendix 1.
8 On the notion of governing strategies, see Bulpitt (1983), Chapters 2–4; Bulpitt and Burnham (1999); Buller (1999, 2000); Kettell (2004), pp.24–6.

9   On the emergence of New Labour, also see Hay (1997); Gould (1999); Coates (2000, 2005); on New Labour in government, see, for example, Brivati and Bale (1998); Driver and Martell (1998); Coates and Lawler (2000); Ludlam and Smith (2001); Rawnsley (2001); Bevir (2005).

10 On the politics of depoliticisation, see Burnham (2001); Kettell (2004).

11 On New Labour's media management, see Jones (2002); Oborne and Walters (2004).

12 Byrne and Weir (2004), pp.458–9; Jones (2004), Chapter 3; Oborne and Walters (2004), pp.289–91.

13 So called after the now-defunct Islington restaurant at which the deal is alleged to have been made. See Peston (2005), pp.60–68.

14 On Blair's predominance as Prime Minister see Heffernan (2003).

15 Jones (2004), Chapter 2; Oborne and Walters (2004), pp.168–9.

16 Mandelson and Liddle (1996), pp.232–6.

17 On these issues, also see Weir and Beetham (2002); Judge (2004); Maer and Sandford (2004); also see Democratic Audit (www.democraticaudit.co.uk); Campaign for Freedom of Information (www.cfoi.org.uk); Charter 88 (charter88.org.uk); Constitution Unit, School of Public Policy, UCL (www.ucl.ac.uk/constitution-unit); Liberty (www.liberty-human-rights.org.uk).

18 See Ignatieff (2003), Chapter 5; also see Kagan (2003), pp.26–7; Shawcross (2004), pp.15–18.

19 On new imperialism, see Harvey (2003); Ignatieff (2003); Wade (2003); Cox (2004).

20 On these issues see the World Development Movement (www.wdm.org.uk).

21 See Lawler (2000); Rawnsley (2001), Chapter 10; Curtis (2003).

22 See Export Credit Agency Watch (www.eca-watch.org) and Campaign Against the Arms Trade (www.caat.org.uk); also see Chalmers *et al.* (2001).

23 See Curtis (2003), pp.102–9; Coates and Krieger (2004), pp.82–3.

Chapter 3: Iraqnophobia

1   See 'The Guidelines: Summary of the Contemporary Documentation', 15/2/96 and 'Government Policy on the Control of Exports to Iran and Iraq 1980–1990', 15/2/96, Federation of American Scientists (www.fas.org/news/uk/scott); also see Curtis (2003), pp.33–8.

2   'The Guidelines...', 15/2/96.

3   On the Scott inquiry, see *Report of the Inquiry into the Export of Defence Equipment and Dual-Use Goods to Iraq and Related Prosecutions*, HC 115, 1996; also see Barker (1997); Norton-Taylor (1995); Phythian (2005), pp.124–5; 'The Scott Report' (www.fas.org/news/uk/scott); A. Puddephatt, 'The Scott report and ministerial responsibility', Violations of Rights in Britain series 3(31), Charter 88.

4   Simpson (2003), pp.210–13.

5   The full title of UNSCOM was the United Nations Special Commission to Oversee the Destruction of Iraq's Weapons of Mass Destruction.

6   The oil-for-food programme was further reformed in December 1999 under UN

Resolution 1284. See Galloway (2004), Chapter 6.

7 Blix (2004), pp.29-30; Rangwala and Plesch (2004), p.27.
8 Tony Blair speech at the Lord Mayor's Banquet, 10/11/97.
9 Ibid.
10 *Review of Intelligence on Weapons of Mass Destruction*, HC 898 (hereafter, 'Butler Report', 2004), section 5.2; *Report on the U.S. Intelligence Community's Prewar Intelligence Assessments on Iraq*, United States Select Committee on Intelligence (hereafter, 'SCI report', 2004), pp.386–8.
11 A. Rawnsley, 'Why war stirs the blood of Tony Blair', *Observer*, 8/9/02.
12 Tony Blair statement in the House of Commons, 24/2/98.
13 The Defence and Overseas Policy Committee was chaired by the Prime Minister and was attended by the Chancellor, the Foreign Secretary, and the Secretaries of State for Defence, Trade and Industry, and Development. The Chief of the Defence Staff, the heads of the intelligence agencies, and other senior advisors were also present.
14 Remarks by Tony Blair during debate in the House of Commons, 17/12/98.
15 R. Whitaker, 'The leaked Foreign Office paper that proves Blair saw caveats a year before the war', *Independent on Sunday*, 1/5/05; Stephens (2004), pp.212, 218–19.
16 SCI report (2004), pp.195–7; Bill Clinton interview, *Breakfast with Frost*, 18/7/04 (BBC1); also see *Iraq: The Debate and Policy Options*, P. Bowers, House of Commons Library Research Paper 02/53 (September 2002).
17 M. Tempest, 'Blair "used intelligence as PR tool"', *Guardian*, 28/10/04.
18 On the Kosovo conflict, see Rawnsley (2001), Chapter 14; Kampfner (2004), Chapter 3; Stephens (2004), Chapter 9; Seldon (2005), Chapter 27.
19 G. Monbiot, 'New findings reveal that NATO's intervention in Kosovo paved the way for a Trans-Balkan pipeline', *Guardian*, 15/2/01; also see R. Harvey (2003), pp.118–19.
20 See Vickers (2000).
21 'Campbell attacks media over Kosovo', *Independent*, 10/7/99; A. Thompson, 'Truth and lies', *Guardian*, 12/7/99; E. Stourton, 'How the Kosovo war was won', *Sunday Telegraph*, 17/10/99.
22 By the end of April, nearly three-quarters of the British electorate professed to be in favour of the military action.
23 'Doctrine of International Community', Tony Blair speech at the Economic Club, Chicago, 24/4/99.
24 Joint memo by Foreign and Defence Secretaries to Cabinet Ministerial Committee on Defence and Overseas Policy, May 1999, cited in the Butler Report (2004), paras.213–17; on the government's assessment of the Iraqi threat to global stability, also see Bluth (2004).
25 'What Did the Leaked Memo Say?', BBC News, 19/7/00.
26 Tony Blair memo to Philip Gould, 29/4/00.
27 On Britain's involvement in Sierra Leone, see Kampfner (2004), p.76; Short (2004), pp.99–102; Stephens (2004), pp.233–5.
28 Leonard and Mortimore (2005), Appendix 1.
29 See Beckett and Hencke (2004), pp.282–3; Stephens (2004), pp.154–5; Peston

(2005), pp.329–31.

30 Cirincione (2003).

31 Open letter to President Clinton on Iraq, 26/1/98; also see ibid.

32 *Rebuilding America's Defenses: Strategy, Focus and Resources for a New Century*, Project for a New American Century, September 2000.

33 See Kampfner (2004), pp.90–7; Riddell (2004), pp.136–8.

34 See Harvey (2003).

35 Joint press conference at Camp David, 23/2/01.

36 Butler Report (2004), paras. 218–58.

37 SCI report (2004), pp.144–5; Woodward (2004), p.194.

38 Clarke (2004), pp.30–2; Ramesh (2004), p.18; Woodward (2004), pp.24–6.

39 'Grasping the Opportunities of an Open World', Tony Blair speech at the Lord Mayor's Banquet, Mansion House, 12/11/01.

40 Tony Blair speech at the Labour party conference, 2/10/01.

41 Tony Blair interview, *Observer*, 14/10/01.

42 'Grasping the Opportunities of an Open World', 12/11/01.

43 Tony Blair interview, *Observer*, 14/10/01.

44 Naughtie (2004), p.4.

45 See Clarke (2004), p.265.

46 George Bush speech to the UN General Assembly, 12/9/02; and at the Hilton Hotel, Washington, DC, 26/2/03.

47 Woodward (2002), p.83.

48 Woodward (2004), pp.26–7.

Chapter 4. The March to War

1 Kampfner (2004), pp.119–21, 157; Seldon (2005), p.499.

2 Evidence by Tony Blair to the House of Commons Liaison Committee (hereafter 'HCLC evidence'), 16/7/02, Q.103.

3 See 'Commentary on the Anti-Terrorism, Crime and Security Bill 2001', *Human Rights Watch*, 16/11/01.

4 *Responsibility for the Terrorist Atrocities in the United States*, Office of the Prime Minister, 4/10/01.

5 See Beckett and Hencke (2004), pp.306–8; Oborne and Walters (2004), pp.279–81.

6 From December 1999 the United Nations Monitoring, Verification and Inspections Commission (UNMOVIC) was established to replace UNSCOM under the terms of resolution 1284.

7 Blix (2004), p.58; Woodward (2004), pp.1–3, chapters 3–9.

8 SCI report (2004), p.453; R. Watson, 'Bush dealt triple whammy on Iraq policy', the *Times*, 6/10/04.

9 Coates and Krieger (2004), pp.26–30, 164 (n. 3); SCI report (2004), p.453.

10 Colin Powell press conference, Cairo, 24/2/01, and testimony to the Foreign Operations, Export Financing and Related Programs Subcommittee of the Senate Appropriations Committee, 15/5/01.

11 George W. Bush State of the Union Address, 29/1/02.

12 Butler Report (2004), para.481.

13 See ibid., sections 5.3, 5.4, and Annex B; also see *Iraqi Weapons of Mass Destruction: Intelligence and Assessments*, Intelligence and Security Committee, Cm.5972 (hereafter 'ISC report', 2003), paras.58–63.

14 'Iraq: Options Paper', Overseas and Defence Secretariat, Cabinet Office, 8/3/02.

15 'Iraq: Legal Background', Foreign and Commonwealth Office briefing paper, 8/3/02.

16 'Iraq: Options Paper', 8/3/02.

17 Tony Blair press conference, 11/3/02.

18 Memo from Manning to Blair, 14/3/02.

19 Memo from Meyer to Manning, 18/3/02.

20 Memo from Ricketts to Straw, 22/3/02.

21 Memo from Straw to Blair, 25/3/02.

22 'Iraq: Conditions for Military Action', Cabinet Office briefing paper (July 2002); reproduced in the *Sunday Times*, 12/6/05.

23 Joint press conference by George Bush and Tony Blair, 6/4/02.

24 On the self-deception of the Blair court, see Hoggett (2005).

25 Tony Blair statement to the House of Commons, 10/4/02; joint press conference with Dick Cheney, 11/3/02; interview with NBC, 4/4/02.

26 Tony Blair speech at the George Bush Snr. Presidential Library, 7/4/02.

27 Tony Blair interview, *Newsnight*. BBC2, 15/5/02.

28 Short (2004), p.150; Evidence to the Foreign Affairs Committee (hereafter 'FAC evidence'), by Robin Cook, 17/6/03; Qs.57–8, the Hutton Inquiry (hereafter THI): FAC2/1–50.

29 FAC evidence (Short), 17/6/03; THI:FAC2/1-50.

30 The key officials at the meetings were Blair, Campbell, Straw, Hoon, Powell, Manning, Scarlett, Dearlove, Admiral Sir Michael Boyce (the Chief of Defence Staff), and Sally Morgan.

31 Butler Report (2004), paras.607–8.

32 Evidence to the Public Administration Committee (hereafter 'PAC evidence'), by Sir Andrew Turnbull, 4/3/04. Q.38.

33 FAC evidence (Cook), 17/6/03, Q.39.

34 Cook (2004), pp.115–16; Short (2004), pp.142–51, 247.

35 Private information.

36 HCLC evidence (Blair), 16/7/02, Q.9; interview with Jeremy Paxman, BBC 1, 20/4/05.

37 FAC evidence (Straw), 24/6/03, Qs.812–13, THI:FAC2/208–248; 25/6/03, Qs.1043, 1117, THI:FAC1/326–349.

38 Kagan (2003), p.35 (n.23).

39 J. Hardy, 'Blair in the doghouse', *Daily Mirror*, 3/7/02.

40 See Stothard (2003), p.87.

41 HCLC evidence (Blair), 16/7/02, Qs.1–7.

42 Ibid., Qs.89–93; Naughtie (2004), p.125.

43 Cook (2004), p.135.

44 Sands (2005), pp.183–4.

45 'Iraq: Conditions for Military Action', Cabinet Office briefing paper, reproduced in *Sunday Times*, 12/6/05.

46 Memo from Matthew Rycroft to Manning, published in *Sunday Times*, 1/5/05.

47 Ibid.; British and US attacks in the Iraqi no-fly-zones were now also intensified, reaching their highest levels for more than two years. See M. Smith, 'RAF bombing raids tried to goad Saddam into war', *Sunday Times*, 29/5/05; and Curtis (2003), pp.25–6.

48 On this see ISC report (2003), paras 68–78.

49 Remarks to the FAC by Ricketts, 24/6/03, THI:FAC2/208–248, Q.742; oral evidence given to the Hutton Inquiry (hereafter 'THI evidence') by Alastair Campbell, 19/8/03, para.88; by Scarlett, 26/8/03, para.33; and by Blair, 28/8/03, paras.1–2.

50 THI evidence (Blair) 28/8/03, paras.1–2, 9, 17; Butler Report (2004), para.316.

51 Tony Blair news conference, 3/9/02.

52 THI evidence (Campbell), 19/8/03, paras.10, 123; (Scarlett), 26/8/03, paras.38–42; S. Powell to J. Powell, 5/9/02, THI:CAB11/17; Campbell to Scarlett, 9/9/02, THI:CAB6/2–4; the draft dossier as it presently stood was entitled: 'Iraqi chemical, biological and nuclear programmes—the current threat'. THI:CAB23/5–14.

53 'Government Briefing Papers on Iraq', 20/6/02, THI:CAB23/16–67; JIC extracts, THI:CAB17/2–5; Butler Report (2004), paras.289–307 and Annex B.

54 ISC report (2003), paras.49–57; Butler Report (2004), section 6.5; JIC papers, THI:CAB17/2–5; THI evidence (Dearlove), 15/9/03.

55 'Iraqi use of chemical and biological weapons—possible scenarios', JIC assessment, 9/9/02; extracts from the Butler Report, Annex B.

56 Tony Blair speech to TUC conference, 10/9/02.

57 Draft dossier, 10–11/9/02. THI:DOS2/2–57.

58 Bassett to Smith, Pruce, and Campbell, 11/9/02, THI:CAB11/23-26; Smith to Pruce and Campbell, 11/9/02, THI:CAB11/23–24; Kelly to Campbell 11/9/02, THI:CAB11/27.

59 Pruce to MM, 10/9/02, THI:CAB11/21; Pruce to Campbell, 11/9/02, THI:CAB11/25-26.

60 Sedwill to Charles Gray, 11/9/02, THI:CAB11/30–31; and to various, 11/9/02, THI:CAB11/34; Campbell to Scarlett, 9/9/02, THI:CAB6/2–4; THI evidence (Campbell) 19/8/03; (Scarlett) 26/8/03, paras.52–5.

61 ISC report (2003), paras.73–5; anonymous e-mail, 11/9/03, THI:CAB23/15; Morrison in 'A failure of intelligence', *Panorama*, BBC1, 11/7/04; David Kelly conversation with Susan Watts, 30/5/03, THI:BBC1/58–63.

62 'Iraq's Programme for Weapons of Mass Destruction', draft dossier 16/9/02, pp.13ff; THI:CAB11/56–58 and THI:DOS2/58–106.

63 THI evidence (Dearlove), 15/9/03; David Kelly conversation with Susan Watts, 30/5/03, THI:BBC1/58–63.

64 'Note on Iraq Dossier' (unnamed), 20/9/02. THI:CAB33/114–115; untitled and unsigned document, 19/9/02, THI:MOD22/1–2; 'Iraqi WMD Dossier—Comments on Revised Draft (15 Sept 2002)', untitled document, 17/9/02; 'Interview with Bryan Jones', *Independent*, 4/2/04; P. Waugh, 'Jones breaks cover

again : Blair raised "false expectations"', *Independent*, 10/2/04; *Panorama*, BBC1, 11/7/04.

65 THI evidence (Hoon), 22/9/03, paras.1–3, 85, 89; (Scarlett), 26/8/03, paras.60–1, 66, 77–8, 89–90; Blair in House of Commons debate on the Hutton Report, 4/2/04.

66 *Panorama*, BBC1, 11/7/04; interview with Bryan Jones, *Independent*, 4/2/04; B. Russell, 'Intelligence expert says Scarlett's MI6 appointment raises "issue of credibility"', *Independent*, 21/7/04.

67 Powell to Scarlett, 17/9/02, THI:CAB11/69; Powell to Campbell and Manning, 17/9/02, THI:CAB11/53; Powell to Campbell and Scarlett, 18/9/02, THI:CAB11/77.

68 Campbell to Scarlett, 17/9/02, THI:CAB11/66–68.

69 THI evidence (Campbell), 19/8/03; (Scarlett), 26/8/03, paras.75, 82–4.

70 Scarlett to Campbell, 18/9/02, THI:CAB11/70–71; and 19/9/02, THI:CAB23/1; 'Iraq's programme for weapons of mass destruction', draft dossier 19/9/02, THI:CAB3/22–78.

71 Powell to Campbell and Scarlett, 19/9/02, THI:CAB11/103; ISC report (2003), paras.76–8; 'Iraq's Weapons of Mass Destruction', final draft dossier, 20/9/02, THI:CAB33/56–113.

72 *Iraq's Weapons of Mass Destruction: The Assessment of the British Government*, 24/9/02.

73 Weir and Beetham (2003).

74 Tony Blair statement to House of Commons, 24/9/02.

75 Butler Report (2004), paras.573–8.

76 See Rangwala and Plesch (2004), pp.27–9.

77 N. Rufford and N. Fielding, 'Tracked down: the man who fooled the world—and was duped himself', *Sunday Times*, 1/8/04.

78 N. Watt, 'Weapons claim: the dossier, the PM, and the headlines', *Guardian*, 6/2/04.

79 *The Decision to go to War in Iraq*, Foreign Affairs Select Committee, Ninth Report of Session 2002–03, HC 813 (hereafter 'FAC report', 2003), paras.61–71; ISC report (2003), paras.84–6; THI evidence (Campbell), 19/8/03, paras.62–4; (Hoon), 22/9/03, paras.80–1; (Dearlove), 15/9/03; (Scarlett), 26/8/03, para.144; FAC evidence (Cook), 17/6/03, THI:FAC2/1–50; evidence to the Intelligence and Security Committee (hereafter, 'ISC evidence'), by Alastair Campbell, 17/7/03, THI:ISC1/36–47; R. Norton–Taylor and P. Wintour, 'Hoon dismissed 45–minute claim as insignificant', *Guardian*, 6/2/04.

80 ISC report (2003), para.iii.

81 Butler Report (2004), paras.327, 331, 466.

82 *Report of the Inquiry into the Circumstances Surrounding the Death of Dr David Kelly*, Lord Hutton, January 2004, HC.247 (hereafter 'Hutton Report'), para.228; THI evidence (Scarlett), 26/8/03, para.91.

Chapter 5. Engulfed

1 THI evidence (Campbell), 19/8/03, para.63; G. Jones, A. Sparrow, and R. Sylvester, 'Iraq dossier "has failed to convince the public"', *Daily Telegraph*, 26/9/02.

2 Tony Blair speech at Labour party conference, 2/10/02.

3 In contrast to the British dossier, however, the US version was never published. See SCI report (2004), pp.146, 286–97.

4 BBC News, 30/5/03.

5 George W. Bush speech to the UN General Assembly, 12/9/02.

6 Coates and Krieger (2004), pp.31–5; SCI report (2004), pp.453–4; Woodward (2004), pp.164–9, 188–90; J. Bookman, 'The President's real goal in Iraq', *Atlanta Journal Constitution*, 29/9/02; *The National Security Strategy of the United States of America*, September 2002; speech by George W. Bush, 17/9/02.

7 On the negotiations behind Resolution 1441, see Coates and Krieger (2004), pp.37–42; Kampfner (2004), pp.215–20, 301–2; Naughtie (2004), pp.142–7; Woodward (2004), Chapter 21.

8 Tony Blair press conference, 13/1/03.

9 S. Ritter, 'The inspections process was rigged...', *Independent on Sunday*, 10/10/04.

10 Statement by Jack Straw in the House of Commons, 25/11/02.

11 *Saddam Hussein: Crimes and Human Rights Abuses*, Foreign and Commonwealth Office, 2/12/02; E. MacAskill and N. Watt, 'Anger over Straw's dossier on Iraqi human rights', *Guardian*, 3/12/02.

12 Blix (2004), p.86.

13 Naughtie (2004), pp.148–9; Riddell (2004), p.241; satisfaction ratings from www.MORI.com

14 Tony Blair speech at the Foreign Office conference, 7/1/03.

15 Blix (2004), pp.117–20, 138–41.

16 Coates and Krieger (2004), p.39; SCI report (2004), pp.461–4; Woodward (2004), pp.253–75, 294–6; C. Rice, 'Why we know Iraq is lying', *New York Times*, 23/1/03.

17 Tony Blair press conference, 13/1/03.

18 FAC evidence (Campbell), 25/6/03, Q.930.

19 'Iraq—Its Infrastructure of Concealment, Deception, and Intimidation', February 2003.

20 See al–Marashi (2002).

21 See FAC report (2003), pp.35–40; memo to the ISC from Dr Glen Rangwala, 16/6/03, THI:FAC3/178–183; FAC evidence (Campbell), 25/6/03, Q.1013; Oborne and Walters (2004), pp.322–7.

22 FAC evidence (Cook), 17/6/03, Q.10; (Straw), 24/6/03, Q.818; R. Norton-Taylor and M. White, 'Blunkett admits weapons error', *Guardian*, 9/6/03.

23 FAC report (2003), paras.108–139; ISC report (2003), paras.8, 129–35.

24 YouGov poll for Blakeway productions and Channel 4 News, 7–10/2/03; 'Polls find Europeans oppose Iraq war', BBC News, 11/2/03; M. Easton, 'The propaganda war', Channel 4 News, 11/2/03.

25 HCLC evidence (Blair), 8/7/03, Qs.154, 185.

26 Ramesh (2003), pp.31–4; Blix (2004), pp.129–31, 147; Woodward (2004), Chapter 28.

27 'US plan to bug Security Council', *Observer*, 2/3/03; N. Cohen, 'I had no choice, says GCHQ whistleblower', *Observer*, 29/2/04; M. Bright *et al.*, 'Whistleblower', *Observer*, 29/2/04.

28 Speech by Colin Powell to the UN General Assembly, 5/2/03.

29 Statement by Jack Straw to the UN General Assembly, 5/2/03; statement to the House of Commons, 10/3/03.

30 T. Mangold, 'How Straw deceived the UN, but was Blair in on it too?', *Mail on Sunday*, 1/2/04; Blix (2004), pp.198–203; also see Rangwala and Plesch (2004), pp.17–24.

31 'Iraq: a challenge we must confront', speech by Jack Straw to the International Institute of Strategic Studies, 11/2/03.

32 Blix (2004), pp.152–6; Coates and Krieger (2004), p.40; Kampfner (2004), pp.271–2; SCI report (2004), pp.242, 253.

33 Blix (2004), pp.178ff; 'Unresolved Disarmament Issues: Iraq's Proscribed Weapons Programmes', UNMOVIC, 6/3/03.

34 'Blix accuses coalition over Iraq weapons', BBC News, 6/6/03; Blix (2004), p.156.

35 Hans Blix interview on *HardTalk*, BBC News 24, 15/7/04; Cook (2004), p.299; Short (2004), pp.168–9; private information.

36 ISC report (2003), paras.125–8.

37 Butler Report (2004), paras.362–4.

38 'Battle of the rival texts', *Guardian* 25/2/03.

39 'Polls find Europeans oppose Iraq war', BBC News, 11/2/03.

40 Kampfner (2004), pp.278–9; Naughtie (2004), p.151; Woodward (2004), pp.337–8.

41 Stothard (2003), p.42.

42 FAC evidence (Campbell), 25/6/03, Q.956; Stothard (2003), pp.5–11.

43 Kampfner (2004), pp.268, 273.

44 Tony Blair statement to the House of Commons, 25/2/03; Riddell (2004), pp.246–7.

45 Ramesh (2003), pp.74–5.

46 Tony Blair press conferences, 19/2/03, 25/3/03.

47 Ramesh (2003), pp.37–8; Riddell (2004), pp.252–3; Stephens (2004), pp.319–20.

48 A request to see the relevant instructions under the Freedom of Information Act elicited the response that 'the Prime Minister's office does not hold any information in relation to this request'. See M. Woolf, 'Was PM trying to cover up his requests to Goldsmith?', *Independent*, 27/4/05.

49 This and the following quotations are from 'Memo from the Attorney-General to the Prime Minister', 7/3/03.

50 R. Whitaker, 'The A4 war: What had the Attorney General and the Prime Minister got to hide?', *Independent*, 13/3/05; A. Barnett and M. Bright, 'British military chief reveals new legal fears over Iraq war', *Observer*, 1/5/05.

51 R. Norton–Taylor, 'Revealed—the rush to war', *Guardian*, 23/2/05.
52 See Short (2004), p.227.
53 See Ramesh (2003), pp.39–41; Cook (2004), p.320; Riddell (2004), pp.250–1; Short (2004), pp.224–32; J. Kampfner, 'The five deceptions of Tony Blair', *Guardian*, 20/10/04.
54 Blix (2004), Chapter 8, pp.243–8; Woodward (2004), Chapters 31–2.
55 Butler Report (2004), paras.379, 383–6; Short (2004), pp.254–5.
56 Sands (2005), p.198.
57 Butler Report (2004), para.386.
58 Short (2004), p.185.
59 Riddell (2004), pp.259–60; Sands (2005), pp.188–93.
60 E. MacAskill and J. Borger, 'Iraq war was illegal and breached UN Charter, says Annan', *Guardian*, 16/9/04.
61 V. Dodd, 'Iraq war illegal, says FO adviser who quit', *Guardian*, 14/6/04.
62 Stothard (2003), pp.46–50; Kampfner (2004), pp.295–7.
63 On the Azores summit see Stothard (2003), pp.45, 66–70; Riddell (2004), pp.254–5; Woodward (2004), pp.357–60.
64 See Cook (2004), pp.321–2 and Appendix; Stothard (2003), pp.84–5.
65 Short (2004), Chapter 5.
66 Ramesh (2003), pp.43–55; Kampfner (2004), pp.306–9; Short (2004), pp.187–91.
67 Private information.
68 Cook (2004), pp.203–4, 312.
69 Tony Blair speech to the House of Commons, 18/3/03.
70 Byrne and Weir (2004), p.455.
71 *Government Response to the Public Administrations Select Committee's Fourth Report of the 2003–4 Session*, July 2004; also see P. Bowers, *Parliament and the Use of Force*, House of Commons Library, 2003.

Chapter 6. Whiter than White

1 Kampfner (2004), pp.322–3; Woodward (2004), pp.403–5.
2 Statement to the nation by Tony Blair, 21/3/03; monthly press conference, 26/3/03; on the war aims of the coalition, also see the Butler Report (2004), Annex C.
3 Ramesh (2003), pp.77–8; Kampfner (2004), p.315.
4 See Stothard (2003), pp.102–3, 132–6, 178–9.
5 Kampfner (2004), pp.313–14.
6 See Ramesh (2003), pp.89–90; Stothard (2003), pp.139, 157, 214–15; Kampfner (2004), pp.313–14.
7 Dyke (2004), pp.253–5; also see *Sunday Times*, 1/2/04.
8 See Beckett and Hencke (2004), pp.308–10.
9 Tony Blair monthly press conference, 26/3/03.
10 Ibid.
11 Kampfner (2004), pp.316–18.

12 Ibid.; Riddell (2004), p.266; Short (2004), pp.197–8.

13 Opinion poll results from MORI; Coates and Krieger (2004), pp.3, 164 (n.52).

14 On these issues see Chatterjee (2004).

15 Cook (2004), pp.332–5; Kampfner (2004), pp.323–6; Shawcross (2004), pp.178–9.

16 Short (2004), pp.216–22.

17 Kampfner (2004), pp.337–8.

18 Andrew Gilligan, 6:07 broadcast for *Today* (BBC Radio 4), 29/5/03, THI:CAB1/144–147.

19 A. Gilligan, 'I asked my intelligence source why Blair misled us all...', *Mail on Sunday*, 1/6/03.

20 PAC evidence (Turnbull), 4/3/04, Q.52.

21 FAC report (2003), paras.1–7.

22 See, for example, comments made by Tony Blair on Sky News, 1/6/03; and at a press conference in Warsaw, 30/5/03, THI:CAB1/158–159.

23 FAC evidence (Gilligan), 17/7/03, THI:FAC5/2–55, Q.259.

24 Kelly conversation with Susan Watts, 30/5/03, THI:BBC1/58–63.

25 THI evidence (Blair), 28/8/03, para.21.

26 Shevas to M. Damazer, 29/5/03, THI:CAB1/154–155; also see Dyke (2004), pp.263–6.

27 THI evidence (Campbell), 19/8/03; Campbell to Sambrook, 6/6/03, THI:CAB1/244–7; 12/6/03, THI:CAB250–2; Oborne and Walters (2003), pp.331–2, 371 (n.7); Dyke (2004), pp.264–8.

28 THI evidence (Scarlett), 26/8/03, paras.97–8.

29 FAC report (2003), Appendix 1; Rangwala and Plesch (2004), pp.25–6; Tony Blair press conference, 2/6/03.

30 See ISC report (2003), p.iii; THI evidence (Blair), 28/8/03, paras.22–3.

31 Remarks by Tony Blair to the House of Commons, 18/6/03; also see THI evidence (Campbell), 19/8/03, paras.113–114.

32 FAC report (2003), para.6; HCLC evidence (Blair), 8/7/03, Q.183.

33 THI evidence (Omand), 26/8/03, para.171; (Scarlett), 26/8/03, paras.105–8; FAC evidence (Straw), 27/6/03, Q.1193.

34 FAC evidence (Cook), 17/6/03, Q.6, THI:FAC2/1–50.

35 FAC evidence (Short), 17/6/03, Q.145, THI:FAC2/1–50.

36 THI evidence (Smith), 20/8/03, para.144; (Tebbit), 20/8/03, paras.15–17; (Campbell), 19/8/03, paras.133–4; 26/9/03, para.92.

37 THI evidence (Campbell), 19/8/03, paras.110–112; (Blair), 28/8/03, para.38.

38 FAC evidence (Straw), 24/6/03, THI:FAC2/208–248. Qs.735, 738.

39 FAC evidence (Campbell), 25/6/03, THI:FAC2/260–325. Qs.1057, 1095, 1131.

40 THI evidence (Campbell), 19/8/03, paras.116–121; 26/8/03, para.118.

41 Campbell to Sambrook, 27/6/03, THI:CAB1/352–4; 29/6/03, THI:CAB1/373.

42 Sambrook on the *Today* programme, 26/6/03, THI:CAB1/335–340.

43 Transcript available at THI:CAB1/368–372; THI evidence (Campbell), 19/8/03, para 126.

44 'Notes of a Meeting...', 4/7/03, THI:MOD1/30–33.

45 Extract from Campbell's diary, 4/7/03, THI:CAB39/1–2.

46 THI evidence (Hoon), 22/9/03, paras.62, 102–4; 27/8/03, paras.79–80.

47 THI evidence (Hoon), 27/8/03, paras.30–5.

48 THI evidence (Hatfield), 17/9/03, para.209; (Tebbit), 20/8/03, paras. 44–5, 58–60.

49 THI evidence (Omand), 26/8/03, paras.186–9.

50 THI evidence (Powell), 18/8/03; (Hoon), 27/8/03, paras.13–14; (Tebbit), 20/8/03, paras.50, 70.

51 THI evidence (Campbell), 19/8/03, paras.145–50, 157; (Hoon), 27/8/03, paras.48–9; (Blair), 28/8/03, paras.55–7; extracts from Campbell's diary, 6–9/7/03, THI:CAB39/ 1–2.

52 THI evidence (Blair), 28/8/03, paras.55–7; extracts from Campbell's diary, 6–9/7/03, THI:CAB39/1–2.

53 THI evidence (Tebbit), 20/8/03, paras.42–3.

54 THI evidence (Omand), 26/8/03, paras.167–8.

55 Among the various discrepancies, for example, was a statement in the summary that Iraq had 'continued' to produce chemical and biological agents, while the main text stated only that Iraq 'could' produce chemical and biological weapons. For a comprehensive analysis, see FAC report (2003), Appendix 2.

56 FAC report (2003), para.90, p.98.

57 Ibid., paras.122, 135, 140, 185.

58 Statements by Campbell and Straw, 7/7/03, THI:CAB1/413–14; BBC response, 7/7/03, THI:CAB1/415–416.

59 Note of Meetings, 7/7/03, THI:CAB11/3–4; (Scarlett), 26/8/03, paras.118–26; Scarlett to J. Muir, 7/7/03, THI:CAB1/46; D. Wilson to R. Hatfield, 7/7/03, THI:MOD1/44–5.

60 'Notes of a Meeting...', 7/7/03, THI:MOD1/46–51; Tebbit to Omand, 7/7/03, THI:CAB1/100–103.

61 THI evidence (Tebbit), 20/8/03, para.72.

62 Ibid., para.82.

63 THI evidence (Blair), 28/8/03, paras.42–3; Dyke (2004), pp.278–9; Oborne and Walters (2003), p.338.

64 S. Powell (on behalf of Campbell) to C. Sumner, 9/7/03, THI:CAB1/86.

65 Note of Meetings (Powell), 8/7/03, THI:CAB11/3–4.

66 THI evidence (Omand), 26/8/03, para.187.

67 Ibid., paras.184–190.

68 THI evidence (Campbell), 19/8/03, paras.151–2.

69 Extracts from Campbell's diary, 8/7/03, THI:CAB39/1–2; THI evidence (Omand), 26/8/03, paras.190–2; 'Record of meetings...', 7–9/7/03, THI: CAB7/9–13.

70 THI evidence (Smith), 20/8/03, para.172.

71 Extracts from Campbell's diary, 8/7/03, THI:CAB39/1–2; Note of Meetings (Powell), 8/7/03, THI:CAB11/3–4.

72 'Record of meetings...', 7–8/7/03, THI:CAB7/9–13; Note of Meetings (Powell), 8/7/03, THI:CAB11/3–4.

73 THI evidence (Kelly), 20/8/03, para.189; Tony Blair interview with Jeremy Paxman, BBC 1, 20/4/05.

74 THI evidence (Tebbit), 20/8/03, paras.86, 98.

75 See Powell to various, 8/7/03, THI:CAB1/59; also see THI evidence (Howard), 16/9/03, paras.104–12.

76 THI evidence (Teare), 18/8/03, paras.42–6; on the drafting of the Q&A material, see THI:CAB21/3–7 and THI:CAB1/64–7.

77 THI evidence (Hatfield), 18/9/03, para.44; (Howard), 16/9/03, paras.36–7; (Tebbit), 20/8/03, paras.88–89; (Hoon), 22/9/03, paras.0–8, 60.

78 THI evidence (Campbell), 19/8/03, paras.149–52, 165–66.

79 For draft versions of the MoD press statement and accompanying notes see THI:CAB1/48–58.

80 MoD press statement, 8/7/03, THI:CAB1/501; BBC press statement, 8/7/03, THI:CAB1/502.

81 THI evidence (Tom Kelly), 23/9/03, paras.3–20, 43–9; (Hoon), 22/9/03, paras.25–33; press briefing, 9/7/03, THI:CAB1/506–510.

82 P. Watkins (on behalf of Hoon) to Davies 9/7/03, THI:CAB1/81.

83 See Hoon to Davies, 8/7/03, THI:CAB1/80; Davies to Hoon, 8/7/03, THI:CAB1/82; THI evidence (Hoon), 27/8/03, paras.55–8, 63, 72–3; Oborne and Walters (2003), p.341.

84 Extracts from Campbell's diary, THI:CAB39/1–2.

85 THI evidence (Tom Kelly), 20/8/03, paras.197–8; Kelly to Powell and C. Sumner, 10/7/03, THI:CAB1/93; P. Watkins to K. Wilson, 9/7/03, THI:MOD44/15.

86 THI evidence (Howard), 16/9/03, paras.49, 65; (Hoon), 22/9/03, paras.25–8, 43, 62, 102–4; 27/8/03, paras.79–80.

87 THI evidence (Hatfield), 18/9/0/3, paras.73–4, 81.

88 V. Dodd, 'MoD clues led papers to Kelly as source', Guardian, 22/8/03; Powell to C. Sumner, 10/7/03, THI:CAB11/12; Tebbit to Hoon, 10/7/03, THI:MOD1/75–76; P. Watkins (on behalf of Hoon) to D. Anderson, 11/7/03, THI:FAC1/7–8; Hoon to Ann Taylor 11/7/03, THI:CAB1/99; Hoon to D. Anderson, 15/7/03, THI:CAB1/97–98; THI evidence (Hoon), 27/8/03, paras.82–5; (Howard), 16/9/03, paras.76ff.

89 FAC evidence (David Kelly), 15/7/03, THI:FAC/4/1–27.

90 ISC evidence (Omand), 16/7/03, THI:ISC1/48–50.

91 Tony Blair speech to the US Congress, 17/7/03.

92 PAC evidence (Falconer), 25/5/04. Q.197.

93 Hutton Report (2004), para.1; BBC News, 20/7/03; also see Oborne and Walters (2003), pp.348–51; Beckett and Hencke (2004), p.319.

94 YouGov poll for the Daily Telegraph, 19–20/7/03.

95 HCLC evidence (Blair), 8/7/03, Q.161.

96 Foreign Policy Aspects of the War Against Terrorism, FAC, Tenth Report of Session 2002–3, HC 405, July 2003.

97 ISC report (2003), paras.94–116; THI evidence (Hoon), 22/9/03, para.87; also see memo by M. Howard, 18/7/03, THI:MOD4/6–8.

98 Figures calculated from MORI.

99 Stephens (2004), p.381.

100 Peston (2005), p.335.

101 Campbell to Blair, 19/8/03, THI:CAB15/1–4.

102 Tony Blair speech to the Labour party conference, 1/10/03.

103 M. White and P. Wintour, 'The new routes to social justice', *Guardian*, 28/11/03.

Chapter 7. Business as Usual

1 Tony Blair interview for the British Forces Broadcasting Service, 16/12/03; BBC News, 17/12/03.

2 BBC News, 28/1/04; Dyke (2004), p.22; Oborne and Walters (2004), p.4.

3 D. Smith, 'Voters savage Hutton verdict', *Sunday Times*, 1/2/04.

4 Hutton Report (2004), paras.407, 411; PAC evidence (Hutton), 13/5/2004, Qs.20, 37.

5 Butler Report (2004), section 5.9; K. Sengupta, 'How judge was misinformed about Iraq's WMD threat', *Independent*, 17/7/04.

6 C. Brown, K. Sengupta, and A. Grice, 'No 10 admits Hutton cover–up'; B. Russell, 'Downing Street forced into the open on discredited spies', *Independent*, 17/7/04.

7 P. Barkham, 'Ex–BBC Chief says failures on Iraq are a blow to democracy', *Guardian*, 11/10/04.

8 PAC evidence (Hutton), 13/5/04, Qs.19–20; Hutton Report (2004), para.274.

9 PAC evidence (Hutton), 13/5/04, Qs.17, 21, 81, 83, 103.

10 Ibid., Qs.39, 86, 92.

11 Riddell (2004), pp.280–1; Woodward (2004), pp.434–5.

12 BBC News, 1/2/04.

13 Butler Report (2004), para.1.

14 B. Russell, 'Ex–cabinet secretary to head WMD intelligence inquiry', *Independent*, 4/2/04; M. Woolf and B. Russell, 'Frantic calls behind Kennedy's "political" decision to stay out', *Independent*, 4/2/04.

15 *Independent* 4/2/04.

16 Private information.

17 Butler Report (2004), para.3.

18 G. Palast and S. Weir, 'The government's FoI proposals: Evidence on behalf of the democratic audit' (1999), Charter 88; Phythian (2005), p.135.

19 The Tory MP Michael Mates, however, refused to stand down and continued as an independent member of the inquiry.

20 NOP poll in *Independent*, 4/2/04; 'A Year After Iraq War', Pew Research Centre, 16/3/04.

21 Short (2004), pp.242–6; R. Cook, 'It will be a gross injustice if the intelligence services get the blame', *Independent*, 4/2/04.

22 BBC News, 4/2/04.

23 M. Bright, A. Barnett and G. Hinsliff, 'Army chiefs feared Iraq war illegal just days before start', *Observer*, 29/2/04.

24 D. Cracknell, 'British fears on US tactics are leaked', *Sunday Times*, 23/5/04.

25 M. White, 'Loyalist ministers shrug off poll gloom', *Guardian*, 14/6/04; A. Grice, 'Blair tries to reassure MPs but rules out apology', *Independent*, 15/6/04; Seldon

(2005), p.652.

26 S. Castle, 'President is triumphant as Blair hopes for democracy', *Independent*, 29/6/04.

27 Interview on *Breakfast with Frost*, BBC 1, 4/7/04.

28 HCLC evidence (Blair), 6/7/04, Qs.237–8.

29 Ibid., Qs.242, 267–8.

30 Ibid., Qs.275–82.

31 Ibid., Q.245.

32 See in particular the separate addendum by Senators Carl Levin and Richard Durbin, as well as the SCI's own Vice Chairman, John D. Rockefeller.

33 *Report on the U.S. Intelligence Community's Prewar Intelligence Assessments on Iraq*, United States Senate Select Committee on Intelligence, Washington, D.C. July 2004.

34 Interview for *HardTalk*, BBC News 24, 9/7/04.

35 *Review of Intelligence on Weapons of Mass Destruction*, Lord Butler, HC 898, July 2004, sections 5.9, and 6.9.

36 Ibid., paras.464, 466.

37 Ibid., section 7.4.

38 Ibid., para.450.

39 Ibid., paras.469, 597.

40 Tony Blair statement to the House of Commons, 14/7/04.

41 Ibid.; remarks during the House of Commons debate on the Butler Report, 20/7/04.

42 *Review of Intelligence on Weapons of Mass Destruction: Implementation of Conclusions*, Cm.6492, March 2005; *Intelligence and Security Committee: Annual Report 2004–2005*, Cm.6510, April 2005.

43 *Guardian*, 20/7/04.

44 BBC News, 16/7/04.

45 BBC News 24, 14/7/04; N. Morris, 'BBC report on "sexed up" dossier is vindicated, says Dyke', *Independent*, 15/7/04; P. Barkham, 'Ex–BBC chief says failures on Iraq are a blow to democracy', *Guardian*, 11/10/04.

46 R. Cook, 'Britain's worst intelligence failure, and Lord Butler says no one is to blame', *Independent*, 15/7/04; interview with BBC Radio 5 Live, 4/8/04.

47 Interview with *HardTalk*, BBC News 24, 15/7/04.

48 *Government by Inquiry*, Public Administration Select Committee, First Report of Session 2004–05, HC 51–1, February 2005.

49 BBC News, 18/7/04.

50 *Guardian*, 20/7/04.

51 Peston (2005), pp.324–6, 343–4, 349.

52 See *Taming the Prerogative: Strengthening Ministerial Accountability to Parliament*, Public Administration Committee, Fourth Report of Session 2003–04, HC 422, March 2004; *Government Response to the Public Administration Select Committee's Fourth Report of the 2003–4 Session*, July 2004.

53 J. Smith, 'Blair dismisses "secret Iraq warnings" leak', *Scotsman*, 18/9/04; G. Hinsliff, 'Iraq leak has Blair back in firing line', *Observer*, 19/9/04; 'UN Secretary

General's speech', *Guardian*, 21/9/04.

54 Joint press conference with Ayad Illawi, 19/9/04.

55 P. Wintour and K. Maguire, 'Blair refuses to apologise for Iraq war', *Guardian*, 14/9/04; 'A sorry affair', *Independent*, 14/10/04.

56 Tony Blair speech to the Labour party conference, 28/9/04.

57 Ibid.

58 Patricia Hewitt on *Question Time*, BBC 1, 7/10/04.

59 Calculated from MORI statistics; also see D. Cracknell, 'Blair's own spin gurus savage No 10', *Sunday Times*, 26/9/04; *Annual Report of the Committee on Standards in Public Life*, 2004.

60 *Comprehensive Report of the Special Advisor to the DCI on Iraqi WMD*, 30/9/04.

61 H. Blix, 'Will President Bush apply the lessons from Iraq...?', *Independent on Sunday*, 10/10/04; M. Woolf, 'The 45–minute claim was false', *Independent*, 13/10/04; P. Barkham, 'Ex–BBC chief says failures on Iraq are a blow to democracy', *Guardian*, 11/10/04.

62 BBC News, 7/10/03.

63 Prime Minister's Official Spokesman (PMOS) press briefing, 12/10/04; Lord Falconer on the *Today* programme, BBC Radio 4, 14/10/04.

64 Tony Blair in the House of Commons, 13/10/04.

65 BBC News, 19/10/04.

66 Channel 4 News, 12/11/04.

67 BBC News, 20/1/05.

68 BBC News, 6/1/05.

69 A. Travis, 'Support for war plummets', *Guardian*, 25/1/05.

70 D. Cracknell and D. Leppard, 'Campbell accused of dirty tricks campaign', *Sunday Times*, 6/2/05.

71 BBC News, various dates.

72 *Intelligence and Security Committee: Annual Report 2004–2005*.

73 D. Hencke, 'Falconer backs war advice secrecy', *Guardian*, 4/1/05; R. Evans, 'Blair refuses FoI request for Iraq war legal advice', *Guardian*, 26/1/05.

74 PAC evidence (Butler), 21/10/04.

75 PAC evidence (Turnbull), 4/3/04, Q.17.

76 BBC News, 9/3/05; W. Woolf, 'Blair broke code to keep war advice from Cabinet', *Independent*, 9/3/05; A. Grice, 'Fresh doubts are raised over the legality of Iraq conflict', *Independent*, 24/2/05.

77 C. Brown and K. Sengupta, 'Blair faces backbench backlash as pressure mounts to publish war advice', *Independent*, 25/3/05.

78 C. Brown, 'Labour believes Opposition is to blame for leaks', *Independent*, 30/4/05.

79 'The paper trail', *Independent*, 13/3/05; J. Rozenburg, 'Reports of Washington leaning on me are conspiracy fantasies, says Attorney General', *Daily Telegraph*, 26/5/05.

80 Sands (2005), pp.195–200.

81 BBC News, 5/4/05.

82 Downing Street statement by Tony Blair, 6/5/05.

83 A. Travis and M. White, 'Labour lead drops by five points', *Guardian*, 5/4/05.

84 'Labour support would soar if Brown were PM', *Independent on Sunday*, 17/4/05.

85 Labour party manifesto 2005.

86 Tony Blair interview with Jeremy Paxman, BBC 1, 20/4/05.

87 Joint press conference, 28/4/05.

88 Statement by the Attorney-General, 27/4/05.

89 Michael Howard on *Question Time*, BBC 1, 28/4/05.

90 J. Curtice, 'Lib-Dem advance would hit Blair – but still leave Howard without hope', *Independent*, 30/4/05.

91 *5th May 2005: Worst. Election. Ever.* Electoral Reform Society, 13/5/05.

92 Election analysis compiled from various sources, including ibid., BBC News, *Guardian*, *Independent*, and *The Times*, 7/5/05.

93 'A partnership for wider freedom', speech by Jack Straw at the Center for Strategic and International Studies, Washington, 18/5/05.

94 BBC News, 8/7/05, 17/7/05; R. Cook, 'The struggle against terrorism cannot be won by military means', *Guardian*, 8/7/05; interview with Hans Blix on *HardTalk*, BBC News 24, 28/8/05.

95 *Security, Terrorism and the UK*, Chatham House report, 18/7/05.

96 M. Bright, 'Leaks shows Blair told of Iraq war terror link', *Observer*, 28/8/05.

97 Home Office briefing paper, 22/2/05.

98 M. Evans, 'MI5 analysts admit link between Iraq war and bombings', *The Times*, 28/7/05; *Threat to the UK from International Terrorism*, Joint Terrorism Analysis Centre, 28/7/05.

99 Statement by Tony Blair at the G8 summit, 7/7/05; joint statement by G8 leaders, 7/7/05; BBC News 24, 9/7/05.

100 BBC News, 17/7/05; G. Jones, 'Ministers reject claim that Iraq war made UK a target', *Telegraph*, 18/7/05; J. Sturke, 'Straw rejects war link to bombings', *Guardian*, 18/7/05.

101 Comments by Charles Clarke in the House of Commons, 20/7/05.

102 Tony Blair press conference, 26/7/05.

103 BBC News, 9/7/05; M. White, A. Travis, and D. Campbell, 'Blair: uproot this ideology of evil', *Guardian* 14/7/05; Tony Blair speech at the Labour party conference, 16/7/05; Tony Blair press conference, 26/7/05.

104 BBC News, 9/7/05; Tony Blair press conference, 26/7/05.

105 Tony Blair speech at the Labour party conference, 16/7/05; Tony Blair press conference, 26/7/05.

106 BBC News 24, 24/8/05.

107 Tony Blair press conference, 5/8/05.

108 See *The Times*, 26/7/05; also see 'Blaming Blair', *Guardian*, 20/7/05.

Bibliography

Official documents

Report of the Inquiry into the Export of Defence Equipment and Dual-Use Goods to Iraq and Related Prosecutions, Lord Scott, HC 115, HMSO, London, 1996.

Rebuilding America's Defenses: Strategy, Focus and Resources for a New Century, Project for a New American Century, September 2000.

Responsibility for the Terrorist Atrocities in the United States, Office of the Prime Minister, October 2001.

The National Security Strategy of the United States of America, September 2002.

Iraq: The Debate and Policy Options, P. Bowers, House of Commons Library Research Paper 02/53, International Affairs and Defence Section, September 2002.

Iraq's Weapons of Mass Destruction: The Assessment of the British Government, HMSO, London, September 2002.

Saddam Hussein: Crimes and Human Rights Abuses, Foreign and Commonwealth Office, HMSO, London, December 2002.

Iraq—its Infrastructure of Concealment, Deception and Intimidation, HMSO, London, February 2003.

Parliament and the Use of Force, P. Bowers, House of Commons Library, International Affairs and Defence Section, SN/IA/1218, February 2003.

Unresolved Disarmament Issues: Iraq's Proscribed Weapons Programmes, UNMOVIC, United Nations, March 2003.

The Decision to go to War in Iraq, Foreign Affairs Committee, Ninth Report of Session 2002-03, HC 813. HMSO, London, July 2003.

Foreign Policy Aspects of the War Against Terrorism, Foreign Affairs Committee, Tenth Report of Session 2002–3, HC 405, HMSO, London, July 2003.

Iraqi Weapons of Mass Destruction: Intelligence and Assessments, Intelligence and Security Committee, Cm.5972, HMSO, London, September 2003.

Annual Report of the Committee on Standards in Public Life, 2004.

Report of the Inquiry into the Circumstances Surrounding the Death of Dr David Kelly, Lord Hutton, HC.247, HMSO, London, January 2004.

Taming the Prerogative: Strengthening Ministerial Accountability to Parliament, Public Administration Committee, Fourth Report of Session 2003–04, HC 422, HMSO, London, March 2004.

Report on the U.S. Intelligence Community's Prewar Intelligence Assessments on Iraq,

United States Select Committee on Intelligence, Washington, D.C, July 2004.

Review of Intelligence on Weapons of Mass Destruction, Lord Butler, HC 898, HMSO, London, July 2004.

Government Response to the Public Administration Select Committee's Fourth Report of the 2003–4 Session, July 2004.

Government Response to the Intelligence and Security Committee's Annual Report 2003–2004, Intelligence and Security Committee. Cm.6241. July 2004.

Comprehensive Report of the Special Advisor to the DCI on Iraqi WMD, 30 September 2004.

Government by Inquiry, Public Administration Select Committee, First Report of Session 2004-05, HC 51–1, February 2005.

Review of Intelligence on Weapons of Mass Destruction: *Implementation of Conclusions*, Intelligence and Security Committee, Cm.6492, HMSO, London, March 2005.

Intelligence and Security Committee: *Annual Report 2004–2005*, Cm.6510, HMSO, London, April 2005.

Websites

BBC News: www.news.bbc.co.uk
Campaign Against the Arms Trade: www.caat.org.uk
Campaign for Freedom of Information: www.cfoi.org.uk
Charter 88: www.charter88.org.uk
Constitution Unit: www.ucl.ac.uk/constitution-unit
Democratic Audit: www.democraticaudit.co.uk
Department for Constitutional Affairs: www.dca.gov.uk
Export Credit Agency Watch: www.eca-watch.org
Federation of American Scientists: www.fas.org/news/uk/scott
Hutton Inquiry: www.the-hutton-inquiry.org.uk
Iraq Body Count: www.Iraqbodycount.net
Liberty: www.liberty-human-rights.org.uk
Market and Opinion Research International (MORI): www.MORI.com
Ministry of Defence: www.mod.uk
National Priorities Project: www.costofwar.com
Number 10 Downing Street: www.number10.gov.uk
World Development Movement: www.wdm.org.uk

Books and articles

Barberis, P. (1996), *The Elite of the Elite* (Dartmouth; Aldershot).

Barker, A. (1997), 'Practicing to Deceive: Whitehall, Arms Exports and the Scott Inquiry', *Political Quarterly*, 68(1).

Beckett, F., and Hencke, D., (2004), *The Blairs and their Court* (Aurum; London).

Beer, S. (1982), *Modern British Politics* (Faber and Faber; London).

Bevir, M. (2005), *New Labour: A Critique* (Routledge; London).

Birch, A. H. (1979), *Representative and Responsible Government* (George Allen &

Unwin; London).

Blackburn, R. (1995), *The Electoral System in Britain* (Macmillan; London).

Blix, H. (2004), *Disarming Iraq: The Search for Weapons of Mass Destruction* (Bloomsbury; London).

Bluth, C. (2004), 'The British Road to War: Blair, Bush and the Decision to Invade Iraq', *International Affairs*, 80(5).

Brivati, B., and Bale, T. (1998), *New Labour in Power* (Routledge; London).

Budge, I., Crewe, I., McKay, D., and Mewton, K. (2001), *The New British Politics*, 2nd ed. (Longman; London).

Buller, J. (1999), 'A Critical Appraisal of the Statecraft Interpretation', *Public Administration*. 77(4).

—— (2000), 'Understanding Contemporary Conservative Euro-Scepticism: Statecraft and the Problem of Governing Autonomy', *Political Quarterly*, 71(3).

Bulpitt, J. (1983), *Territory and Power in the United Kingdom: An Interpretation* (Manchester University Press; Manchester).

Bulpitt, J., and Burnham, P. (1999), 'Operation ROBOT and the British Political Economy in the Early 1950s: The Politics of Market Strategies', *Contemporary British History*, 13(1).

Burnham, P. (2001), 'New Labour and the Politics of Depoliticisation', *British Journal of Politics and International Relations*, 3(2).

Byrne, I., and Weir, S. (2004), 'Democratic Audit: Executive Democracy in War and Peace', *Parliamentary Affairs*, 57(2).

Chalmers, M., Davies, N., Hartley, K. and Wilkinson, C. (2001), *The Economic Costs and Benefits of UK Defence Exports*, Centre for Defence Economics Research Monograph Series 13, University of York.

Chatterjee, P. (2004), *Iraq, Inc. A Profitable Invasion* (Seven Stories Press; New York).

Cirincione, J. (2003), 'Origins of Regime Change in Iraq', Carnegie Endowment for International Peace, *Proliferation Brief*, 6(5).

Clarke, R. A. (2004), *Against All Enemies: Inside America's War on Terror* (Free Press; New York).

Coates, D. (2000), 'The Character of New Labour', in D. Coates and P. Lawler (eds.), *New Labour in Power* (Manchester University Press; Manchester).

—— (2005), *Prolonged Labour: The Slow Birth of New Labour in Britain* (Penguin; London).

—— and Krieger, J. (2004), *Blair's War* (Polity Press; Cambridge).

—— and Lawler, P. (eds.) (2000), *New Labour in Power* (Manchester University Press; Manchester).

Cook, R. (2004), *The Point of Departure: Diaries From the Front Bench* (Pocket Books; London).

Cox, M. (2004), 'Empire by Denial? Debating US Power', *Security Dialogue*, 35(2).

Curtis, M. (2003), *Web of Deceit: Britain's Real Role in the World* (Vintage; London).

Dearlove, J. and Saunders, P. (2000), *Introduction to British Politics*, 3rd ed. (Polity; Cambridge).

Doig, A. (2005), '45 Minutes of Infamy? Hutton, Blair and the Invasion of Iraq', *Parliamentary Affairs*, 58(1).

Driver, S. and Martell, C. (1998), *New Labour: Politics after Thatcherism* (Polity; Cambridge).

Dyke, G. (2004), *Inside Story* (HarperCollins; London).

Galloway, G. (2004), *I'm not the Only One* (Penguin; London).

Glees, A. (2005), 'Evidence-Based Policy or Policy-Based Evidence? Hutton and the Government's Use of Secret Intelligence', *Parliamentary Affairs*, 58(1).

Gould, P. (1999), *The Unfinished Revolution* (Abacus; London).

Hall, P. and Taylor, R. (1996), 'Political Science and the Three New Institutionalisms', *Political Studies*, 44.

Harvey, D. (2003), *The New Imperialism* (Oxford University Press; Oxford).

Harvey, R. (2003), *Global Disorder* (Robinson; London).

Hay, C. (1996), *Re-Stating Social and Political Change* (Open University Press; Buckingham).

—— (1997), *The Political Economy of New Labour* (Manchester University Press; Manchester).

Heffernan, R. (2003), 'Prime Ministerial Predominance? Core Executive Politics in the UK', *British Journal of Politics and International Relations*, 5(3).

Hennessy, P. (2000), *The Prime Minister: The Office and its Holders Since 1945* (Allen Lane, London).

—— (2005), 'Informality and Circumspection: The Blair Style of Government in War and Peace', *Political Quarterly*, 76(1).

Hoggett, P. (2005), 'Iraq: Blair's Mission Impossible', *British Journal of Politics and International Relations*, 7(3).

Ignatieff, M. (2003), *Empire Lite: Nation-Building in Bosnia, Kosovo and Afghanistan* (Vintage; London).

James, S. (1992), *British Cabinet Government* (Routledge; London).

Jones, N. (2002), *Control Freaks: How New Labour Gets its Own Way* (Politicos; London).

Judge, D. (1993), *The Parliamentary State* (Sage; London).

—— (2004), 'Whatever Happened to Parliamentary Democracy in the United Kingdom?', *Parliamentary Affairs*, 57(3).

Kagan, R. (2003), *Paradise and Power: America and Europe in the New World Order* (Atlantic Books; London).

Kampfner, J. (2004), *Blair's Wars* (Polity; London).

Kavanagh, D. (2000), *British Politics: Continuities and Change*, 4th ed. (Oxford University Press; Oxford).

Kerr, S. (2001), *Postwar British Politics: From Conflict to Consensus* (Routledge; London).

Kettell, S. (2004), *The Political Economy of Exchange Rate Policy-Making: From the Gold Standard to the Euro* (Palgrave; London).

Kingdom, J. (2001), *Government and Politics in Britain*, 3rd ed. (Polity; London).

Lawler, P. (2000), 'New Labour's Foreign Policy', in D. Coates and P. Lawler (eds), *New Labour in Power* (Manchester University Press; Manchester).

Leonard, D. and Mortimore, R. (2005), *Elections in Britain: A Voter's Guide*, 5th ed. (Palgrave; London).

Ludlam, S. and Smith, M. (2001), *New Labour in Government* (Palgrave; London).

Mackenzie, R. T. (1955), *British Political Parties* (Heinemann; London).

Maer, L., and Sandford, M. (2004), 'The Development of Scrutiny in the UK: A Review of Procedures and Practice', The Constitution Unit, University of Central London.

Mandelson, P. and Liddle, R. (1996), *The Blair Revolution: Can New Labour Deliver?* (Faber and Faber, London).

al-Marashi, I. (2002), 'Iraq's Security and Intelligence Network: A Guide and Analysis', *Middle East Review of International Affairs*, 6(3).

Marsh, D., and Tant, A. (1989), 'There is No Alternative: Mrs Thatcher and the British Political Tradition', Essex Papers in Politics and Government (69), University of Essex.

Naughtie, J. (2004), *The Accidental American: Tony Blair and the Presidency* (Macmillan; London).

Norton-Taylor, R. (1995), *Truth is a Difficult Concept: Inside the Scott Inquiry* (Guardian Books, London).

Oborne, P., and Walters, S. (2004), *Alastair Campbell* (Aurum Press Ltd.; London).

Peston, R. (2005), *Brown's Britain* (Short Books; London).

Phythian, M. (2005), 'Hutton and Scott: A Tale of Two Inquiries', *Parliamentary Affairs*, 58(1).

Pilkington, C. (1999), *The Civil Service in Britain Today* (Manchester University Press; Manchester).

Ramesh, R. (ed). (2003), *The War We Could Not Stop: The Real Story of the Battle for Iraq* (Faber and Faber, London).

Rangwala, G., and Plesch, D. (2004), *A Case To Answer: A First Report on the Potential Impeachment of the Prime Minister for High Crimes and Misdemeanours in Relation to the Invasion of Iraq* (published by Adam Price MP, House of Commons, London).

Rawnsley, A. (2001), *Servants of the People* (Penguin; London).

Riddell, P. (2004), *Hug Them Close: Blair, Clinton, Bush and the 'Special Relationship'* (Politicos; London).

Rogers, R., and Walters, R. (2004), *How Parliament Works*, 5th ed. (Longman; London).

Rose, R. (1985), *Politics in England Today* (Faber; London).

Sands, P. (2005), *Lawless World: America and the Making and Breaking of Global Rules* (Allen Lane; London).

Seldon, A. (2005), *Blair*, 2nd ed. (Free Press; London).

Shawcross, W. (2004), *Allies: The United States, Britain, Europe and the War in Iraq* (Atlantic Books; London).

Short, C. (2004), *An Honourable Deception? New Labour, Iraq, and the Misuse of Power* (Free Press; London).

Simpson, J. (2003), *The Wars Against Saddam: Taking the Hard Road to Baghdad* (Macmillan; London).

Stephens, P. (2004), *Tony Blair: The Price of Leadership* (Politicos; London).

Stothard, P. (2003), *30 Days: A Month at the Heart of Blair's War* (HarperCollins; London).

Tant, A. P. (1993), *British Government: The Triumph of Elitism* (Dartmouth; Aldershot).

Tyrie, A. (2004), *Blair's Poodle Goes to War: The House of Commons, Congress and Iraq* (Centre for Policy Studies; London).

Vickers, R. (2000), 'Blair's Kosovo Campaign: Political Communications, the Kosovo War and the Battle for Public Opinion', Paper for the Political Studies Association, UK 50th Annual Conference, London, 10–13 April.

Wade, R. H. (2003), 'The Invisible Hand of the American Empire', *Ethics and International Affairs*, 17(7).

Webb, P. (2000), *The Modern British Party System* (Sage; London).

Weir, S. and Beetham, D. (2002), *Democracy Under Blair: A Democratic Audit of the UK* (Routledge; London).

—— (2003), *War and Peace: Executive Democracy in Action*, Democratic Findings No.6, Democratic Audit of the United Kingdom.

Woodward, B. (2002), *Bush at War* (Simon & Schuster; London).

—— (2004), *Plan of Attack* (Simon & Schuster; London).

Wright, T. (ed) (2000), *The British Political Process* (Routledge; London).

Index